the
broken biscuit

the
broken biscuit

john cowell

JOHN BLAKE

Published by John Blake Publishing Limited,
3 Bramber Court, 2 Bramber Road, London W14 9PB

Published in paperback 2001

ISBN 1 90340 2 45 X

British Library Cataloguing-in-Publication Data: A catalogue record for this book
is available from the British Library.

Cover design by Graeme Andrew

3 5 7 9 10 8 6 4

Papers used by John Blake Publishing Limited are natural, recyclable products made
from wood grown in sustainable forests. The manufacturing processes conform to
the environmental regulations of the country of origin.

contents

Dedicated to Winifred by her son John.

The following verse is in dedication to my beloved, dearly missed partner Ann, who sadly passed away on May 17th 1999. I am proud to say that she has shared with me in this book at every step of the way.

My Gentle Ann

Despite your illness ... your sorrow and pain,
Not once to me did you e'er complain.
Each morning you greeted me like the morning dew,
Never again will the sky appear quite so blue.
Just as the planets revolve around the sun,
We mingled ... we laughed ... we became as one.
In my heart you'll remain with me till life's end,
My love ... my life ... my true devoted friend!

The reason why I started to write this book is quite simple. When I was a young boy, my mother used to tell many tales of her own childhood and that of her own parents and grandparents. I was always intrigued with what she had to say and found her tales both fascinating and poignant. She is quite a good writer in her own right, having won various competitions for "Amateur writer of the year" including one in the Lancashire area. For this reason, I tried many times to persuade her to write her autobiography, but to no avail.

When I was a pupil at St Thomas's Junior School, the headmistress, Miss Gordon was very impressed by some of the many letters that my mother wrote to the school. She too, tried to persuade my mother to write her own story, saying that it would make wonderful reading.

My mother's answer was simple, "Yes, maybe it would, Miss Gordon, but there are too many hurtful things that I wouldn't want people to know."

This is the same answer that she always gave to me, and sadly, she never would put pen to paper. I thought it rather sad to let such stories go untold, feeling that they should be passed on to future generations. All the same, I didn't want to hurt my mother in any way, so I tended to let it go. However, as the years passed, the stories still remained within me and the need to write them persisted. So I broached the subject with my mother once more. She was still adamant that she wouldn't do it, but to my surprise she said she wouldn't mind if I wrote it myself.

"But, Mum, what about all the hurtful things that you wouldn't want people to know about?" I asked her.

"Listen, son, I've always brought you up to do what you think is right; you're your own person, if you want to write the story, then write it."

I felt rather excited; she'd actually given me the go ahead.

"There's just one snag," I thought to myself, "I've never done anything like this before and I certainly don't possess the same writings skills as Mum." Still, not to be put off, I started to scribble things down as I recalled them from the stories my mother told me as a child. I don't profess to be a writer but I think it would be a terrible waste not to pass these stories on to my children and future generations. This need in me compelled me to write on, despite the outcome.

I do not wish to offend anyone by my book, and for this reason I have changed the names of some of the characters. Notwithstanding, I have written everything as honestly and truthfully as it was told to me, or as I witnessed it with my own eyes.

1: *the* war years

Bacup is a small Lancashire town in the Rossendale Valley close to the Yorkshire border. Surrounded by high moorland hills and intersected on the valley floor by the River Irwell, the staple industry at the turn of the century was cotton. Ross Mill was by far the largest of the many factories, which, over the years, had transformed a quaint rural village into a bleak industrial town. The smoke from the factory chimneys, which hung over the town like a shroud, together with the damp climate, contributed to the high incidence of bronchitis and other chest complaints amongst the local folk; but the main factor in the poor health of the inhabitants was poverty.

Winifred was born in this little town on January 29th, 1913. She was the third child of Matthew and Mary Walsh, her two older siblings being Catherine, better known as Katie, and Martin.

They lived in a very humble neighbourhood in the heart of the town, where dwellings were notorious for being cold and damp. Their home was built into a steep hillside, known as a back to earth house. Shoddily built and full of rising damp, it was typical of the houses thereabouts. There were only two rooms, a small downstairs room, and an even smaller bedroom.

The main feature in the downstairs room was a cast-iron fireplace built into the chimney-breast. Standing on a thick hearthstone, it was capped by a mantelpiece where the family photographs were displayed and lovingly dusted every day. Pans could be placed on top of, and into, a built-in oven with a big heavy door. A water boiler, with a hinged lid, rested below a shelf on which kitchen utensils were stored. Nearby, wooden cupboards and drawers, also built into the wall, and always warm from the heat of the fire, provided the ideal place for the storage of bedding and clothes. The only daylight in the room entered through a single window, a stone slop sink on cast-iron legs lay directly underneath it.

Water had to be collected from a standpipe in the street directly opposite the communal toilets.

It was a cold house, for the stone flag floor retained no heat, but in spite of being a draughty house the ventilation was poor, and the sweet smell of mildew constantly filled the air. The house was overlooked by factories, which cast large shadows and cut off much of the natural light from the cramped room, leaving it in permanent semi-darkness. The only lighting to offset the gloom was supplied by an old paraffin lamp, or candles. But the kettle, kept constantly on the bubble to make a welcome cup of tea to raise the spirit, offset the gloom. The fireplace emitted a little light and a little warmth, and tantalising smells danced in the nostrils when meals were being cooked above the red-hot coals, or when bread was baking in the oven.

The family washed themselves in the sink. On bath night, a tin bath, which hung on the wall outside, was brought within and placed in front of the fire. Bathing was a laborious task, as all the water had first to be carried from the standpipes, heated in the water boiler, and then decanted into the bath. Washdays were no less of a drudge, as the dolly tub was filled with boiling water in the same tiresome manner. After the wet clothes had been put through the mangle they were draped over a rack, which hung suspended from the ceiling above the fireplace.

Right from the start Winifred made her mark on the world, and it soon became apparent to her parents that she was altogether different from their other two children. She wasn't a fretful baby but she certainly let them know when she was hungry or needed changing, especially so during the night. She slept in a make-do crib by their bedside, whilst the two older children slept together in a small bed in the same tiny bedroom.

Matthew, her father, wasn't the most patient man in the world, and more so when his sleep had been disturbed. He was something of a chauvinist, and strongly believed that he was the breadwinner, and his wife Mary's place was to look after the children.

He'd complain to Mary, then growl at her, "See to that baby wilta?" and would then add, "I don't know, them other two were ne'er like this ún." He would then go back to sleep as Mary tended to the baby's needs.

Winifred was only a tiny baby, and in her future years she was only to be a slight girl, but *always* with a mind of her own. When she had just turned five months old, Bacup was preparing for a memorable event; bunting and flags could be seen decorating all the houses in the town. The preparations were for an official visit by King George V and Queen Mary on Tuesday, July 9th. After visiting other neighbouring towns including Burnley, they would then make their way to Bacup.

On the day most firms and shops closed at noon, and all schools were granted a public holiday. People started waiting from early morning in order to get a good place, and by noon thousands, from Stacksteads through to Bacup and along Whitworth Road, lined the streets; everyone was in a happy mood, the atmosphere was wonderful. At certain points along the way there were sections reserved for different groups of children. The school authorities had made arrangements for school children over seven years, but there were many more there under that age who evidently didn't want to miss out on the occasion. Mat, as Winifred's father was better known, and Mary got the three kiddies ready and took them along to Whitworth Road. They were lucky enough to get a place near one of the groups of children, which guaranteed them a good view of the King and Queen as they passed by on their way to Rochdale. Mary was holding little Martin in her arms and Katie was on Mat's shoulder; Winifred was in a pram and quite unconcerned by all the activity around her.

Bacup Council had just acquired a new visitor's book, and was very proud that the royal couple would be the first to sign it. One could tell when the royal car was approaching, because scattered along the route were different bands, and each one in turn struck up the National Anthem as the royal cortége passed them by. It was about twenty past five when the car drove up Whitworth Road. The King and Queen passed along the route at a very slow pace; they were most considerate in this respect, giving Mat and Mary an excellent view of the royal couple. Katie was going on four now and quite appreciated the goings on, but Martin was too young; as for Winifred, she'd fallen asleep and wasn't aware of anything. The day had gone well and the weather stayed fine; on the way home many neighbours were at their doors chatting away about the royal occasion.

As they were strolling along, Matthew turned to Mary and announced, "I'll tell thi what it is, luv, them Royals make a right bonny couple in all their finery, but that's how I picture thi all the time anyroad. Mind you, tha doesn't need fancy clothes for t' beauty to show through; to me; tha'll allús be MY QUEEN," and after a slight pause, "MARY."

"Oh don't be so daft," she replied, "stop tha kiddín'!"

"No, I means it, mí luv … I don't know what I'd do without thí. Nay, Lass, I wouldn't swap thee for all tay in China."

On nearing home, Katie became all excited as she heard the hustle and bustle of lots of happy children. There were street parties going on all over town for the children, known as a "Jacob's Join." Mary was a very good baker and had contributed scones, buns and biscuits. The celebrations went on into the small hours with people dancing and singing, and the day's events provided a constant source of conversation in the following weeks. Gradually though, Bacup settled back into its normal routine, and within a few months the royal visit was just a memory.

Winifred was only eighteen months old when, in September 1914, her brother James was born; he was to become a Godsend and a real love to his mum.

About a month later World War One broke out and Matthew volunteered to join His Majesty's Forces. On enrolment he was given the King's Shilling, a symbol of military recruitment dating back many centuries. Feelings of patriotism were high, and Matthew, like many others, went to war confident of early victory. Little did he know that he would be away from home for four years, and most of that time was to be spent on the front line in the trenches.

Mary received a small pension from the army, but it was not enough to support the family; she had to work evenings part-time at the mill, and leave the children in the care of a neighbour. During the next four years she was to live off her wits doing everything possible to ensure the well-being of her family; she was rather naive at first but gradually learnt all the tricks of survival. Market days were Wednesday and Saturday, and trading finished at nine o'clock or even later. She always waited until nearly closing time, when the stallholders sold lots of fruit and vegetables at knockdown prices; she also obtained cheap meat from the butcher's stall. Mary was not always successful, as many other people living in similar conditions to her had the same idea. Sometimes, she resorted to retrieving fruit and vegetables that had been discarded as unfit for sale, but after cutting away the perished parts, she soon had a basketful of edible produce. These methods were her main source of obtaining fruit and vegetables throughout the war years. She also went to the bakers where she could buy mis-shaped loaves or slightly stale bread for ha'penny. No matter, cut into small chunks they went down well with broth mix made from salvaged vegetables and bits of corned beef.

Another way of coping, and in some cases making a few coppers, was to go to jumble sales where she picked up clothes, shoes, etc. for the children and even overcoats for use as bedding. Her way of making a little extra cash was to buy trinkets and other oddments, which in turn she pledged at the pawnshop in Union Street with no intention of redeeming them. However, she also pledged many items which she later redeemed, as these helped her get by till payday and the pledge cost was minimal.

Like most housewives, she had a regular set pattern of events. Monday was washday, she'd fill the dolly-tub and whilst possing some clothes, others would be boiling over the fire in a double-handled pan; after rinsing they'd be put through the mangle, then hung on the rack. Rather than waste the sudsy water, she'd ask a neighbour if she wanted to use it whilst it was still hot, or collect a few oddments from an elderly neighbour and wash them through for her, indeed, nothing was wasted. The ironing, using the old type flat iron that had to be heated on a grid, was usually left till later in the week.

Saturday, being cleaning-up day, was also the day for donkey-stoning the front doorstep, with white or yellow stone. This latter task was a tradition passed down from generation to generation and a must for every household. Every woman strove to have the cleanest and best donkey-stoned step in the street. They were never prouder than when theirs was gleaming; no matter what it was like inside the house, the doorstep was always immaculately donkey-stoned.

A local joke at the time was:

> The local bobby copped a man climbing out of the back window of a house.
> "Right mi lad!" he said. "Now I've copped thí."
> "It's all reight, officer, this is mí own house ... the wife's just donkey-stoned the front step!"

At times when hard up for cash, Mary would borrow from a

neighbour and pay it back on payday, and if unable to, nobody bothered too much; it could always be repaid in kind by a bowl of broth or a day's washing. When she went shopping she would always ask a neighbour whether they wanted something bringing whilst she was in town, and vice versa. Everyone was poor but the community spirit was very close knit. If anyone was short of tea, sugar or such, it could always be exchanged for another commodity.

Meal times were difficult, as food was always hard to come by, but Mary improvised every way that she could. The main diet consisted of a little corned beef cut up into small pieces, with a combination of potatoes, onions, carrots, cabbage, cauliflower, all boiled up in a pan into a hash, then served with a crispy crust on top. Mary used her baking skills to make delicious biscuits, scones, buns and bread. Specialities for afters were apple pie or mixed fruit pie made from the salvaged cut fruit.

On bath night, she bathed the kiddies in the stone sink, dried them in front of the fire then dressed them in nightwear that had been aired on the rack. To bath herself she had to wait till the children were in bed, then use the old tin bath.

She wrote regularly to Mat to help boost his morale, and she received many letters in return. At first they were filled with humour, but as the war went on bitterness revealed itself. In the first year he would joke about the awful conditions.

> You know, luv, our CO is dead keen on personal hygiene, but I think he's goín a bit o'er top. Last week it were throwín' it down and trenches were flooded out. Now he's gone and put one ó lads on a charge for washing hisself in water that we have to sleep in.

He went on to say that spirits were high and how men used to sing the song, 'Oh what a lovely war'. Later she received a letter saying he'd been made up to Corporal, but a couple of months later he'd been demoted for fighting. In the latter years, the letters became much sadder.

One of these read something like this:

> You know, love, they're sending young lads o'er here

now straight from cradle. On nites afore action, thá can hear
many of ém crying for their mums.

He couldn't go into more detail, as his letters were censored; but
even if they hadn't been, he wouldn't have written about the true horrors
of the war for fear of upsetting Mary. However, after the war when the
children were older he would on occasions open his heart, and here is
more or less what he talked about.

The cold wet conditions of the trenches were
atrocious, and especially so during the winter months, most
of the time men had to just bivouac down on the spot, many
died of pneumonia or simply froze to death. Many
wounded needed medical attention with wounds that were
festering and becoming gangrenous; they died through lack
of attention and had to be put outside the trenches along
with many other corpses. Men broke down and cried
openly without shame for the stupid, senseless loss of so
many young lives and comrades.

Being bivouacked on the spot for days at a time, and
constantly bombarded by gas bombs and shellfire night
after night was unbearable. It was impossible to sleep
properly, even when it was quiet, because of smarting eyes
caused by the gas bombs, in spite of wearing gas masks.
Many had to remove their sodden clothing, not only to try
and dry them, but because they were ridden with fleas and
bugs; there was no peace forthcoming because of the
constant itching. The place really was like Hell on Earth!

Orders and counter-orders were forever being received
from command headquarters. Men lived in constant fear
and torment, either waiting for something to happen or all
hell being let loose; they were either being attacked or on
the offensive themselves. Battalions were ordered to attack
carrying full battle pack, including grenades, gas masks,
and rifle with fixed bayonet; many men hesitated but
followed the others like sheep knowing that they may never

see another day, and thought that even that would be a relief. Some men even hoped they would be injured just enough to be medically discharged. Bullets from machine guns whistled everywhere with many men dying instantly, others were severely wounded, whilst many were pinned down. Still some managed to go forward under a barrage of artillery enveloped in smoke.

There were foul-smelling corpses of men and horses alike with legs, arms and torsos lying everywhere in coagulated blood. Many men were unrecognisable, either with badly blackened burnt faces or no face at all; it was total carnage!

"Forward! Forward!" came orders shouted by senior officers. That they did, very slowly on their bellies; this resulted in many more being killed or maimed. Many times, some arrived at no-man's land, where no one could either go forward or back unless under cover of smoke or darkness.

Badly injured men tried desperately to drag themselves to the safety of the trenches moaning, "Please help me! ... Ple ... ease don't leave me here please! ... Please! ... Ple ... ease!" Stretcher-bearers were courageously doing their job but many died alongside the injured.

Still more orders came ... "Onwards!" "Defend your post at all costs!"

Many men were stuck in terrible positions for days until backed up by reinforcements. Ironically, they sometimes got Jerry on the run, and took over some trenches, only to discover more misery, as the Germans had left many booby traps. It's a miracle that any of us survived!

One of the greatest morale boosters for the soldiers was to hear news from home about their family, but sadly this occasionally could be quite devastating. The following is a quote from a local newspaper about a young priest who had just been visiting the front lines:

The preacher gratefully bore testimony to the loyalty of the soldier to his family. He found on his visit to the front, that one of the greatest pleasures they could give the soldier was to talk to him about his children. As he talked to them, he could see that their minds wandered home and saw visions of their children at the fireside with their mother, and oh, how they longed to be there!

He could never forget the agony of the soldiers out yonder when they received news of betrayal by their wives or sweethearts. One felt that the measure of their pain was the measure of their loyalty to their home. What seemed to him to be the most extreme sorrow to such men was that there was no home for them to return to when they had finished their grim task in the front line.

The soldier would return to England with a new passion for home. Most of them would love their home as never before.

With regard to Mat's letters, there was a very good reason for his change in mood and it wasn't just what he had to endure in the trenches.

He had served one year in the forces when he received very bad news from home; his eldest son, Martin, had died! He was completely devastated.

The letter informed him of the following:

His wife Mary had been called home from her evening job at the mill because Martin was ill. The doctor arrived about an hour later and after examining the little lad, he asked Mary whether he had fallen or been dropped, as he appeared to have something wrong with his neck. She didn't know, and the truth of what actually happened never came to light. Despite all the care and attention given, Martin's condition deteriorated rapidly, and he died within a couple of days.

After reading the letter, Matthew went to see his Commanding Officer about compassionate leave, but his request was turned down, as by now his son was already buried.

The conversation went something like this, "I am very sorry, Private Walsh, and I offer you my condolences but I cannot spare even one man, and I have no alternative but to order you to remain at your post."

Matthew's first impulse was to go AWOL, but being rational, he knew that this wouldn't do him or his family any good, also the sentence for desertion under fire was to be shot. He got lots of support from his mates in the trenches, but was still visibly grief-stricken and deep in shock.

"Oh Mary," he kept thinking to himself, "if I could only but put mí arms about thi and gí thi a cuddle, and thee me." That night and every night after, he knelt down and prayed, "Oh please, God in heaven, I ask Thee to accept my little lad into Your Heavenly Kingdom, and to shine Thy holy light down on mi wife and young uns back home. Aye, and also on to mi friends and miself out here, so that this terrible war may soon be over then we can all return home safely to our loved ones."

It's just as well he didn't know then that the war was to last another three years; the thought of that would have been just too unbearable. He was to see many of his young friends badly injured and killed. Three and a half years into the war he himself was wounded; a bullet passed through his right shoulder fracturing his clavicle and damaging his shoulder joint. He was taken to a field hospital where his arm was kept hoisted in a sling for several months.

Meanwhile, back in Bacup, Mary had been trying to cope with her sad loss the best way that she could, and she put on a brave face for the children's sake. Times didn't get any easier. In fact, by April 1918, inflation had more than doubled from what it had been at the onset of war. Mary had to constantly live off her wits in order to survive. She did most of her shopping at the corner shop where almost everything was sold loose: sugar, salt, flour and other basic commodities would be weighed on a scale, using different-sized brass weights, then put into strong paper bags, which cost a ha'penny for four. Because of the cost they were saved and used over and over. Much larger iron weights and scales were used for weighing vegetables like potatoes and onions. The shops stayed open till quite late but for emergency shopping for things like teething powders, medicine, rheumatism pills, and painkillers the backdoor was often used. Many people used these commodities and most of them had a slate, which allowed them to buy things on account and settle up on payday. The shopkeepers were quite happy with the arrangement, as they were assured of the custom, plus they also charged a little extra for the service. Mary was allowed credit up to twenty-two shillings, and if she hadn't spent that much by Tuesday, she would then often borrow money from the shopkeeper up to her allotted amount. If she couldn't repay the total amount on payday, then the balance was carried forward to the following week. Things carried on much like this, and Mary coped in whatever way she could to make life bearable and comfortable for the children.

On October 3rd, 1918 it was Katie's ninth birthday and although she hadn't much money, Mary took her and the other two children for a little treat in a small cafe in Bacup.

Just over a month later and after four years of conflict, the news was broadcast that everyone all over the world had been waiting for: THE WAR WAS OVER!

It was announced at 11 a.m. on November 11th. This is the reason for the famous saying, "The eleventh hour of the eleventh day of the eleventh month."

Meanwhile Armistice Day in the trenches caused a lot of excitement, but also some confusion. On first hearing the news many men didn't know whether to believe it or not, and wouldn't stand up in the trenches for fear of being shot.

You'd hear the lads saying, "Aye it's all right, mate, tha knows, and I knows, but does Jerry know it's o'er?"

Only next morning were they certain, when leaflets were dropped from their own planes, and German delegations drove over the battlefield waving large white flags. Then, many thousands of men from both sides congregated together in no-man's land and, even though they couldn't understand each other, there was loud cheering and laughter everywhere. The strange feeling that struck everyone was actually being so close to the so-called enemy, who was so much like themselves, with all the same human frailties.

"Home! Home to our loved ones!" was the cry that resounded throughout the camps from all the exhausted soldiers.

Like everyone else, Mat just wanted to leave that rat-hole and make his way home as quickly as possible, but it wasn't so straightforward. The transportation of thousands of men had to be arranged and this was no easy task, as all the makeshift roads were mud-pits and completely congested for miles. They had no option but to wait their turn to move out, and for Mat, it was a couple of weeks or so, which meant it was going to be mid December before he actually arrived home.

The Armistice back home was celebrated spontaneously, as the news spread rapidly throughout the town. Thousands of people from all over Bacup, Stacksteads and Whitworth flocked into Bacup square where there was loud singing and rejoicing and laughter filled the air. People danced in long lines throughout Union Street, Stacksteads Road, and Todmorden Road and even the local policemen joined in.

Bands seemed to magically emerge from nowhere; they played the National Anthem and happy tunes like "Knees up Mother Brown" and many more. Never had so many people congregated together since the visit of King George V and Queen Mary, which was now more than five years ago. Mary was there with her three children, as were many more mothers. All the children were really excited with the goings on, and on this occasion, Winifred was fully aware of everything and enjoyed every minute. Bunting and flags were once again dug out from the drawers to decorate all the houses throughout the streets in celebration of the peace and the homecoming of their loved ones.

Over the next few weeks special receptions were arranged for the returning soldiers; the reason for separate receptions was because some men arrived home much sooner than others on account of the transport situation. On arrival home it was obvious to everyone that Mat had really been through it; he looked ashen and his face was quite drawn, and he had lost at least two stone in weight. His shoulder still wasn't right and obviously troubled him; in fact he was never again able to use it at an optimum level. He appeared a little round shouldered and had a notable limp due to rheumatic in his knees caused by constantly crouching in the cold damp trenches. On top of that, he was suffering from acute bronchitis and his breathing was quite laboured.

He looked round the little room that he had left what seemed a lifetime ago; it was all trimmed up with paper-chains, silver tinsel and balloons, and on the back wall was a large hand-painted sign saying, "Welcome Home Daddy." Mary was standing by the fire looking every bit as lovely as he'd pictured her over the last four years, and the three children were by her side.

He walked slowly towards her and gently clasped her hands, and for a few moments, he just gazed at her saying nothing. "Oh those beautiful blue eyes and black hair that shines like silk," he thought to himself, "them's what's bín keepin me goín all these years."

A wonderful tingling sensation flowed right through to his nerve ends, and he could feel the hairs standing up on the nape of his neck. "Eh, Mary, mí luv, come here and let mí luv thí," he said taking her into his arms, and then he started to sob. "Oh Mary … Mary, if tha only knew how much I've missed thí; I've dreamt o this moment for four years, and I even got to thinkín I'd ne'er see thee or mí kids e'er again."

"Oh, Mat," she responded tenderly kissing him over and over, "Please don't tell me I'm dreamín … it is true, isn't it, you've really come home?"

Meanwhile Katie was tugging at his jacket on one side and Winifred, who was now nearly six, was tugging on the other.

First he picked Katie up saying, "My, who's a big girl then? By eck tha's grown; I hope tha's bín a good lass for tha mum while I've bín away?"

Katie, who was a very loving child, threw her arms around her daddy's neck asking excitedly, "Are you going to live with us again Daddy? Please say yes, Daddy!"

"I am that, luv," he replied quite touched, "by gum I am!"

"And will you not be leaving us again, Daddy?" she enquired adding, "I want you to stay with us for ever and ever."

He looked at her little inquisitive face and smiled, "My first-born," he thought to himself, then answered, "No, Luv, don't fret thasél, Daddy won't leave thí ever agén. I'm here to stay, and I'm gonna look after thee and tha mum and tha brother and sister till tha's all full grown."

She responded by throwing her arms around his neck again and giving him a big kiss.

He hugged her lovingly for a moment, then turned and knelt down facing Winifred, he was immediately taken aback to see how much she resembled her mother. "And how's my little Win then?" he asked. "By éck tha'd just started to walk the last time I saw thí afore I left, and now look at thí."

Unlike Katie, her response was quite restrained; she only half looked at him with her head slightly bowed, and she kept looking downwards. He sensed her unease and after a moment, he added, "Well then, are you gonna give your daddy a big hug ó what?"

Hesitantly, and with tight lips, she replied, "Umm ... oh all right, Daddy," and then she cautiously put her arms around his neck and gave him a little peck on his cheek.

But as he tried to cuddle her, she pulled herself away and went back to clutching her mum's dress. He was a little bewildered by her response but understood why; but what he didn't realise at the time, was that he'd done quite well really, as Winifred was never a demonstrative child or free with her affections at the best of times.

Finally he turned to look at little Jimmy, who was now four years and three months old; the little lad was clinging to Mary's dress and partly hiding behind it.

Mat wondered what sort of response he would get this time. "Hello, young fella," he said, "do you know who I am then?"

At first the young lad looked rather shyly at his dad, then a big broad grin spread across his little face, as he replied in a childish voice, "Ye-es, you're my daddy, and you've bín away and cúm back again."

Mat was overcome by his son's reply, and the tears welled up in his eyes. "My little lad," he muttered all choked up, "when I left thí, tha was just a babe in arms, and now look at thí." He paused for a moment before saying, "I know tha's a little boy, and little boys are not softies like girls, but wud ya like to give your daddy a big luv?"

Little Jimmy looked deep into his daddy's eyes, then glanced up at his mum as if asking for approval, she smiled at him and gently nodded her head. No sooner said than done, the little lad ran eagerly into Mat's outstretched arms and gave him as good a welcoming as anyone could ever have hoped for.

After the greetings, Mary approached Mat saying, "Right now, my luv, I want you to sit thesén down in your favourite chair and make thasel comfortable, because toníte tha gonna be really spoilt cós I've got a little surprise in store for thí."

All the neighbours had chipped in small assortments of food so that Mary could give him a welcome home party. Everything had been prepared and stored in one of their houses so as to keep it a surprise, not only for Mat, but for the kiddies as well. Mary timed it well; the table was laid and the kettle had just started to boil when there was a knock on the door ... the neighbours were there with the goodies. They stayed just long enough to offer their welcomes, knowing only too well that Mat would want to be alone with his family on this special night. When the children realised what was going on, the house was full of excitement and laughter; all three were elated and especially so the two younger ones as never before in the whole of their young lives had they ever had a party. For the first time in four years, the humble house was alive with happiness and echoed to the laughter of the delighted children. During the little feast, Mat looked on in admiration; it was awe inspiring to be back home again amongst his loved ones. Every now and again, he would put his hand under the table and gently clasp hold of Mary's; she gently squeezed back in response.

To add to the occasion, after they'd eaten their puddings, Matthew turned to Mary and said, "Na-then, Mary, luv, before I forget, I've brought thí a present." He gave her two little parcels wrapped in brown paper and tied up with string; one contained exotic perfume from Paris and the other, a beautiful woollen shawl.

"Oh, these are really beautiful, mí luv," she said, "and me, all I've bought thi is a pair of slippers."

"That's all reight, luv," he replied with a smile, "just to see thí and mi kids again is the best present any man cúd ask for."

"Oh that's nice, Mat ... come here and give me another cuddle!" The children had watched excitedly as their mum opened her presents, and were now looking expectantly at their daddy.

He looked at them knowing exactly what was going through their little minds, and gently teased them, "Umm ... now let me think ... I'm sure there's somét else, but I just can't think for the life in me what it is." The two girls looked at him coyly with their bottom lip under their top teeth not quite knowing just how to take him.

However, little Jimmy let everybody know, in no uncertain terms, what he was thinking, as he blurted out excitedly, "Is it a prezzie for me, Daddy?"

Mat turned to the little lad with a smile on his face, "By gum, my little lad, I believe it is! Now let's see if I can find it." He started to rout through his kit bag, and to the young lad's amazement, he pulled out a tin clockwork car and handed it to him; the little lad's face said it all, and once again the tears welled up in Mat's eyes.

"And now it's your turn," he said looking at the girls; to each one, he gave a rag doll, the like of which they had never seen before, each with long plaited golden hair. Both of them accepted their gifts with sheer delight, but Winifred even more so than Katie, she'd never before had a doll of her own and she stared at it in wonderment, marvelling at the happy expression on its face.

"This is really mine," she thought, "my very, very own." It was only a rag doll, but to Winifred, it was the most beautiful dolly in the world and it gave her lots of comfort and joy; for that very reason, she chose to name her just that ... Joy. To Winifred that little dolly was her very own little baby, and she was to keep and treasure it for many years to come, right into her adult life.

She approached her dad with the doll cuddled to her chest, and, with slightly shrugged shoulders, she murmured, "Thank you, Daddy, I love my dolly, she's beautiful," adding, as she gently touched his hand, "And I love you as well, Daddy, and I'm glad you've come back home to us."

Mat looked down at her and was almost stuck for words. "Eh ... my little Win," he murmured, "and now is there any chance ó givín Daddy a cuddle?"

This time she responded with affection, and even though she wasn't as effusive as the other two, Mat knew he had the love of all his three children. That night the children went to bed happy and contented; little Jimmy kept excitingly leaning out of bed to peek at the place where he'd put his toy car; Katie and Winifred chatted away for quite a while until they finally fell asleep cuddling their new dolls. Mat and Mary chatted downstairs, and reminisced into the small hours before finally going to bed along with their children. The little house had been full of happiness and laughter; it had been a day they would all remember for the rest of their lives. The next few days were the run-up to Christmas, which meant that the trimmings were now serving a double purpose.

Mat had received a small gratuity on discharge from the army, but it wasn't much and he was already feeling concerned about getting a job. Even though he wasn't a well man, he tried to conceal his feelings but there was no way that he could hide them from Mary.

"Now you listen here, Mat Walsh," she said to him in an encouraging tone, "stop tha worryín wilta? We'll get by somehow; besides, I don't want thí to even think about it till after Christmas and the New Year. I know that the little money they gave thí won't go far, but it's more important that tha gets thasél better first. At least we'll be able to give the kids a little treat and still have enough left over to make this the best Christmas we've ever had."

"But, Mary, I ..."

She raised her hand and stopped him in mid-sentence, "No buts, Matthew Walsh, I know what tha thinkín, tha's a right worrit." She then put her arms around his neck and added lovingly, "Eh, luv, all that matters is that you're back with us, and we're a family again."

"Aye all reight, Mary, mí luv," he responded, "tha's a goodún, what would I do bout thí? I promise thí, I'll try not to worry about it again."

2: *the* ancestry

Christmas 1918 was the best one that they had ever had, but now the family had to face up to the reality and hardship that lay ahead.

The war left an everlasting mark on many men and Matthew was no exception. He tried his hardest to be the kind, loving husband and father he wanted to be but too much had been asked of and taken from him. He was never again the fit young man who had marched away so very long ago, but this was the fate of many young men returning home from the horrors of war. When the first group of soldiers arrived back in their hometowns they were given a hero's welcome and treated like celebrities, and so they should have been; but it was soon forgotten. Every man, having endured those long years of torment should have been able to come home and expect a decent standard of living, but this was not to be, and many of them had to live in atrocious conditions. The social distinctions that had blighted their lives before the war were still very much apparent, and the upper class just didn't give a damn. Because of the squalid and degrading conditions many of these young ailing men died like paupers .... forgotten .... unloved! Many of them were single men without a family, and, much against their pride, ended up in the Workhouse. One man in Burnley, for example, was suffering very badly from the effects of gas poisoning, and was bleeding from his ears and nostrils and, after being refused treatment from at least four doctors, was taken to Burnley Victoria Hospital, which was full, and then to the Workhouse.

People were bewildered because this was supposed to be the war to end all wars, and make the country a land fit for heroes. Many men returned with only one leg or arm, their nerves completely shattered. Others were suffering from gas poisoning, bronchitis, pneumonia, influenza and other ailments, only to be met with a seemingly don't-care attitude from the government.

It wasn't just the single men who were suffering; the aftermath of the war brought with it many grave consequences, including a severe epidemic of influenza, which affected many of the civilian population. The condition and immune system of many demobilised soldiers was so low that they had no defence against any virus for months afterwards, so countless many died of pneumonia and other complications.

Because of the dreadful situation, the nation as a whole became outraged, and the pressure of public opinion forced the government to provide help centres. A large community soup kitchen was set up in Burnley, with smaller ones in places like Bacup. There were write-ups in various newspapers highlighting just what the soldier had gone through, stating that he should at least be able to expect justice for himself and his family. Another sad event was that for weeks afterwards, there were photographs of young men in the local newspapers, who had been killed in action just a few days before the end of the war, much to the despair of their families who had been living in hope.

Most of the men were eager to resume work even though they perhaps wouldn't be as efficient as before. But there was no doubt that by and by they would do their civil work as well as they had carrried out their military duties.

Propaganda to raise public morale throughout the country was high on the government's agenda. Showing in Burnley at the Mechanic's Institute was the film, *My Four Years in Germany*. It was advertised as the greatest film ever made and the slogan was, "Every man, woman and child should see this film".

Peace processions would take place throughout the country every year thereafter to commemorate the peace. They were to take place on November 11th each year, commence at eleven o'clock, and to be called Armistice Day. On the first occasion a gun was fired followed by two minutes silence when everything came to a complete standstill. Anyone who participated in the first commemoration received a medal embossed with the face of King George V.

Mat got a little stronger and, although not fully fit, he returned to his job as a labourer in the building trade. He was a very stubborn man, and despite being unable to use his shoulder efficiently and suffering constant pain in it, he was too proud to apply for an army war pension to help support his family. Mary urged him many times to make a claim but his obstinate pride always got in the way.

"I'm the man in this house," he would say, "and I don't need handouts from anybody to help raise mi kids!"

"But, Mat," Mary would plead, "just look what you've been through and how it's left you. It's not as though you're not entitled to it, and by éck, we could use it!"

He'd snap back in an angry voice, "Mary! If I've told thi once, I've told thi a dozen times, I'm not gonna beg off nobody and that's final!"

"But, Mat! Why can't … ?"

"No!" he'd interrupt. "I don't want to hear another word on the subject …. right!"

That was all very well but his shoulder didn't improve, he was constantly struggling and found work very hard. Consequently, he was always tired which caused him to be bad-tempered and grumpy, hence he took it out on the family. The army life must have rubbed off on him because in the home he became a strict disciplinarian and his word was law. As the children grew older he set them tasks that had to be strictly adhered to and woe betide if they did not. Mary, a more sensible person, bit her lip and bent to his will. The hard times remained and nothing much changed for the better. Mary kept her part-time job at the mill and the couple pulled together striving to make ends meet. Katie took over the chore of going to the market for the cut fruit and other cheap produce and her mum kept up all the other schemes just as before so as to earn a few extra coppers.

Because Mat had to start work early in the morning he employed a knocker-up, who charged sixpence a week. It wasn't very much, but all the same, so as to save money the expense was shared with the next-door neighbour. It worked on the principle that after Mat got up, he would then knock on the party wall of his neighbour's bedroom, who in turn would knock back in acknowledgement. Incidentally the knocker-up was himself a weaver and it was just a sideline to earn a few more bob.

the **broken biscuit**

A popular joke at the time:

> What a short week! The Monday morning blues.

> If someone had a hangover from Sunday night and wouldn't get out of bed, the knocker-up would shout,
> "COME ON LAD, - day after tomorrow's Wednesday, then tha's only Thursday to géd o'er an it's payday."

Winifred was seven years and two months old when her sister Annie was born on March 27th, 1920. Annie was a healthy child but was slightly mentally impaired, and although she understood almost everything that was going on, she always had the mental age of a child. Mat was much more tolerant, patient and protective towards her than to any of his other children.

One year and nine months later on December 17th, 1921, Mary was born. Katie, being the eldest, got lumbered with the responsibility of having to look after her two younger sisters. During out of school hours, she had to take them with her wherever she went.

Winifred and Jimmy took over the chore of going to market, and between them they had to do the washing up and make the beds. Another job that all three had to share and particularly disliked was emptying the gerry pot. It was emptied into a slop bucket, which in turn had to be carried to the end of the block, down stone steps, then emptied down one of the community toilets. The toilets had to be cleaned daily, a joint effort shared by all the households. When it was the turn of the Walsh household, the task fell to the three children.

As they got older, Jimmy got a weekend job on one of the market fruit stalls ensuring that he was not only able to earn a little money, but was also assured of cheap fruit at the end of the day. He was a very cheerful, likeable lad and was very popular with everyone, including the local bobby. He got on with and liked everybody, but one thing stood out above everything else: he really loved his mother and thought there was no one else like her on God's earth. He was never happier than when he could give her a little money to help towards paying the bills.

He'd say to her in a loving voice, "Eh, Mum, I think you are the best mum in the whole wide world, and when I grow up and start working, you won't have to worry about anything ever agen."

On one occasion he came home all excited and told her, "Do you know, Mum? I've just got another job selling papers at night after school for the *Evening Telegraph*, so from now on I'll be able to give you another two shillings a week to help you."

She looked at his little beaming face and replied, "Oh, Jimmy, mi luv, tha shouldn't have, tha never has time for playin wí tha friends as it is."

"Oh please, Mum, please let me! I'm not bothered about playing out so long as I can help thí ... honest!"

"Oh, Jimmy!" she exclaimed. "Come here and give your mum a big hug, you're a right little luv."

He certainly didn't need any encouragement for that. He still kept his market job and on top of that, at the end of the day he would collect discarded wooden boxes, drag them home, then chop them up and make bundles of firewood.

He really enjoyed his paper job and did it for a few years becoming quite a well-known character around town as he stood in a corner of the square shouting in a loud Bacup twang, "*Telegraph*! .... *Telegraph*!"

Jimmy and Katie seemed to accept the strict discipline without question but Winifred, having a more rebellious nature, never came fully to terms with it and clashed with her father on many occasions, despite the consequences. From a very early age, it became apparent that she was quite high-spirited and strong-willed.

"By éck," Mat would comment, "I don't know who that ún téks after, she's not a bít like any ó t'others."

All the same, she still had to do her chores like the others, and, every day after school, she had to go out selling the bundles of firewood from door to door. One dirty job, which she hated, was having to rout for coal from a tip near to Old Meadows Pit where sometimes she'd have to scratch away for hours to find half a bucketful. Technically, it was stealing because it was private property, but the authorities turned a blind eye to it so long as no one pinched coal from the slow-moving Ginny Tubs.

There was a lack of good quality teaching in the schools and what facilities there were left a lot to be desired. Most families were poorly educated and living in squalid conditions; parents, unmindful of the implications, did not encourage their children to study. Consequently, on leaving school, many children were illiterate, leaving them with no option but to follow in their parents' footsteps and seek work in the mills or in any other kind of humdrum work. What applied to most families also applied to Winifred's family, but somehow she and her sister Katie rose above it; they attended St Mary's Roman Catholic School on Dale Street and both had a natural flair for reading. In any free time that Winifred had she would go to the public library. At first she used to read children's books, but quickly adapted to more mature ones. Due to her natural aptitude and a hunger to learn, she also became quite a fluent writer, but was never as bright at other topics.

Winifred's best friend was a girl called Mary MacDevit, who the same age, and from a similar background; in fact, she lived on the same block, and there were eight in her family living in a one-up-one down house like Winifred's. Mary was not a good reader and sometimes they would go to the library together where she loved to listen as Winifred read stories to her.

They went everywhere together including the Saturday matinee at the Empire, which showed silent Western movies and other films – the admission price was just ha'penny per child. Afterwards they liked to walk around the Town Square and Market Place, as both were intrigued by the many street traders.

There were lots of handcarts, and the vendors would ring bells shouting, "Roll up, roll up! Come and see what's on offer today, bargains galore!"

The pie man would walk around with a large basket on his arm and people stopped him to buy meat pasties, meat and potato pies and torpedoes. What excited them most was watching the muffin man as he walked about skilfully balancing the basket on his head as he sold muffins, crumpets and an assortment of oven bottom cakes. There were many more real characters like the Mussels and Cockles Man, Fish-man and others. Another thing that delighted them was the many door-to-door salesmen who peddled many assortments of small-ware; they carried battered old suitcases containing packets of needles and thread, cards of buttons, lotions, razor blades, elastic and lots of other knick knacks.

Mary was kind of sweet on Jimmy, even though he was a little young for her and rather shy, so she'd often go out of her way, saying to Winifred, "Oh look, there's your Jimmy over there selling the *Telegraph*! Let's go and have a chat with him before going home."

As usual, he'd give them both a hearty greeting, "All reight, Mary, how's it goín, hasta bín enjoying thasel then?" They'd chat away for a while, then just prior to them going home, he'd hand Winifred a paper saying, "Here, our Winnie, wilta ték *Telegraph* home withee for Dad and while tha at it, can ta give this here two bob to Mum for mi?"

On January 8th, 1923, Winifred's mum gave birth to another little girl ... Teresa.

Times remained hard and the poor conditions took their toll. Teresa was a very tiny, frail baby and Mary was unwell after the birth and found it difficult to cope. Within five weeks the baby girl was taken ill with pneumonia and died leaving all the family devastated. Mary was on the verge of a nervous breakdown and the family tried their hardest to comfort her, especially Jimmy who stayed constantly by her side in an effort to console her.

He'd hold her hands and stroke her hair. "Please, Mum, please don't cry, baby Teresa has gone to Jesus in heaven like you've always taught us; she's looking down at you right now from the sky and doesn't want you to be unhappy."

Mary looked at him with watery eyes. "Eh, my Jimmy, you're such a kind little boy and so very wise for your years," adding, "Mind ... you were born older than most other children."

He looked puzzled by that comment but just smiled and gave her a big hug.

Matthew had also taken his daughter's death badly, and was grieving very deeply but tried to hide his feelings, as he felt he had to be the strong one to support the rest of the family. Winifred was just like him in this respect; therefore, she understood better than anyone else in the family why he was reacting the way he was.

She put her arms around his neck and reassured him, "I know how you're feeling, Dad, and how much you're hurting inside and I love you for it."

He took hold of her hand saying, "Thanks, our Win," and after a pause, "Yes, and I know exactly how you feel as well, you're just like me. Anyroad, we're a family and we've got to pull together and try to get through this somehow."

Katie was listening to everything and the tears rolled down her face. She took her two little sisters under her wing and tried to keep them happy, and with Winifred's permission, she let them play with the two rag dolls that their dad had fetched back as presents from the war.

The funeral arrangements had to be made and as Mat didn't have any proper clothes he contacted the Tallyman, who was the local tailor and a kind of moneylender. He came to the house and measured Mat up for a suit and made it within two days. The price was three pounds, eighteen shillings and had to be paid for at two shillings a week. Another expense was for the funeral arrangements and that was eighteen pounds, that also had to be paid for weekly; however the cost was spread over two years.

Little Teresa spent her last days in her own home amongst her loved ones. The undertaker set up two small trestles with boards covered in linen on to which she was gently laid. On the morning of the funeral a service was held at St Mary's Church before burial in Bacup cemetery alongside her brother Martin.

That night, before Winifred went to sleep, she knelt down by her bed and prayed, "Dear God, I don't fully understand why You gave us little Teresa and then took her from us so quickly; but I feel in my heart as if I'm to blame. Did I not love her enough, cuddle her enough, care for her enough? I promise You that if You ever give me another little sister again, or any children of my own, I will always love and care for them till I die." She paused for a moment before adding, "Also, please shine down Your holy light on to Mum and Dad so as to ease all their pain and sorrow."

Ironically, in June, just three months later, her mum, Mary, found out she was expecting again.

In October, Katie was fourteen years old and started working at

Ross Mill as a doffer. Doffing was usually the first job that young starters were assigned to; although they were also the general runabouts, having to fetch and carry for the more experienced workers. The pay was only seventeen shillings a week, but as far as the family budget was concerned, every little helped and was gratefully accepted.

On February 9th, and almost a year to the day since Teresa's funeral, Mary gave birth to yet another baby girl ... Nellie. Once again, there were six children in the house. Conditions were still poor but the atmosphere in the humble house was much happier now.

Winifred had missed her other little sister very much and was determined to make up for it this time with Nellie. It was as if she had been given another chance; she remembered how she had prayed for her little sister Teresa ... it was as if her prayers had been answered. She really kept to her promise and helped her mum every way she could. Besides her normal chores, she enjoyed helping to bath little Nellie and changing her nappies, and loved nursing her on her knee whilst bottle-feeding her; the constant nearness formed a close bond and a strong affinity between them. Katie also loved her new little sister and used to care for her, but not quite as much as Winifred, as she always had her hands full with the other two youngsters. Little Nellie was a very happy baby with quaint mannerisms and used to make everyone laugh. Winifred's mum was much more content now so things were beginning to improve.

However, Mother Nature can be very cruel and does not take into account what is fair or unfair; for something unbelievable happened! Little Nellie was just eight months old when she too was taken ill and suffered the same fate as her sister Teresa!

There was something quite untoward about this little house with so much sorrow. To lose another sister in this way was just too much for Winifred; she spent the whole of the first day in the bedroom crying her heart out, as she clutched Joy, her rag doll to her chest. She could only remember the love and joy that the baby girl had brought into the home, and especially to her personally. The times she had helped to feed her, bath her, play with her and all the other things. Little Nellie had occupied a very special place in her heart and now it felt as though it was broken into a thousand pieces and all that remained was an empty void. She knew only too well just how the other members of the family were feeling; still, she couldn't bring herself to console them, speak to them or be with them. She just sat there with tears rolling down her cheeks staring at her little rag doll pretending she was Nellie.

The little doll's expression appeared to be saying, "I still love you Win; I won't ever leave you."

Winifred's bottom jaw was quivering and her teeth were chattering when her father came into the room. "Come on, luv!" he encouraged. "Come downstairs where it's warmer and get somét in your belly, we don't want anything happening to thi, do we?" He gave her a loving cuddle, then gently took her hand and led her downstairs.

She went over to her mum who was sat in a chair and knelt down in front of her and looked at her kind face. "I'm so sorry, Mum, I don't mean to hurt you; it's just that I can't stand it."

"Yes, I know that, mí luv ... your mum understands exactly how tha feels," she replied stroking Winifred's long jet-black hair as she lay her head on her mother's lap.

Once more the two small trestles were set up with boards laid on them covered with linen just like they had been for baby Teresa. On this occasion, Winifred stayed up all night and scarcely left little Nellie's side for a moment, at one point, overcome with emotion, she actually took her dead little sister into her arms and lovingly cuddled her. After gently replacing her back on the boards she carefully wrapped her back up and tenderly kissed her on the cheek. She knew that Nellie shouldn't have been picked up like this but couldn't seem to help it and just wanted to say her good-byes in the only way she knew how.

Next morning, none of the family seemed to notice anything amiss; however, when the undertaker arrived, it was apparent to him that the child had been moved. After realising what had happened, he informed Winifred's parents and she was given a good telling-off. Winifred was just eleven years and nine months old when it happened but the memory was to remain with her for the rest of her life.

Mat didn't have to buy a suit this time but they had to bear the expense of yet another funeral. The cost was added to what they already owed and the total balance was now spread over three years.

It was now December with the festive season fast approaching, so everyone had to show willing for the sake of the younger children, but inside, the overall feeling was sadness. As usual, Jimmy was very loving and supportive towards his mum; and whenever possible, he remained by her side.

Notwithstanding, there is nothing truer than the saying, "Life goes on" and the following Christmas, Mary discovered she was pregnant once again. Consequently, there were mixed feelings; they didn't know whether to be pleased or shocked.

On July 12th, 1926, Mathew was born. Just like Katie had had the responsibility of looking after Annie and Mary, this time the chore of looking after Mathew fell on to Winifred.

Like many other schools, St Mary's did not have a canteen for dinners; the children had to take their own sandwiches and the main diet for Winifred and her brother and sisters was bread and dripping and sometimes jam. Before leaving home for school in the mornings, breakfast consisted of just two slices of bread and a cup of tea. On returning home after school the main meal of the day was the corn beef hash with the crust on top.

Sunday morning was the only day when eggs were served in the home and each of the school children received half an egg. Winifred longed for the day when she would leave school and start work because then she would be able to have a full egg all to herself. She used to go to school very sparsely dressed in hand-me-down clothes from her sister Katie, which had been bought from a jumble sale or a second-hand stall in the first place. The clothes were always clean, but in comparison to the way other girls from more well-to-do families were dressed, she looked shabby. The clothes had also worn quite thin and were not suitable for the winter months as they didn't keep out the cold. At break time she would often seek shelter in the boiler house in order to keep warm. Her friend Mary MacDevit would shelter there too, as would lots of other kids in a similar situation. They took a risk, as it was strictly out of bounds to pupils and the punishment was the cane. To overcome this, they would take turns to keep watch and warn the others if anyone was coming. Mary and Winifred had such a lot in common with each other, they drew comfort from this and their friendship just grew and grew.

In spite of the discipline in the home, Winifred loved her parents very much, but there was one aspect of her father's nature that she never agreed with; he would never allow his children to tell their side of things. If any of the neighbours came to the house complaining that one or other of them had done something wrong, especially if they had been fighting, then he would chastise that child without listening to his/her side of the story. Winifred was determined that should she ever have children of her own, she would always listen to both sides and then sort it out accordingly.

There was one particular event that stuck out in Winifred's mind more than any other. Because of the way she was dressed, she was prone to being picked on by girls from well-off families. There were three girls in particular, who always went around together; their names were Sally McGough, Margaret Brennan and Emily Freeman. All three were notorious throughout the school for fighting; most of the other girls, including Winifred, were afraid of them. Sally McGough was the ringleader and the main culprit when it came to handing out insults; she was a tall well-built girl with a deep voice and wore glasses. Being from a more well-to-do family than Winifred, Sally did not understand her circumstances, and being a bully, she didn't really care. Winifred was only small and slim, but very wiry and strong with a quick temper.

One day, after being constantly mocked, she retaliated calling Sally "Goughy", a nickname she hated; Sally was furious and reacted immediately, saying that she would get Winifred after school on Smithy Back.

The news spread quickly through the classrooms.

"A fight! A fight! Sally McGough's gonna beat up Winnie Walsh ... everybody's gonna wait outside the gates after school."

Winifred's friend Mary was worried. "Oh, what are you going to do, Winnie, are you going to fight her?"

"Am I eck as like," she replied. "I've got to go straight home to sell t' firewood; if I don't get home on time my dad'll kill me."

"Oh éck, Winnie, you shouldn't have said that though, should you? You know how much she hates that name."

"Yeah I know," shuddered Winifred, "but it's too late now, isn't it?

I've already said it."

"Why don't you just tell her you didn't mean it?" asked Mary.

This didn't appeal to Winifred at all. "You're joking! Besides, she wouldn't take any notice, she's wanted to have a go at me for ages. Anyway, I did mean it; she's been calling me names long enough." She started to falter, her nerves were getting the better of her. "Oh bloomín éck! I'll just have to tell her t'truth that I've got to get home."

Mary screwed up her face. "Umm, that's all very well, Winifred, but I don't think she'll take any notice of that either; you're gonna have to be careful because I think she'll clonk you one."

By now, Winifred was so nervous she couldn't stop shaking, and her tummy seemed full of butterflies. "Oh, I hope not, we'll just have to wait and see," adding, "Anyway, Mary, thanks for being on my side."

Mary looked a little hurt by that remark. "Whaddaya mean, being on your side, we're best pals, aren't we?"

"Oh I'm sorry," Winifred replied, "I didn't mean it like that, it's just that I'm a little scared of what's going to happen; you know I wouldn't hurt you for anything."

They were interrupted by the sound of the bell and had to fall into line and march into their classroom. That afternoon during lessons, Winifred was extremely nervous and couldn't concentrate on anything; she was actually reprimanded by the teacher for daydreaming, which gave the rest of the class quite a laugh. When lessons finished a large crowd of children gathered outside the school grounds and Sally McGough, along with her two friends, was waiting by the gates for Winifred to come out. Winifred had no option but to pass through them, whilst attempting to do so she was pushed and shoved by Sally and told to fight.

She was now shaking more than ever. "Please leave me alone! I can't fight; I ... I've got to go home to do my chores, if I'm not there on time I'll get in trouble with my dad."

"Chores? That's a laugh!" mocked Sally. "You mean you've got to go out selling firewood like a beggar." The remark created quite a lot of laughter amongst the now rowdy children.

Sally's two friends also taunted her and then all the others started jeering and chanting, "Fight! .... Fight! .... Fight!"

Winifred looked at Sally's aggressive face and pleaded with her once more. "Please let me by, if I'm not home shortly I'll be in trouble with my dad." Everyone laughed and carried on jeering as Sally kept shoving her. Then Sally made a big mistake; she actually struck Winifred in the face! Winifred was absolutely fuming; the thought of her dad's wrath or anything else no longer mattered!

All her fears just vanished, the only thing she could think of was, "Right, Sally McGough, it's either you or me!" She lunged at Sally with the ferocity of a wildcat, striking her and pulling her hair with a strength from deep within that she didn't know she had.

When Sally's two friends saw that she was getting the worst of it, they intervened, but both finished up with scratched faces and torn dresses. After the fracas Sally had a split lip and deep scratches on her face; her glasses were also broken. Winifred had been helped a little because when her friend Mary had seen Sally's two friends intervene, she'd also joined in to help her; Winifred and Mary had certainly come out on top and both walked home in a rather buoyant mood. Be that as it may, that evening, Sally McGough's parents went to Winifred's house to have a word with her father, complaining of her unruly behaviour.

Without asking any questions, Mat gave Winifred a good hiding and sent her to bed for the night.

She tried to protest, "But, Dad, I was only...."

He cut her short, he just didn't want to know; all he could think of was that she had disobeyed him. That was not the finish either, as she knew that the Headmaster, Mr Cassidy, was also very strict, and that he had a ruling that should anyone fight within the school grounds, the punishment was four strokes of the cane. For this reason she dreaded going to school the following day. Her fears were confirmed, as directly after assembly all five girls were summoned to the Headmaster's study. The children entered nervously. There was a lady present who lived in one of the adjacent houses on Dale Street, which overlooked the school. She informed Mr Cassidy that she had witnessed the whole episode, alerted by the loud jeering and chanting of the children.

She walked over to Winifred and put her hand on her shoulder saying, "I saw everything, and this young girl is blameless. She tried her very best to avoid a fight but was left with no alternative, and was only defending herself." She then pointed to Mary saying, "And this young girl only tried to help her friend who was being attacked by three at once." Finally she turned to the other three and pointed them out. "It was these three girls here who were the culprits".

Mr Cassidy turned to Winifred and Mary, told them they were free to go, but ordered the other three to remain, and they were chastised accordingly. Later that day during playtime, lots of schoolgirls gathered around Winifred and Mary singing their praises; they had become celebrities. Sally McGough and her two friends never ever picked on Winifred again, in fact their notoriety throughout the school was now ineffective, as they now found themselves ostracised, and on the receiving end of ridicule and insults from the other children.

Afterwards Mr Cassidy sent for Winifred's parents, and informed them of everything that had happened, and how she had been the innocent party. No matter, Mat did not relent; he was too proud and stubborn to admit he had made a mistake, and there was no apology forthcoming.

Winifred understood only too well that her father had to be strict and lay down certain ground rules, but she felt strongly that he sometimes went too far because of his silly pride. She didn't like the way that he was constantly grumpy and bad tempered; his moods were the cause of many a row in the house. He was forever raising his voice to Mary and upsetting the household. During the constant rows, he would throw out insults; and one of these used to really confuse Winifred.

Amongst other things he would shout at Mary, "Yeah! Why don't you get back to your bloody orange mother?"

As a child, Winifred couldn't understand it at all, and in her confusion lots of thoughts would run through her tiny mind. "I wonder what Dad means, mi grandma doesn't look orange, she's the same colour as everybody else." The more she thought about it, the more intrigued she became. "Perhaps," she thought to herself, "this is why I haven't seen Grandma for such a long time."

the *broken biscuit*

Some of her thoughts were quite bizarre. "I wonder if my grandma Anna has turned into an orange monster or something." A burning curiosity began to consume her, and she was determined to find out what her father meant by "orange mother".

She pondered on the fact that her grandmother Anna spoke with a different accent to her mum and dad. Another thing that puzzled her was that her grandma hardly ever came to the house any more, and when she did there always seemed to be tension in the air. It was as though Winifred's mother Mary didn't like her own mother; the older Winifred grew, the more curious she became. Being the inquisitive girl she was, she decided to visit her grandmother, who lived in Stacksteads, to solve the riddle for herself. Much to her delight, on arriving there, Anna, who was going about her everyday chores, looked just as normal as anyone else.

As always, her grandmother gave her a hearty greeting, "Eh it's our little Winnie, this is a nice surprise ... what have I done to deserve this honour then?"

Winifred, being wily enough not to mention the real reason straight away, just brushed the comment aside answering, "What do you mean, Grandma? I've come to see you because I haven't seen you for a long time, and I was wondering how you were going on."

"Eh that's nice of you to think about your old gran in that way, I was beginning to think that nobody cared any more."

"Of course we care, Gran, it's just that you live such a long way from our house and it's not all that easy to get here."

"Yes fair enough, my dear, I'll go along with that, especially for a young girl like yourself. Right now, sit yourself down, our Winnie, and I'll make you a cup of tea, and you can have a nice piece of cake."

They got settled comfortably beside the fireside and had a nice heart to heart chat. Winifred was waiting for the opportune moment before bringing up the subject of being orange but felt rather awkward, as she didn't want to hurt her grandmother's feelings.

Trying to be tactful, she asked politely, "Grandma, why don't you come to our house much any more?"

"Ah well!" replied Anna as she screwed up her eyes. "It's a little bit awkward to explain but at the present time, your mum and I don't exactly see things eye to eye and we both feel that it's best that we don't see each other quite so often."

"But, Gran," protested Winifred, "you've got to come, you can't stay away from our house; you're mí mum's mum."

"Yes I know that, my dear, but it's not as straightforward as all that."

"Why not, Gran, what's happened, that can be so bad as to keep you from coming to our house? I've got to admit that I did notice there was friction between you both and I've been wondering for a while what it was all about."

"All right! All right, fair enough, our Winnie, there is something else which I think you ought to know, you're a sensible girl and certainly entitled to know the truth. First of all though I'd just like to say that I'm not laying the blame on anyone, it's just the way that life's worked out. You're right when you say there's some friction between your mum and me, but I can assure you that no ill-will is intended. Your mum just can't seem to accept me but it's not entirely her fault; if anything, the fault really lies with me. Anyway, I'll let you decide that for yourself." She then asked Winifred to relax and began to tell her a fascinating story:

"I was born in a small country village about a hundred miles west of Dublin in County Mayo in the beautiful country of Ireland in the year 1869. I was christened Joanna but as time passed I became better known as Anna. I was a very fortunate girl and throughout my young life I lived in a world of luxury and never knew what it was like to want for anything. My parents were very wealthy landowners and descended from many generations of gentlemen farmers. They were also strong practising Protestants and were known as Orange People because it was William of Orange who defeated the Catholic Rebellion of 1690.

They had many workers in their employ and each one knew his place, from the labourers on the land to the head butler of the household. The house was large like a

stately home with many rooms and was surrounded by
the most beautiful countryside. They employed servants
and I was waited upon hand and foot. However, my
father, though kindly towards me, was very strict and he
set house rules that everyone had to strictly adhere to.

Unlike my father, I was very easy-going with a very
caring and sensitive nature and I made many friends
amongst the more unfortunate workers during my numerous
visits to the land. As a teenager, I had long flowing dark hair,
a rosy complexion with a warm spirit to match; life was
good, it felt as though the world was made just for me.

I was just a slip of a girl of seventeen when I met and
fell in love with your grandfather; he was a tall young
Catholic man called John Callaghan and was three years
older than I. He was a hard-working young fellow, and had
worked for my father for six years since being fourteen
years old. On many of my rambles around the estate we
would often talk to each other and we became very good
friends; our friendship soon blossomed into a deep affection
for one another and unbeknown to us, it became obvious to
onlookers that we had fallen in love. We met many times but
always in secret for fear of our romantic affair being
discovered. However, it all came to the ears of my father
who immediately sought out John, whom he sacked on the
spot, ordering him off the land. Next he summoned me to
his study, where he gave me strict instructions never to see
Callaghan again and warned me that should I do so, there
would be serious repercussions. In spite of the warning,
John did encroach on to the land again and we carried on our
affair in secret; it was wonderful, we were so much in love.

Despite trying to be discreet, my father once again got
to know about it, he was absolutely furious. On this
occasion, he sought out John with a loaded shotgun and
threatened to shoot him, should he ever set foot on the land
again.

Once more, he summoned me to his study. This time

he was much more serious and he gave me this warning, "If you ever disobey me and see that lout Callaghan again, I will make you leave this house and all its comforts never to return. Also you will be written out of my will and your inheritance will be gone forever."

He looked at me with deep piercing eyes adding, "Take heed of my words, Joanna, I mean every single word, my girl!"

I tried my utmost to make him understand, but to no avail. With this threat hanging over our heads, you would have thought that it would have caused our love to cool. On the contrary, being a high-spirited girl with a mind of my own I defiantly refused to give up my young man. Your grandfather John Callaghan felt the same as I did, so without giving it too much thought, we both decided to elope to England where we were married. We arrived in England in early autumn and settled in the Yorkshire town of Kingston-upon-Hull on the East Coast of the country.

Within the next few months, I started to realise the gravity of my situation as I experienced poverty for the first time in my life. After trudging around the town for many hours looking for somewhere to stay, we finally found a small two-roomed apartment, which was damp and without any form of heating. Even so, it was a luxury in comparison to what we were going to have to endure in the future as our little money ran out. As John was only a labourer without a trade or qualifications of any kind, he discovered that work was very hard to find; hence, he just wandered endlessly around the town every day looking for any type of work but with little success. Eventually after a month of seeking, he got a job working in a foundry where the work was hard, the hours long but the pay very poor.

Just thirteen months after landing in Hull, I gave birth to a little girl, your mother Mary. I wrote home to my parents in Ireland to give them the news but my letter was returned unopened. Within the next five years I gave birth to another three children being James, Alice and Thomas respectively; on each occasion I wrote home to my parents in Ireland but each time the letter was returned unopened.

Your mum Mary was always John's favourite; he doted on her but he never showed much affection to any of the other children.

The poverty put a great strain on our relationship and there was constant quarrelling, which caused us to split up. John had some relatives, Mr and Mrs Tiddy, who lived here in Stacksteads and he decided to leave us and went to stay with them. He only took little Mary with him and left the other three children with me.

After that, I only remained in Hull for a short while. I felt so terribly alone, as I didn't know many people in that town; besides, I missed John and my little Mary a lot and I wanted to be near to them. For that reason, I decided to follow them to Stacksteads in the hope that we may be reunited, but alas, it was not to be. John and I were later divorced and I had no option but to settle down and bring up the other three children on my own. I was lucky enough to get a small terraced house to rent that was about half a mile from the Tiddys."

Joanna looked down at Winifred remarking, "There! Now you know where you come from, what do you think about that?"

Winifred didn't say anything for a moment, as she was so impressed, also intrigued.

After regaining her thoughts she responded, "Grandma, that was really interesting and enlightening; I just don't know what to say, I'm absolutely flabbergasted."

"Flabbergasted or not, our Winnie, that's the truth of it, every single word, so help me."

"I've got to say, Gran, that you were very brave, you must have really loved my grandfather."

"Aye, lass, that I did ... in fact very much so."

"Eh, Grandma, I always knew you were a little different from other people, but I just couldn't figure out why," remarked Winifred. "I know now who I take after and who I get my stubborn streak from." She paused for a moment, then added, "You know, Gran, I've always felt that I was from better stock and now I know why."

At that remark, Anna gently scolded her, "Now that'll do, our Winnie, you can't come from better stock than your mum and dad; money's not everything you know."

"Yes, I know that, Grandma, I love Mum and Dad very much, but you know what I mean ... you've got to admit that there must be a better way of life to the one that we're living right now."

"Yes, my love, I can assure you there is but in the meantime, your mum and dad are doing the best they can under very difficult circumstances."

Winifred had to agree with her there but knew in her heart that she personally couldn't settle for that. After another cup of tea, she bade her grandmother goodbye, then made her way back to Bacup on a tram. During the journey, she was quietly pleased with herself as the day had been quite eventful.

She smiled as she thought to herself, "Well I certainly know now what my dad means when he throws out his nasty remarks to my mum." Her smile turned to a little snigger as she said to herself, "Orange Mother indeed!" On arriving home, she couldn't wait to tell her sister Katie about her grandmother Joanna and how brave she thought she was.

Katie was as surprised and intrigued as Winifred had been, she also found it quite amusing. "Eh by éck, our Winnie, I must have heard mí dad throw that out at Mum loads ó times and I've always wondered what the flamín éck he was on about!"

Just then, their mum walked in the house carrying a basketful of groceries and the first thing she said was, "Eh by éck, but I'm glad to be home. Right girls, what dusta think ó puttín kettle on and we'll have a nice cuppa tay?"

They all got settled around the fire and were feeling nice and cosy when Winifred broached the subject with her mum. She told her of her visit to Joanna and finished by saying, "I'm sorry, Mum, I didn't mean to go behind your back, or anything like that, it's just that I didn't like asking you about it."

Mary smiled to herself at first and then answered, "Don't worry thasel, I should have told thí about it myself a long while ago. Your grandma is right about one thing, though, there's definitely no ill-feeling intended. However, I think she was being rather kind and protective of me when she tried to take the blame for the friction that you've obviously noticed between us. It is true that I just can't seem to bring myself to be loving towards her … I suppose it's because I was brought up by Mr and Mrs Tiddy and as a child I seemed to develop a deep resentment for my own mother. I know that I shouldn't still feel like this now, but I do; however, for your sake, I promise that from now on, I'll try my best to put it behind me and greet her well."

Both Winifred and Katie were pleased to hear this, but their curiosity was by now greater than ever.

Katie made this quite clear as she excitedly blurted out, "Oh, Mum, tell us some more! Please tell us how you met Dad and how we came to live in this house?"

"Yeah, why not, you're both sensible girls and certainly entitled to know the truth. Now mék thasel comfy whilst I try to carry on from where tha grandma left off. Right, where do I start?" She stroked her chin in thought, then began:

I only have a slight recollection of living in Hull with my mother and dad, as I was only six years old when Dad took me to live with the Tiddys. They were a respectable couple with a nice comfortable little house and they treated me very kindly, and I came to look upon them as my parents.

My father, John Callaghan, only stayed there two weeks because of the work situation; he decided to join the Grenadier Guards and set off for London. As I recall, he was quite tall and rather handsome with dark hair. He sent the Tiddys a good allowance for looking after me and he also used to send me gifts at Christmas and birthdays. It carried on in a similar way for three years and then one morning the Tiddys received a telegram from Her Majesty's Forces informing them that my father John Callaghan had collapsed and died whilst on guard duty; he had had a heart attack for no apparent reason.

After that, they legally adopted me and raised me in the Catholic faith. As I grew older, they told me about my real mother Joanna and my brothers and sister who lived close by in Stacksteads. I visited them many times and a strong bond was formed between myself and my younger siblings; however, I never felt the same affinity for my real mother Joanna, as what I did for my adoptive parents, whom I'd grown to love and respect.

I was always a very happy little girl, quietly spoken and very pretty with long black hair. I left school at fourteen and like many young girls, I went working in the mill as a weaver; the hours were long, the job very hard and I worked there all my teenage years. Although I say it myself, by then I had blossomed into a pretty young lady with a beautiful complexion, and the most gorgeous blue eyes. I wasn't very tall but I did have a neat trim little figure and, like my mother Joanna, a warm loving nature.

In Stacksteads there was a well-known pathway which was nicknamed "the Bridleway" because it was frequently used by courting couples. However, it was also a very popular spot where lots of young single people congregated, especially so at weekends or summer evenings. In this way, many young people met and got to know each other, and your dad and I were no exception. Boys and girls usually walked the path in separate groups. There was one certain young man called Matthew Walsh, your dad, who walked the path regularly with his friends and he used to exchange greetings with me. I really liked him and it was quite obvious that he liked me too, for when I smiled at him, he became all dithery; he told me later that his legs used to feel like butter, and that his heart would beat rapidly on seeing me. It became obvious to his mates that he was smitten, so they encouraged him to ask me out. He was a very shy person, therefore it was quite a while before he finally plucked up enough courage to do so, but to my delight he did, and I gracefully accepted. We both had very strong feelings for each other and we got on very well together. After just a short courtship we were married at St James the Less Church in Rawtenstall in the year 1908.

For the first year we lived in lodgings, then we were offered this small house to rent. The Corporation informed us by letter of a place, which was situated in the middle of a block of houses on Spring Gardens. It didn't mention that it was on a steep section of Todmorden Road below the Flowers Inn. Our enthusiasm was overwhelming, especially so mine, I just couldn't wait to move into our new home. The name Spring Gardens sounded very nice and appealing, but on reflection, this was not the case; humble as this little house was, though, it was our new home.

"We might be poor," I would say, "but that's no reason for not being clean." I'd been brought up with the saying, "Cleanliness is next to Godliness" and I firmly believed this. I was very house proud and especially so about the fireplace. It was my pride and joy and every Saturday afternoon I would black-lead and polish it till it shone. I also scrubbed the flag floor till, as they say, you could eat off it. Another must for Saturday afternoon was white-stoning the front doorstep. I'd also put a hearthrug down but I always rolled it up and put it away on Sunday evening for the following weekend. I continued to work full-time at the mill until I had my first child.

. Like your grandfather, John Callaghan, your dad was a labourer in the building trade; he'd been working for the same employer for three years, which in those days was very good. Both your dad and I worked five and a half days a week and finished on Saturday dinner for the weekend. Whilst I was busy doing the housework this was your dad's time to go out for a couple of pints at the local pub. Afterwards he would go to the Market off Bankside Lane for the weekend shopping.

On the Sabbath, we both donned our Sunday best and went together to the local church service; on Sunday afternoon, we'd sometimes go for a walk along Bridleway and talk about how we met.

In 1909 the electric tramway was introduced, it was quite a novelty at first and we quite enjoyed taking little trips on the trams. This was the regular pattern of events until October 3rd, 1909, the day you were born, our Katie. You were a beautiful child and never an ounce of bother; your dad absolutely doted on you.

Two years later Martin was born. Your dad couldn't have been happier; he was as proud as Punch.

"By éck!" he'd say, "God's good, life couldn't be better, a little girl, a little boy, and a beautiful wife … who could ask for more?"

He was right too, life couldn't have been better; we were just one little happy family. Your dad was a kind and gentle man and he just lived for his family. He was never prouder than when we were out walking; I'd push the pram with little Martin in it, and he would carry you, our Katie, in his arms,

During those early years, lots of families fell upon hard times; many firms in the building trade were struggling and the one that your dad worked for was no exception, and like many other men he was made redundant. He was the breadwinner and as we could not live on the pittance he received on the dole, he had no alternative but to go out looking for work every day. He trudged around town from site to site looking for an odd day's work wherever he could get it. When there was no work to be had in Bacup he went to Burnley or Rochdale. When he did work the maximum wage for a day's work was two shillings. He worked in all weathers and sometimes would come home soaked to the skin.

Mary finished her tale by saying to Winifred, "It was about this time that you came on to the scene our Winnie, so you know the rest. Maybe now, girls, tha'll be able to understand better why tha dad gets a bit grumpy at times, what with the war and all. Aye, allus keep in mind that he loves every one of us very much, no matter how he acts."

"Oh yeah, Mum, we do understand, honest!" the girls said in unison. Katie and Winifred were once again intrigued by what they'd just heard, and eagerly discussed it.

"Bloomín éck, our Katie," blurted Winifred, "they've had a hard life have Mum and Dad, haven't they? Like I said about Grandma though, I just knew that we must be from better stock, I've always had a funny feeling about it."

"That may be so, our kid," replied Katie, "but it doesn't alter the fact that we're stuck with our lot, there's not much we can do about it, is there?"

"Oh I don't know so much about that," said Winifred quite indignantly, "there's one thing for sure, I'm going to do whatever I possibly can to improve things."

During the rest of her schooldays there were many times when Winifred tended to clash with the school authorities because she didn't always agree with their strict ruling. If she had done something wrong she would accept her punishment without question, however if she thought she was in the right and a slight injustice was afoot, she would adamantly stand her ground in defence of her rights.

In spite of everything the Headmaster, Mr Cassidy, had a soft spot for her because of her upbringing, and how she had risen above it educationally. On her fourteenth birthday, just before she left school, he called her into his study to have a little chat and then gave her some friendly advice. She was to start work the following week at Ross Mill doing a labouring job and he felt sad for her, because he knew she was capable of far better things. The job she was due to start was as a carrier and doffer for the spinners in the mill, and he knew only too well that her future would be very hard and full of drudgery.

Looking at her with a reassuring smile he said, "Winifred, I'm very pleased with your reading and writing skills and I implore you to keep them up and put them to good use like I know you can. Will you promise me this?"

"I certainly will, Mr Cassidy," she answered sincerely, "I love my reading, and it gives me great pleasure to be able to tell stories to my little sisters before they go to sleep."

"That's good, Winifred, very good, because with your knowledge and command of the English language, you could go anywhere in the world. Oh, just one more thing before you go, I know we haven't always seen eye to eye, have we, Winifred? But no matter, I have always respected your strong moral views and the way you stick to your principles; if you go through life like that you won't go far wrong."

He smiled at her, then said something that was very uplifting. "Finally, Winifred, I just want to say that you have just two days left at school. Now when you leave this room, go out there and make them the happiest days of your life, you deserve it!"

Those kind words created a deep impression on Winifred and she was to remember them all the days of her life; to think that a man of such high standing as Mr Cassidy actually had belief in her; it gave her inner confidence and a wonderful feeling.

3: *the* accident

The following Monday morning Winifred proudly set off for work at Ross Mill alongside her sister Katie, who had now progressed to working in the card room where the cotton was compacted and prepared for spinning.

Winifred, like her sister before her, started work on the top floor of the six-storey building as a doffer. She was also the general skivvy, and was continually at the beck and call of the more experienced workers having to run errands, brew up and perform other menial tasks.

As a doffer, she was basically a labourer for the spinners and her job was to make sure they were kept going. With another young girl, they worked as a pair on one side of a large spinning machine that contained many bobbins, which were constantly being filled. The machine took about an hour to fill the bobbins, then stopped for approximately five minutes; during the stoppage, the two girls had to remove all the full bobbins and replace them with empty ones. To achieve this, they had to work very fast, taking empty bobbins from a large metal can with one hand, whilst removing the full ones with the other; the full bobbins were then placed into another can. If they weren't quick enough, the machine would start up again and the remaining full bobbins had to be removed whilst it was in motion. When the cans were full, they were carried through to the winding department, which was hard work, as they were very heavy.

Winifred found it a very difficult operation; on one occasion she cut the first two fingers on her right hand quite badly. They really needed stitching and she should have gone off sick, but she wasn't shown much sympathy; the fingers were quickly cleaned and dressed. Then she had to return to work. The damaged fingers and even part of her hand became quite swollen and very painful, which made the job even more cumbersome; still she had to struggle on and at times got told off for being too slow. She was also constantly reprimanded by the Gater-up for causing too many loose ends in the cotton; the Gater-up was a man who followed the doffers repairing any loose ends that had been made. Both fingers took a long time to heal and to this day she still bears the scars.

The morning and afternoon breaks brought her little respite because she had to run up and down the steps making brews for workers on other floors. In addition to this, in between doffing time when the machine was running, she had to take messages and other things from one department to another. The only time she could relax was during the dinner hour when she met up with her friend Mary, who worked in another part of the factory. They would go for a stroll or sit on a wall outside the factory gates, but sometimes they just liked to frolic on the large bales of cotton that were heaped up in a large warehouse.

Her working hours were Monday to Friday from seven o'clock in the morning till five-thirty at night with an hour break for dinner, and Saturday from seven o'clock till twelve noon. For that the gross pay was one pound, one shilling and tuppence, the wages were always paid on Thursday during the dinner break. On receiving her wage, she would immediately run a distance of more than a mile and hand over the unopened wage-packet to her mother, then sprint back to work.

For pocket money she received one shilling and eightpence a week, out of which she had to buy her own underwear. She was also expected to buy her own dinners throughout the week. Just like her school days, she took the same boring sandwiches but, on Fridays, she used to treat herself to a tuppenny mixture of chips and peas from the local fish and chip shop, which stood just outside the factory gates.

Times didn't improve any and the hardship took its toll of many families; one dreadful event happened in the winter of 1927. TB (Tuberculosis) was rife about town and many people were dying, including the young. The MacDevit household suffered a terrible loss, including Winifred's best friend Mary. Mary, her sister Alice and brother Tommy, aged fourteen, sixteen, and seventeen respectively, were all taken ill, and died within two months of each other from the terrible disease. Despite the shameful waste of human life due to the unavailability of good health care, the cries of the poor, who were caught in the web of poverty, fell on to the Government's deaf ears; nothing was done to ease their plight.

Poor Winifred was totally shocked and despondent, she'd now lost the only true friend she'd ever had and really loved, someone whom she'd always been able to confide in and feel at ease with. In spite of having her brother and sisters, she still felt so totally alone for being the introverted girl she was Winifred didn't make friends easily.

Lots of thoughts, all jumbled up, were going through her head at the same time. "Oh, Mary, why have you left me all alone? You were my best friend and the only one who really liked me. Oh what am I going to do without you?" Her mood changed from sadness to anger, "God! ... If You're up there in Heaven, why do You let these things happen? It's not fair, first my little sisters and now my best friend; it's as though You don't want me to have anyone to love."

In her confused state she repented once more, and with tears rolling down her face said, "I'm so sorry, I don't mean to be disrespectful, but I feel so lonely and vulnerable. I don't know what I'm going to do without my friend; everything seems so empty, I miss her so much already. According to everything I've ever been taught and believe in, she must now be alongside You in Your Heavenly Kingdom. I know we got into mischief many times, but mostly she was very good and kind. Please I ask that You let her remember me; yes, and when it comes my time to die, I want us to be friends again for ever and ever."

Her thoughts were interrupted by the shrill sound of the factory whistle, followed by the clatter of clogs as the mill-workers made their way home. It seemed strange that amongst death there was life; the world was carrying on as though nothing had happened. Winifred's parents knew how close the two friends had been and how badly she was affected and tried their best to comfort her.

Katie was very kind and supportive; she loved her sister and didn't like seeing her upset. "Eh, our Winnie," she said tenderly, "I'm so sorry about your little friend Mary; I know how close you both were, and how much you must be missing her." She put her arms around her and hugged her saying, "Look, our kid, I know I'm quite a bit older than you but if you ever want to come out with me anywhere, you can do." After that, Katie took Winifred under her wing and they went to the pictures together quite a lot.

Young Jimmy was also very sympathetic towards her, in spite of being cut up about it and feeling low himself. He put his arms around her, trying his best to comfort her in his simple way. "Eh, our Winnie, I don't like seeing thí like this, is there ówt I can do for thí? It does seem strange dunnit that we won't e'er see Mary agén? I'm gonna miss her too, tha knows, I can't believe that she won't e'er be coming to talk to me any more in the square."

Winifred clasped his hand, and looked up at him. "Oh, thanks our Jim, it's nice to be comforted by my little brother."

"Yeah, and it's about time too, our kid, what about all them there times tha spends reading stories to me and t'other little úns?"

"Oh thanks again, our Jim, it feels nice to be appreciated; anyroad, I'll still come and see you when I'm down town."

Even Mat tended to be more patient and easy-going towards her and not quite so strict. Nonetheless that only lasted for a short time, and as the months went by things returned to normal.

But days became weeks and weeks became years and soon it was Jimmy's fourteenth birthday. The day had arrived for him to leave school and start work. He had already applied for work and been accepted at the local coalmine on Burnley Road – The Old Meadow's Pit. He was only a slight lad, but on his first morning he walked to work with his shoulders back, his chest stuck out and his head held high with a beaming smile on his face. He was wearing a flat cap, which his mother had bought him, and carrying a tin water bottle on his belt and a bait tin under his arm that contained jam butties. Jam and bread was the main diet eaten underground at bait time, as the miners found that they tasted better than anything else in the dusty conditions. There was not a happier lad than Jimmy in the whole of the Rossendale Valley as he proudly walked alongside his fellow pit workers, the sound of his clogs going clip clop, clip clop! He was highly delighted, as now he too was one of the breadwinners earning some money, which would help his mum pay the bills. His first job was as a tackle lad, which involved carrying props, girders, blocks and other materials to the colliers working on the coal-face; because of his cheerful disposition, he was very well liked by all his fellow miners. At the end of the week he used to receive some pey brass, just a few coppers from the colliers, which helped boost his meagre pay.

By the time he was sixteen he had grown stronger and was promoted to a drawer, a more strenuous job which involved pushing tubs of coal from the coal-face to the pit bottom; it was a much harder job but he didn't mind because the money was better. When the tubs were full they weighed between three and four hundredweight. They had to be shoved over a long distance on a small railway type track through tunnels that were about five feet high. Water seeped in throughout the tunnel from the layers above and the lighting was poor; in spite of this, many tubs had to be drawn in the course of a shift. The method used was to bend down behind the tub, dig in the feet against a wooden sleeper and place the head against the back of the tub. To start the tub rolling, it was necessary to grasp the steel tracks, dig the feet well in against the sleeper, and then start shoving with all of one's strength, using the head, neck, shoulder, back, arm and leg muscles. The drawers would roll up a piece of cloth, a jersey or something similar, and place it within their flat caps to protect their heads; the rolled-up piece of cloth was known to the colliers as a pusher. Part of the journey had a slight downhill gradient and a partly uphill one; when going downhill the drawers tried to gather as much speed as possible so as to help the tub run part way up the uphill gradient.

It was very hard work and at the end of the shift Jimmy would be extremely tired; to make matters worse, there were no pit top showers, which meant he had to walk home in all his muck. The ordeal of filling the tin bath was beyond him in his exhausted state, and many a time he would fall asleep in the chair and still be there in his muck when the others came home, and for that he'd get a rollicking.

His working hours were Monday to Friday starting at six o'clock in the morning till three o'clock in the afternoon. He still kept his Saturday jobs working mornings on the market and selling the *Telegraph* in the evenings. Four full-time workers in the house now but money was still scarce, and they were still living from hand to mouth;

however, taking everything into account, their mum Mary put on a brave face and was grateful for small mercies.

Sunday was the day of rest and the whole family went to Church together dressed in their Sunday best. It was the time when Mum wore her best shawl, which Mat had brought back from the war. After the service, Jimmy liked nothing better than to go to the Town Square where groups of men from pits, mills and other trades would be standing on the street corners or leaning on lamp posts or walls chatting away. The colliers were different and very easy to distinguish, as they had the quaint habit of squatting on their haunches, and appeared quite comfortable as they smoked and chatted away. Jimmy, being the friendly lad he was, would proudly squat amongst them, not only for a chat, but because he wanted to show the whole world that he too was now a mineworker.

The summer of 1931 was warm and sunny and the morale of most families was a little higher than usual, including the Walsh household in Spring Gardens; the four breadwinners were in regular employment and they felt good about this, even though the wages were low.

Katie was now nearly twenty-two years old and quite outgoing with a loving nature. In her leisure time she liked to go to the Village Hall, which was a good meeting place for young people, as regular dances were held there on Thursday and Saturday evenings. Just recently she had met a young man there called Eddie Sweeny, and she was quite smitten; he'd asked her out on a date, they'd been to the pictures a couple of times together and were just taking it one day at a time from there. Winifred, having a more introvert nature, was a bit of a loner and spent most of her free time at the library; she took children's books home and spent many hours reading stories to her younger siblings, including Jimmy, and helping them with their reading and writing. She felt strongly that there was a lot of injustice in society and especially so against the lower class; she knew that there must be a better way of life than the one that she and her family had to endure. On warm summer evenings she liked to walk in the surrounding countryside, and, like many young girls, she would daydream of meeting her knight in shining armour, who would sweep her off her feet and they would live happily ever after.

She'd say to herself, "Yes, when I get married I'm going to have four children, and they will want for nothing, they will have the best of everything, including education; my husband and I will do everything together for them."

Alas this was not to be, and it is perhaps just as well that she didn't know what the future held in store for her. Before that very summer was over, she and her poor family were to suffer another terrible tragedy, which occurred one fateful day in September.

Jimmy got up as usual with his dad and after having a sparse breakfast he bade farewell and set off for work. The morning shift was just like any other, but for some reason Jimmy wasn't quite feeling up to the job and was a little behind schedule; it was just before ten o'clock and he was shoving his third tubful of coal. He had covered half the distance and was part way up a slight gradient when he had to stop for a rest; to do that, he had to put a sprag in one of the wheels. He stopped for a little longer than normal; in the meantime one of the drawers behind him had gathered a good speed on the downhill run and quickly came up the uphill gradient while Jimmy was resting. Although his tub had slowed down on the uphill run, it was still going fast enough to crush Jimmy between the two tubs. He had to be carried out of the pit on a stretcher and was taken to hospital. He had bruises on his head, shoulders and legs, but after being examined by the hospital doctor, he was sent home and told to stay in bed for a few days and that he would be all right after that. Poor Jimmy couldn't rest, all he could think of was missing work and not being able to earn money.

He kept saying to his mum, "Don't worry, Mum, I'll soon be on my feet again."

None of the family was too concerned at first because it was accepted as just an ordinary accident; however after a couple of days it became apparent that his condition was deteriorating rapidly. He hardly complained but kept whimpering on the slightest movement and the odd tear would trickle down his face.

On realising just how ill he was, his father sent Katie to fetch the doctor, but he refused to come, saying, "I'll come later ... there's always somebody ill in your house." He didn't come that night but the following day Winifred saw him in the street and stopped him; she shouted at him saying how poorly her brother was and that he had better come soon. He went to the house later that evening, but the first thing he did on entering was to complain about Winifred's manners; however, his attitude changed when he saw the poor lad. After examining Jimmy the doctor's face was ashen and very serious as he turned to speak to Mat and Mary.

In a quiet voice he said, "I am very sorry but I think that your son is suffering from meningitis; his condition is critical and he is going to need a lot of loving care and attention. My advice to you is to take Jimmy's bed downstairs where there's a fire. First though, I'd like you to get this prescription dispensed immediately at the chemist; give the lad his first dose as soon as possible, and every two hours after that. I'm going now but I will come again to see him after surgery tomorrow morning."

In spite of his condition Jimmy was still aware of what was going on, he kept holding and stroking his mum's hand and repeating, "Oh, Mum, what are you going to do, you are in arrears with the rent, aren't you?"

"That doesn't matter, Jimmy," she kept saying, "all we want is for you to get better, mi lad."

They brought his bed downstairs and Mat and Mary stayed with him throughout the night and slept in chairs; the younger children went to bed at their normal time but Katie and Winifred stayed up till around four o'clock. During the night Jimmy started to hallucinate and kept mumbling in a Bacup twang, different verses from one of his dad's favourite songs that he used to sing to his mother.

Daisy Daisy gimme your answer do,
I'm half-crazy all for the love of you.
It won't be a stylish marriage,
Cós I caint afford the carriage,
But you'll look sweet, upon a seat,
Of a bicycle made for two.

The following day, no one in the household went to work or school; they all remained constantly at his bedside.

The doctor arrived at around a quarter past eleven; after giving Jimmy another examination, he turned to Mat and Mary with a very grim expression on his face. "I am very sorry," he said sympathetically, "but you must prepare yourself for the worst, his condition is deteriorating rapidly, and there is nothing more I can do for the boy; I am afraid that he is going to die!" He knew that they were Catholics and advised them to send for the priest.

The priest came and was actually angry with Mary and Mat asking, "Why have you left it so long before sending for me, this boy is beyond all human aid? Why did you not send for me at the same time that you sent for the doctor?"

He then stood by Jimmy's bedside and administered the last rites, whilst the whole family knelt down in prayer. After this act, he left the house; all the family grouped together in an attempt to comfort each other as emotions were running high and everyone was weeping, including Mat.

Even in his weakened state Jimmy's thoughts were still for his family, but on one occasion, he quietly muttered, "Please don't cry for me ... pray for me." His mum was holding his hand and he kept repeating, "Don't worry, Mum, everything will be all right ... you'll see."

Both Katie and Winifred were heartbroken.

With tears in her eyes Winifred bent over him and asked, "You're going to Heaven, aren't you, our Jimmy?"

To which he replied quietly, "You don't know that, our Winnie ... only God knows that."

During the next few days he kept slipping in and out of consciousness; when he was awake, he was no longer aware of anything.

In his semi-conscious state he kept trying to shout, '*Telegraph*! *Telegraph*!' Then, suddenly, he started muttering, "The birds! The birds!" This went on for just a short while and then his hands started to move as though he was trying to raise his arms; his eyes opened wide as he stared upwards, this time muttering, "Mum ... the babies ... the babies!" His face had a special look about it, then the colour began to drain away, his eyes started to flicker, then close ... he became very limp … then gently passed away.

A strange silent stillness came over the tiny room, as all present were aware that young Jimmy had gone. The hush was broken first by the quivering of jaws, and then the weeping of all, as they could no longer contain their sorrow. The atmosphere in that little room was unimaginable, it didn't seem possible that such a thing could happen … it was unreal.

It was just over a week since the accident; in another few days it would have been Jimmy's seventeenth birthday.

Heartbroken as they were, Mat and Mary tried to put on a brave face for the sake of the children, but that was easier said than done. Mary didn't think she could do it, but knew, in her heart, that this is what Jimmy would want; however, brave face or not, she broke down and cried many times after the younger children had gone to bed. Katie cried more openly no matter where she was or who was there, whereas Winifred and Mat tended to hide their feelings more; but both grieved deeply inside.

Together, the parents had the awful job of making the funeral arrangements; it took place from the home, and his coffin was set up in the downstairs room recalling the terrible events of the past. The room was strewn with the most beautiful flowers from friends and neighbours; there were so many that some had to be placed on the stairs reaching almost to the top.

On the morning of the funeral, Mat helped to carry the coffin, which was placed on to a horse-drawn carriage. Mat took hold of Mary's hand as all the family stood in their appropriate place behind the carriage in preparation for the two-mile walk to the cemetery.

As the carriage pulled out on to Todmorden Road the pavements were lined with people from the neighbourhood, who wanted to give young Jimmy a good send-off; many joined in the procession and walked solemnly behind the family.

They had to walk approximately half a mile down Todmorden Road as they first made their way to the church. When they passed through Bacup town centre there were many more people who had turned out to show their respect. The local bobby was stood in the place where Jimmy used to sell the *Evening Telegraph*, and he courteously raised his helmet as the procession passed by. On reaching the church many colliers and Jimmy's friends were standing outside, all with cap in hand.

After the church service the funeral procession became quite large, and the mourners followed the carriage another one and a half miles along Stacksteads Road almost to the Toll Bar. They finally arrived at Bacup cemetery where young Jimmy was buried alongside his little brother Martin, and sisters Teresa and Nellie.

4: *the* decision

Following the death, the family was in total shock but by the grace of God they found the strength from within to carry on. They had to face the painful reality of life without Jimmy, knowing that never again would they come home from work and find him asleep in the chair or hear any more of his corny jokes. Once again, it seemed strange and unreal to Winifred that other people were just going about their everyday lives as if nothing had happened.

Mary was taking it very hard, and this time she didn't have poor Jimmy to comfort her. Her once jet-black hair had been gradually fading with the passing years, but within one week of poor Jimmy's death, it had turned completely snow white.

She seldom went shopping any more but when she did she would make remarks like, "Eh, my lad, I were walking through t'square today and I kept thinking I cud hear thí shoutín '*Telegraph*!' Lots ó people kept cumín up to me and sayín how sorry they were; I know they were only tryín to be kind, but I just couldn't talk to any of ém."

Both Katie and Winifred could see the agony she was going through and kept fussing over her in an effort to console her.

Katie knelt down in front of her and looked at her with very sad puppy-like eyes, "I know our Jimmy was very special, Mum, and nobody can ever take his place, but we still love you and we always will."

"Yes I know that, my luv; I only wish things were different and I could give thí more."

At that point Winifred intervened, "Oh, please don't say that, Mum; you can't help being poor; you've always loved us and that's all that counts."

Mary put her arms around both her girls. "Oh, come here, the pair of you! In spite of everything I know I've been blessed; you're both good girls even though tha doesn't seem to get a lot of pleasure outa life."

At this remark, Winifred couldn't help thinking to herself just how true it was. She felt that there must be something more than this humdrum existence, and oh, how she longed for it.

A week passed and both girls had to return to their jobs at the mill; their dad went back to his job on the building site.

There was an old lady who lived on Spring Gardens known to the locals as Old Ginny, and Jimmy used to run errands for her; Winifred took over the task and the old lady befriended her. After bringing home the shopping, they would sit and chat over a cup of tea by the fireside. Old Ginny would tell tales of how she used to work as a housemaid in a large house for a Mr Baron until he moved to London for business reasons, also that he still came to see her when visiting his relatives in Bacup.

She went on to say that she had worked in his employ for twenty-eight years and how kindly he had always treated her, and added, "Even now he keeps in touch with me by post."

Almost a year went by, and although things were never the same, other aspects of life remained as before.

Then one evening in August whilst they were walking home together after work, Katie said something that completely took Winifred by surprise. "Our Winnie," she uttered rather sheepishly, "I have something to tell you, I don't know what to do."

"What is it?" asked Winifred rather inquisitively.

In a more timid voice than usual, Katie replied, "I ... I'm three months pregnant!" and went on to say that Eddie Sweeny, her chap, didn't want to know, and that he hadn't been in touch with her since she'd told him.

Winifred was shocked and dismayed to hear this; instead of consoling and giving advice to Katie, she felt panic-stricken. Her thoughts and feelings were all mixed up, and in her confusion she just didn't know what to do. She knew only too well that being pregnant out of wedlock was really frowned upon by society, and that most people would shun Katie. The thought of her father finding out and having to face his wrath made Winifred shudder, even though it wasn't her who was pregnant. She couldn't sleep at all that night, so she made up her mind to do something about it.

Next day at work she told Katie how she felt and said, "I'm sorry, our Katie, but I can't face up to what's going to happen at home; I just can't take any more. I've decided that after I get my wage on Thursday I'm going to leave Bacup and try to make a new life in London. Please forgive me, Katie, I know that I should stay here and back you up, but I'm too scared of what my dad'll do; I promise you though that I'll get in touch with you as soon as I find somewhere to live."

"Aye, all right, our Winnie, don't fret yourself cós I do understand; I'd probably do the same thing if shoe were on t'other foot."

True to her word, after receiving her wage, Winifred said her goodbyes to Katie; they hugged each other, then Winifred caught the one o'clock bus to Burnley, then a train to London. She was very naïve about the wider world and only had a small bag, which contained few possessions, and just a little money in her pocket. However, one thing she did have was the address of the gentleman, Mr Baron, which she had obtained from Old Ginny, who had also given her a letter of introduction. She didn't know exactly what she was going to do on reaching London, but felt that this was her chance of making a better life.

She felt rather anxious as various thoughts passed through her head. "Is this going to be the start of the adventure I have dreamed of since I was a young girl? Maybe so, maybe not, there's only one way to find out, I've got to do it! I've just got to, I'll never find out if I don't." She rummaged through her bag and pulled out ... her little rag doll!

Her thoughts went back to the night her dad had returned from the war. She gazed at its happy expression, it was still unchanged; she remembered all the love and joy it had given her as a child. She just hadn't been able to leave it behind and felt it would bring her luck; it was to be her mascot; besides, it gave her some comfort.

Back in Bacup it was another two months before Katie plucked up the courage to tell her mum, who then had the daunting task of having to tell her father.

As expected, he got angry, shouting and bawling and calling Katie all the names under the sun. "You bloody little so and so, you're nowt else! You can get your bloody bags packed right now and get outa this house."

He was absolutely fuming and Katie thought he was going to hit her and started crying hysterically, "Oh please, Dad, please! Please don't hit me ... oh, mind my baby!"

He clasped his head in his hands. "Mind your baby ... I'll bloody well strangle thí!"

Uncharacteristically for her, Katie's mum stood in between them and intervened, "That'll do, Mat, leave her be! This is her home, and this is where she stays; I don't like the situation any more than thi but what's done is done. Besides, she's our lass, and we have to stand by her."

He looked into her determined eyes knowing that she meant every word; it made him feel a little uneasy, but he was unmoved. "Oh she will, will she?" he growled. "Well I'm telling thí right now, just keep her outa my bloody way! I don't want no more to do with her. Aye, and another thing, whilst we're at it, that baby's not gonna be born in this house ... she'll bloody well have to have it in the Workhouse!"

After the initial shock, things settled down a little, but were by no means normal. Mat didn't raise his voice in anger any more, but became very sullen and refused to talk to Katie at all; not one word passed between them; he wouldn't even take his meals at the same table as her, and ate alone by the sink. The atmosphere in that small house was unbearable. Katie, being the lovable, easy-going person she was, couldn't stand it, and constantly tried to get round him, but to no avail.

The months passed, and the time came when Katie had to finish work, the factory workers had a whip-round and collected some money for her; it wasn't much but with it she went to town and bought some shoes for her dad. When she got home she showed them to her mum and asked what she thought.

"Eh, that's a nice thought, luv; perhaps now, he'll come to his senses and have a change of heart. I'll tell thi what, put ém under his chair, and it'll be a surprise for him."

Katie was a little excited, yet also on edge, wondering how her dad would react to her little scheme. "Oh éck, Mum, I feel ever so nervous waiting for mí dad to come home, I hope this wins him round, then we can be friends again."

Her hopes were raised, but in vain; at first, when he arrived home, he didn't notice anything and just talked in grunts and, as per usual, he took his meal over to the sink.

He'd just finished eating when he spotted the shoes. "What's these then, who's bín out spending?"

Katie said nothing but Mary tried to smooth the way for her, "Eh! Do you know what, lúv? They've had a whip-round for our Katie at work and whaddaya think? She's gone out and trét thí to a new pair of shoes."

"She's done what?" he retorted angrily. "Well tha knows what tha can bloody well do with the flamin shoes!" Without further ado, he picked them up, walked to the door and threw them outside. "There, you can take them to that bloody Eddie Sweeny! He might appreciate them more than me."

The situation didn't ease up and carried on much the same until one very cold stormy wintry night on February 24th, 1933. Temperatures everywhere were well below zero and there was a really fierce blizzard blowing and howling; snowdrifts throughout Bacup were over six feet high, transport was at a complete standstill. The best place for anyone that night was in the home around a nice cosy fire. Of all nights, Katie picked this one to go into labour and from that moment on panic set in. Then, a kind of miracle happened ... her dad became quite calm and mellow.

Bending over Katie, he took hold of her hand, and said in a kind, gentle voice, "Don't fret thasel, mí lass, I'll see tuít that tha gets some help; now just lie thasen down and your mum'll look after thí until I get back wi a nurse."

He had to dig himself out of the house, as the snow had drifted as high as the bedroom windowsills; then he ploughed his way through the snow, over half a mile to the home of a retired midwife. At first she refused to go, as she didn't think she could make the journey because of the terrible conditions, she also dreaded getting stuck in the snow.

Mat was determined and wouldn't take "No" for an answer,

"Look! I'll get thí there if I've to carry thí on mí back, mí lass needs thí; tha's just gotta come." He finally managed to persuade her, and for part of the journey, he did have to actually carry her.

On arriving back at the house, everything went quite smoothly and it was a normal birth ... both mum and baby were fine. Tony had been born bringing a little ray of sunshine and happiness into the lives of that poor family ... their home was to be his.

The bond between Katie and her dad was now rekindled.

Meanwhile, Winifred had arrived in London quite late at night; after making enquiries at the station, she stayed at a Salvation Army hostel. The next morning, after a hearty breakfast, they kindly gave her a map of the underground railway and instructions how to find Mr Baron's address. It was a difficult task, never before having been in a big city or on the underground, but nonetheless, she found it a very exciting experience. She had to change trains and also catch two buses, but eventually, at four o'clock that afternoon, she reached her destination.

On arrival there, she gave Mr Baron the letter of introduction from Old Ginny and explained that she was looking for a job and somewhere to stay; she found him to be just as kind a gentleman as Old Ginny had described him. He said that she could stay that night in his house with him and his wife, and that he would try to help her.

"What kind of experience do you have, my dear?" he asked in a caring voice.

After informing him that the only work she had done was in the cotton mill, he put his hand to his chin in thought. "Umph, that makes it a little more difficult."

Winifred looked at him with her mouth agape feeling rather agitated.

After a pause, he reassured her, "Then again, I should have known, shouldn't I? That's all there is in Bacup, isn't it?"

Winifred was becoming more anxious by the minute as she thought to herself, "Oh dear, is he going to turn me away?"

Mr Baron saw the worried expression on her face and guessed what she was thinking. "It's all right, my dear, don't alarm yourself; I'm sure I'll be able to fix you up with something."

"I'm willing to do any job," said Winifred. "I'll work really hard and I promise you I won't let you down."

"Umm, I was just wondering; how would you like to work in an hotel? The work is extremely ..."

Before he'd time to finish, Winifred blurted out eagerly, "Oh, I'd love to and ..."

"Whoa, girl, just slow down a little! It's not quite so glamorous as it may appear; it's extremely hard work, the hours are long, and besides, I don't know whether I'll be able to get you a job yet ... so don't build your hopes up too much. I will say, though, that I have some good connections, and I'll try my best. Anyway, so much for that; you've been travelling all day and I should imagine you're quite hungry, how would you like to join my wife and me for some tea?"

Winifred gratefully accepted and that evening, they all spent a pleasant time chatting around the fireside. Both Mr Baron and his wife were quite amazed that Winifred had travelled alone all the way from Bacup and admired her spirit. They were also intrigued and enjoyed being able to chat to someone from their hometown.

True to his word, Mr Baron had a few connections and the very next day he fixed Winifred up with lodgings in the house of a lady, who had a blind daughter, and also with a job working in the kitchen of a large hotel. Winifred couldn't believe her luck; her life was about to change.

The house was about two miles from the hotel, but there was a good bus route. She had her own bedroom and there was a bathroom, a luxury she'd never experienced before in her life. Right from the start, she got on really well with the blind girl, who was three years younger, and called Maria. In the evenings, Winifred would sometimes read stories to the young girl, which reminded her of her brother and sisters back home.

On one occasion when Winifred went to Maria's bedroom, she noticed lots of porcelain-type dolls, all in beautiful satin and lace dresses. She couldn't help but compare them to her own little rag one. "Oh what beautiful dolls, have you had them a long time, Maria?"

"Yes, I've had some since I was a little girl; my mum always bought me one every Christmas and birthday till I was fifteen." She felt along a shelf and picked up one with golden hair, and handed it to Winifred. "I've had this one the longest, ever since my sixth birthday … she's my favourite and I call her Belinda." She was a caring sensitive girl and could sense Winifred's admiration. "Oh! I'm sorry, Winifred, did you have any dolls when you were a little girl?"

"Well yes, just the one; in fact I have it with me in my room," replied Winifred, who then went on to describe its happy expression, and how her dad had brought it home after the war; also how much it had always been a comfort to her.

"Oh, Winifred! I think that's a really beautiful story; do you think there's any chance that I could hold her for a minute?"

"I don't see why not," answered Winifred, who then went to her bedroom to fetch it.

She handed the doll to Maria who felt at it all over, then hugged it to her chest. "Oh, Winifred, she's so soft and cuddly, I can really imagine the expression on her face just as you've described to me. Umm, I can really understand why you love her so … it makes me want to cry."

"Thank you, Maria, you're so kind but she really doesn't compare to yours."

"Oh, but, Winifred, she does … honestly! She's so different to any of mine, and that's what makes her so special."

On some of her days off Winifred and Maria went for walks together in Regent's Park and Hyde Park. They also went around many shops and markets where Winifred would describe things to her. The friendship wasn't one-sided though, because when they went to art galleries or museums or places like the Tower of London, then Maria would tell Winifred about all the history and other interesting things.

It cost just one shilling for a daily bus pass, which allowed them to ride on the underground or any bus around London throughout the whole day. They spent many happy hours together doing this, taking in all the many interesting sights. Winifred got to know the complex routes of the underground very well and was really enjoying her new-found freedom.

Like Mr Baron had said, the work in the hotel was laborious, but she didn't mind, as she'd always been used to hard work, and besides everyone treated her with respect. Her job consisted mainly of working in a large kitchen washing pots and pans, and making sure all the units and working top surfaces were scrupulously clean, then she'd scrub the floor. In between times, she was ordered to help clean the bedrooms and make the beds.

Sometimes, she was called upon to serve on the tables, but this only happened when one of the waitresses was absent. She loved doing that, as she had to wear a pretty uniform, which made her feel quite important. She took to the job immediately and very soon became efficient at it, a fact that did not go unnoticed by the proprietors. She had only been working there three months when one of the waitresses left and she was promoted to waiting on the tables permanently. The hours were longer but she didn't mind, as she didn't socialise a lot and enjoyed the work; besides, with the extra hours and tips, she was actually able to save some money.

During her stay in London she wrote many letters to Katie and her parents and was therefore kept in touch with the course of events back home. This made her feel good for two reasons: one, that things were now much happier at home, and two, her parents had forgiven her for leaving home and wished her well.

On occasions, in her free time, she used to walk around the city on her own. She noticed smartly dressed men in bowler hats and pinstriped suits carrying canes and elegant-looking umbrellas. But, all around were many more people very shabbily dressed, who looked as though they hadn't two pennies to rub together. Others were on street corners with begging bowls, and the more well-to-do just walked by as if they didn't exist.

She could feel her hackles rising as her mind started to work overtime. "Rich man, poor man, no matter where you go, there's always the class distinction; it just doesn't seem fair that some have so much, whilst others have so little."

Her thoughts were interrupted by someone pulling at her sleeve, and on looking down, she saw a very pretty little girl with a dirty face and long dark straggly hair.

The little girl looked up at Winifred with pleading eyes and asked,

"Please, Missus ... can ya gimme tuppence for a drink?"

Winifred couldn't help thinking how much the little girl reminded her of herself when she was a little girl. She rummaged through her purse and took out two pennies, then once more looked at the little girl who by now had a big smile on her face from ear to ear.

"What the éck," she thought then put the two pennies back in her purse and took out a shilling piece. "Here you are, my dear, now don't spend it all at once, mind."

The little girl just looked at the coin for a moment dumbfounded, then let out a shout of sheer delight that gave Winifred a wonderful feeling. She thought how nice it would be to be able to raise the little girl as her own and give her a good chance in life. It also amazed her how so little could create so much excitement and joy.

The longer she was in London the more her confidence grew and she found herself venturing into places which in the past she'd always thought were beyond her. To assess the job situation she went into many hotels to enquire about vacancies and, to her surprise, found there were many opportunities if you were experienced. This made her more determined than ever to learn everything about the hotel trade.

She stayed in London for eighteen months, and then decided she wanted to return back up north. She felt the time was right, and that she would now easily be able to get a job as a waitress in Blackpool or Morecambe, from where she would be able to visit her family more easily. She'd enjoyed working in the hotel and her newfound freedom, but overall she missed the friendlier atmosphere of the northern people. She'd found a good friend in Maria and knew she would miss her very much, yet she felt so very lonely. She was actually feeling homesick, and wanted to be near her parents and brother and sisters again, also she longed to see her little nephew Tony. Besides, it was soon to be her twenty-first birthday, and most of all, she wanted to celebrate that with her family.

Her mind was made up; she gave her employers the appropriate one-month's notice. It was just before Christmas and she promised she wouldn't let them down over the busy festive period; this gave her ample time to make preparations and say her goodbyes. She especially thanked Mr Baron and his wife for all their help and gave them a small gift as a token of her appreciation.

"Well, Winifred, it's been very nice meeting you, and certainly an experience; we're both sorry to see you go, but we do understand why," said Mr Baron. "Oh by the way ... don't forget to give our regards to Old Ginny."

On her last day, her feelings were mixed, being both happy and sad. She said her goodbyes and expressed her gratitude to Maria's mother, then finally to Maria herself.

"Oh, Winifred! I'm going to miss you so much, we've been such good friends and I don't want you to go."

"Yes, we have been good friends, haven't we, Maria? I'm going to really miss you too."

With that, they put their arms around each other and hugged one another tightly and affectionately. "Oh, Winifred, please promise you'll write to me, my mum will read the letters to me, I don't want to ever forget you."

"Eh, Maria, how could I ever forget you; you've been a wonderful friend to me." Just then Winifred bethought herself, "Oh that reminds me, Maria, I've bought you a little present. It isn't much, just a small music box, but I thought you'd like it because it plays your favourite tune."

"Oh thank you, Winifred, that's a lovely thought," said Maria, "and now I've got something for you." She handed over a small box wrapped in blue flowery paper tied with a pretty ribbon. On opening it Winifred saw a beautiful gold-coloured bracelet inset with red stones. She just held the bracelet in her hand staring at it, overcome and momentarily stuck for words.

"Oh, Maria," she said stammering with emotion, "I ... I just don't know what to say, this is the nicest present I have ever had."

Maria smiled. "I'm glad you like it; my mum helped me to pick it. Anyway, Winifred, I think you're just trying to be nice; it can't be the nicest one you've ever had ... what about your little rag doll?"

Winifred had to smile at that remark, then, suddenly, she had a wonderful thought. She walked to her bedroom, and, after a few moments, returned with "Joy" and handed the little doll over to Maria.

"Maria!" she said in an affectionate voice. "I would like you to have my doll to remember me by. I've had her now for over fifteen years and she's always been my treasure, but I know if I give her to you she'll have a good home and be appreciated and loved … please accept her."

The tears started to trickle down Maria's cheek. "Oh, Winifred, I can't believe you'd give your little doll to me, she's your pride and joy." She hugged the little doll very tightly and shook her head. "Uum, she feels so lovely and soft; I promise you, Winifred, she will take pride of place amongst all my dolls and she'll always be loved."

"Yes I know she will, and that's why I want you to have her."

They were interrupted by the sound of the taxi that Maria's mother had ordered pulling up outside the door. It was time for Winifred to go. Maria and her mother helped to carry out her two large bags, which contained many more possessions than she had arrived with. To her surprise, Mr Baron and his wife had come to see her off, and once more he asked to be remembered to Ginny. Tearfully, Winifred and Maria hugged each other for the last time, then they had to tear themselves apart. As the taxi drew away, Winifred looked back, and the last sight she had of Maria was with a white handkerchief in one hand and clutching her little rag doll in the other.

As the train pulled out of the station she reflected on the last eighteen months and how her life had changed dramatically. As she looked through her bag for her tickets she pulled out the glowing references she had been given from the proprietors of the hotel.

She had to smile, she felt so happy as she thought to herself, "Winifred, you're going home but this time things will be so different."

On arrival back at her little home in Bacup, baby Tony was now eleven months old and crawling all over the place. All her family gave her a rapturous welcome and her younger siblings fussed all over her. Her mother, Mary, was standing by the fireside just as she had been when Mat had returned from the war.

On approaching her, Winifred was rather sheepish. "I … I'm sorry, Mum, that I left without telling you," she mumbled, "but I didn't know what else to do."

"Eh, my lass, don't worry thasel so, as long as you're all right, that's all that matters. Now come here and give your old mum a luv."

Then came the moment Winifred dreaded … coming face to face with her dad.

But her fears were unfounded, he actually gave her a hug saying, "By éck, our Winnie, tha's blossomed into quite a lady, tha makes tha dad feel real proud."

They embraced for a moment, then finally she turned to her sister, Katie. "All right, our Katie? Eh, but I've really missed you."

"Yes me too, our Winnie, we've a lot to catch up on and talk about, haven't we?"

Now looking straight at Katie, Winifred murmured, "I think your little boy is lovely," then winking and mouthing silently so as not to rouse her dad, she added, "Congratulations!"

Winifred then had the great pleasure of being able to give everyone a present. When she saw the sheer happiness on the young ones' faces after giving them some toys, she realised for the first time how her dad must have felt when he'd just arrived home from the war.

Among other things, she gave her mum a beautiful woollen shawl, "Here you are, Mum, I know how much you love that old one that Dad brought you back, but I thought it was time that you had a new one that you may want to use for best."

She'd bought a new modern dress and earrings for Katie, and a shirt with cufflinks for her dad.

What gave her the greatest pleasure though was being able to give her mum a little money and say, "Here you are, Mum, why don't you just spoil yourself a little? You deserve it."

A couple of days later they had a party for her twenty-first birthday and Winifred thoroughly enjoyed celebrating it in the bosom of her family. Afterwards, the younger ones pleaded with her to read them some stories before going to bed; taking everything into account, it was a memorable day. One of the things that gave her the greatest satisfaction was being able to take her mum and Katie out for small treats.

The family spent the next few evenings chatting together around the fireside; everyone was intrigued and listened attentively as Winifred told of her exploits in London. As she told her stories, she felt good about herself, but also a little guilty, because even though she loved her family, she knew inside that she could never return to her old way of life, having found another. On one of the evenings around the fireside, she told her parents how she felt and that with her new found confidence and experience, she planned to seek work in one of the seaside resorts.

"I can't say as I blame thi, lass," said her mum. "I could tell that tha had itchy feet. All I can say is tha's got our blessing and we both wish you well. But don't forget, our Winnie, keep up tha going to church and remember us in tha prayers."

Winifred then turned to her dad and asked, "And what about you, Dad?"

"Aye, lass, don't worry about it! Like tha mum's just said, I agree with her; both of us realised a long while ago, our Win, that tha's different to most folk around here, and tha'll allus do thy own thing. Whatever tha chooses to do, our Win, just try tha best and tha's got our blessing."

"Thanks, Dad, that means a real lot to me," replied Winifred, giving him a hug. "I'll tell you what it is, Dad ... you put on a hard front but you're just a big softy at heart."

"Now that'll do, don't be so daft, our Win, go on, gedda way withee!"

She smiled as she thought to herself, "Of all my brothers and sisters, I am more like you, Dad, than any of them."

Almost a month passed before Winifred decided that the time had come to move on again. Once more, she said her goodbyes, but this time with her parents' blessing. She had applied for and got a job in the town of Morecambe, which was about fifty miles away on the West Coast. She set off for the seaside resort full of confidence and high expectations.

Little did she know, that this is where she was to meet her future husband, and jump right out of the frying pan and into the fire!

5: morecambe

Once again, Winifred was on her way to a new destination but felt much better about it on this occasion, as her parents had seen her to the bus and both had given her their love. On making her connection at Burnley Central, lots of workers from weaving sheds, who had just finished work boarded at the same time. It was a single carriage train and consequently her compartment was quite full, some people were even standing; however, this was short lived as many disembarked at Accrington and more at Blackburn leaving ample room. Winifred's thoughts were on what her dad had said just prior to her getting on the bus:

"Now don't forget, our Win, what tha mum telt thee, keep up with tha prayers and going to church, and also write home and keep us in touch wí everythín that's goín on. And last but not least, look after yourself, my lass."

These thoughts comforted her; it was nice to have both their blessings. She rested her head back against the seat and could hear the sound of the wheels going, "Rat a tat tat; rat a tat tat."

It made her feel very relaxed and her mind started to wander, "How lucky I am, those poor people who have just got off the train living everyday, humdrum lives, and here's me off on another adventure. U-um and this time with much more experience and enough money to get by on for a short while until I find a suitable position."

Her thoughts were interrupted as the train pulled into Preston station, where she was almost tempted to go to Blackpool. Nevertheless, she thought better of it, as she had been previously advised by a well-wisher, who had worked in hotels, that although Blackpool was more appealing, Morecambe was much better as far as work prospects were concerned.

She arrived in Morecambe about seven o'clock that evening and found lodgings in a small boarding house close to the Pleasure Beach. Next morning, her enthusiasm was high as she went to the hotel to see the lady who had offered her the job; nonetheless, her confidence was a little shaken as there was a shock in store for her.

"I'm very sorry to tell you," said the lady, "but due to unforeseen circumstances I have had quite a setback, and I'm afraid I can now only employ you Saturday and Sunday mornings; however, if you take the job, I can offer you a room at a nominal rent."

Winifred was a little upset at first but soon got over it. "Now come on, Winifred," she told herself, "get your thinking cap on and get your act together, you've been in much worse positions than this." Turning to the lady, she replied, "All right, madam, I'll take the job, but please appreciate that I will have to look for another position besides this one in order to survive."

"Oh yes, that's quite understandable, my dear, I would do the same myself; I can assure you, though, that when the season gets under way I will probably be able to increase your hours."

On leaving the hotel, Winifred immediately set off in search of work but to her dismay it wasn't easy; a fact confirmed all the more after a week of looking. In spite of her setback, she looked on the bright side and kept telling herself that things would improve once the season started.

Her new address was 9 Grafton Street and her working hours from eight in the morning until one o'clock. The job involved waiting on the tables, washing up and cleaning the rooms. She only did the two mornings a week and her wages were low but at least she had lots of free time on her hands. During the afternoons she liked to go for walks, especially on the sea front along the promenade. One particular stretch was a favourite haunt frequented by young folk where they congregated together; it reminded her of the Bridleway in Stacksteads. She noticed one group in particular because a certain young man, with sandy-coloured hair, stood out from the crowd, he appeared to be the centre of attention.

On one occasion whilst passing, he nodded to her and politely asked, "Hello, we've noticed you walking by a few times on your own, are you from around here?"

Winifred was dumbfounded and just looked at him; her legs went all weak and wobbly just like her dad's used to do when Mary talked to him all those years ago. The young man wasn't very tall but there was something very appealing about him; he had the most gorgeous blue eyes that she'd ever seen and when he smiled, his face just lit up.

She felt rather strange, as never in her whole life, had anyone made her feel this way before; somewhat taken aback she stuttered, "Well ... um ... I ... I'm from a little place called Bacup."

"Ah yes!" he reacted enthusiastically, "I know the place, it's only about eight miles from where I live."

She was a little surprised at his response. "Really? And where might that be then?"

"Oh it's a place called Burnley and I live near to the town centre in the Croft Area with my mother and sister."

Winifred's head was in a bit of a spin; her first impulse was to ask, "Oh you're not married then?" But she thought better of it and enquired instead, "And what are you doing here then, are you on holiday or something?"

He gave a little laugh, "No such luck! I'm working over here."

To Winifred's disappointment, a very pretty blonde girl gently tugged at his sleeve asking, "Excuse me, John, are you coming, the others are leaving us."

"Yes righto, I won't be a minute," he replied, then turning to Winifed, "I'm sorry, I have to go, we're going to the boating lake." Then, he added as an after-thought, "By the way, I'm John, how would you like to come with us?" At that, the pretty young girl took hold of his hand giving him another gentle reminder.

Winifred felt her heart beating much faster than normal, as she really did want to go with him but she couldn't see herself fitting in with a crowd, so politely refused, "Oh I'm sorry but I can't; I have somewhere to go this afternoon." It was a white lie but she didn't know what else to say under the circumstances; she only hoped she wouldn't regret it later.

"Oh what a shame! Well never mind, maybe another time, eh?" The young man then very politely said goodbye and set off for the boating lake, linked up to the blonde girl. Winifred started to walk off but couldn't resist looking back until he had gradually disappeared into the distance. On the way back, she decided to have a look on the Pleasure Beach and whilst walking by the office, she noticed a poster displaying a vacancy for a cashier on the Ghost Train.

"Why not?" she thought. "It's not exactly what I want but it's better than nothing, and at least it'll put me on till something better crops up." On making enquiries, she was asked by the manager if she had any experience, to which she replied, "Well no, not exactly, but I am used to dealing with people," she then went on to tell him of her experience in London.

The manager was impressed by her honesty and self-assurance and said to her, "Right, young lady, I'm willing to give you a chance, you can start next Monday. However, for starters, until the season gets under way properly, I can only offer you twenty hours a week working mornings only. Mind you, next weekend is the start of the Easter period; it's usually very busy so you will be expected to work much longer hours on Good Friday and Easter Monday. How do you feel about that?"

"Oh that will suit me fine, sir, and I promise I won't let you down."

Taking everything into account, she actually hadn't done too badly, for although it was still only in the quiet season, at least she felt as if she was on her way. That evening, she stayed in her room and started to read a book but couldn't concentrate, as her thoughts kept floating back to the young man. She couldn't understand why she felt this way; it wasn't as if she'd never been spoken to by a man before, or asked out for that matter. In fact, whilst in London, she'd been asked out several times by good-looking well-to-do gentlemen, but had never been interested and always declined.

"So why this time," she thought as her mind started to wander. "I can't understand it, there's not much about him really; he's only small and slim and ... mind! I never did like big men. Anyway, why am I going on like this? He already has a girlfriend and I have to admit she's quite pretty." Her confidence waned a little and she started to talk to herself, "I know I'm slim and have nice black hair but they are my only redeeming features where as she is so bubbly and attractive. Oh, but he's so nice, and … u-m, that smile and those eyes, he was so kind and … stop it, Winifred! Don't keep going on like this, it's done, finished! You may never see him again." Be that as it may, no matter how she tried, she couldn't get the mixed emotions out of her head.

That week, in the afternoons, she went for walks along the promenade but although she saw the group he had been with, neither he nor the blonde girl were amongst them; subsequently, she started to daydream once again. "Ah well, that's it, he mustn't be interested. Come now, Winifred, you'll just have to forget him."

The following Monday morning she started her new job on the Pleasure Beach and actually found it quite interesting, as it gave her plenty of opportunity to meet different people. The first four days were uneventful, as it was rather quiet; this was good in a way because at least it gave her ample opportunity to learn the job and get herself organised in preparation for Easter. The next day was Good Friday and being forewarned, she expected it to be very busy; however, something happened that took her completely by surprise.

She had just entered the cash box when she heard a voice behind her. "Hello there, mystery girl, what are you doing here?" She turned, and to her amazement there, stood in front of her, was the young man she had been daydreaming about. For a moment she was speechless, as once again she noticed his deep blue eyes and sandy-coloured hair, which was parted to the right with a little quiff and he had the most gorgeous smile.

Finally, she managed to blurt out, "Oh I'm sorry, you took me by surprise. It's funny really, I could well ask you the same question; I work here, how about you?"

"Well now that is a surprise; you're certainly right about one thing, and it sure is funny. You see, I work here too."

Winifred couldn't believe it. "You're joking, then why have I not seen you before?"

Being a smooth talker and very astute, he saw this as his opportunity. "Ah well," he replied, "you see, I only work for the Pleasure Beach during the busy periods, as I am floater; that is to say I work on the Dodgems, the Waltzers, the Big Wheel or anywhere else

I'm needed. But today must be my lucky day because I'm working on the Ghost Train, and with such a charming companion too."

She enjoyed the compliment but felt a little awkward and blushed. "Now now; that'll do! Come on, we'd better start work!"

He sensed how she felt and said with a twinkle in his eye, "Look, I'm sorry if I've embarrassed you, but I certainly didn't mean to. It's just that I've noticed you walking by us on the promenade with your long black hair blowing in the wind, and I've never ever seen anything more beautiful."

"Ah, now I know you're teasing."

"No, honest I'm not, I really think that your hair is absolutely fabulous. Anyway, I'll say no more except that since we have to work together, would you please tell me your name? You've got to admit you have the advantage over me, because at least you know mine."

She had to agree with him there, "Yes, fair enough … my name is Winifred."

"Ah, Win! That has a nice ring to it."

"That's strange," she thought to herself. "No one except my dad has ever called me by that name before." She just had to ask him, "Excuse me but why did you call me by that name? No one in my whole life other than my dad has ever called me Win before."

"No reason except that I think it suits you and from now on it's going to be my pet name for you too … all right, Win?"

She liked that, and from that moment on there was a definite affinity between them.

The day turned out bright and sunny and the Pleasure Beach was packed to capacity. They worked right through till eight o'clock that night with only two short breaks for dinner and tea, but John fetched her a few drinks of tea in between, and chatted with her for brief moments.

At the end of the shift, he deftly wiped a little sweat from his brow, then approached her. "Well, Win, that's the end of our first working day together, and I must admit I've really enjoyed it, how about you?"

"Yes, I've got to admit I enjoyed it too, John; in fact, very much so."

"In that case, Win, how would you like to go for a drink to celebrate the occasion?"

"Oh I'm sorry, I don't think that would be a very good idea; besides, you already have a girlfriend."

"Oh you mean Sally, the blonde girl I was with on the day I talked to you on the promenade? Ah well, you've got it wrong there, Win; she's just a good friend from the group that I meet up with. I can assure you there's nothing serious between us."

She was quite pleased about that, but then started to ponder on what to say; he could see the bemused look on her face and prompted her for a reply, "Well, what do you say?"

"Well all right; but only on the condition that we go to the bar close to the Pleasure Beach, because I don't want to be out too late with having to work early tomorrow."

"Righto, you're on," he said offering his hand, "come on then, let's go before you change your mind." She readily accepted and they walked off together like a courting couple.

Inside the bar, she felt a little nervous but he soon put her at ease. "Well, Win; what would you like to drink? Just say the word and it's yours."

"Could I just have a plain orange drink please?"

"Certainly, how would you like a small gin as well, just to liven it up a little?"

"Oh no thank you, I've never had an alcoholic drink before and, besides, you're not trying to get me tipsy, are you?"

He gave her a cheeky grin. "Now come on, Win; give me a little more credit than that … it's just that you seem so uptight, and I thought it would relax you a little."

She looked into his laughing eyes and was soon won over. "Yes all right, go on then, I'll just have the one; I have to admit I am a little on edge."

They had a couple more drinks after that and just talked the evening away; she had never in her whole life been able to talk so freely to anyone before; she went on to tell him of her life in Bacup and her exploits in London.

He was really smitten with her and expressed it openly. "You know something, Win? I'm really impressed and I think you are a very brave and courageous woman to do what you have done … you are indeed a very special kind of lady."

"No I'm not really, anyone living in those conditions would have done the same."

"I'm sorry, Win, I can't agree with you there, I think you're too modest; what about all the thousands who do, and yet they do nothing to improve their situation. Once again, I have to say I think you are somebody very special." He certainly treated her like a lady and made her feel very special.

"Like you, Winifred, I'm from a big family too; I have a half brother called Ted, who is the eldest, and five sisters, all older than me except for Lily; so you see, I have been rather spoiled. My father had his own prosperous fruit business, but he died four years ago and as yet, I haven't come to terms with it. He left the business to me but I acted rather irresponsibly and let it run down; the only excuse I can make is that I wasn't interested at the time; I was devastated by his death."

"Oh that's understandable, John; he couldn't have been all that old, could he?"

For the first time, she noticed a hint of sadness in his face, "No, he wasn't – just fifty-eight in fact – and the tragic thing is that, with insight, his death could have been avoided. You see, all that happened was that he got a spell in one of his fingers whilst lifting a wooden box and he didn't have it attended to straight away. He wasn't too concerned at first as he thought he'd removed the entire splinter himself; but later it became infected and started to fester badly, and despite having hospital treatment, gangrene set in and the finger had to be amputated. In spite of this, the gangrene spread even further into his hand, and then he was informed that it too would have to be amputated. He adamantly refused to have another operation and sadly his condition deteriorated and he died. His name was James Albert and I've missed him so much, and should I ever have a son of my own, I would dearly love to call him James after my dad."

His expression changed once more to cheerfulness. "Anyway, why am I going on about sad things? We're here to enjoy ourselves."

"Oh that's all right, John, I enjoyed you telling me about your family, besides, I've talked plenty about mine, haven't I?" At that moment, they were interrupted by the sound of the bell ringing for last orders.

"My goodness," quipped Winifred, "I didn't realise it was that time already, doesn't time fly when you're enjoying yourself?"

"Oh I'm glad to hear that, Win, at least you've enjoyed yourself then?"

"Yes I have, John; very much so, thank you. Now could I buy you a drink to show my appreciation?"

"Oh no, Win! I wouldn't hear of it; anyway, I can assure you the pleasure's been mine. All it leaves now is for me to walk you home."

"Oh that doesn't matter, I only live a couple of streets away, I can ..."

"I wouldn't dream of it," he interrupted, "when I take a lady out I always escort her home." He then gently took her hand and they walked back to her lodgings together. On the way, he reflected on the day saying how much he was looking forward to working with her again the following day.

Just then, she realised something. "Oh I'm sorry, John, I haven't told you yet, have I?" she said. "But tomorrow and Sunday, I'm working in a hotel; I'm only employed to work from Monday to Friday on the Ghost Train."

"Oh, what a let down!" he exclaimed. "I thought it was too good to be true; I was so looking forward to working with you again tomorrow." He looked a little despondent then said, "In that case, I'd better ask you now; can I take you out tomorrow evening? I'd love to take you to a dance."

"Yes, I'd like that very much," replied Winifred all excited, "except for one little snag ... I can't dance."

"Oh that's no problem, I've been dancing since before I could walk." He gave her a reassuring smile. "No, seriously, Win, all joking aside, I love dancing and I know most of the dances, and it would be my pleasure to teach you some of them."

He looked at his watch then gently teased her, "Well, what do you know, it's almost Cinderella time already. I'd best be on my way." He gently squeezed her hand, gave her a little peck on her cheek, then bade her goodnight before leaving.

Back in her room as she was getting ready for bed, she couldn't help but reminisce over the wonderful day, and just couldn't believe her luck.

"I've never been so happy in the whole of my life; this John is all I've ever wanted in a man, he's such a gentleman. The way we met, it must be fate and ... u-um, he's so lovely."

She didn't get much sleep that night, as she was just too excited; she tossed and turned endlessly before eventually nodding off in the early hours. She'd wanted so much to sleep so that the next morning would come quickly, then the evening, when she would see John again.

On awakening, the light was shining through her bedroom window. "Oh what a beautiful morning," she said to herself, "and in more ways than one ... I've so much to look forward to." She worked heartily doing all her chores in the hotel and enjoyed it, but couldn't help wishing she was working with John on the Pleasure Beach.

She kept thinking how well they worked together. "Oh, with a man like him, both of us pulling together; I feel we could conquer the world." After finishing her shift, she was in two minds about visiting him for a little chat, but thought better of it. "No, I'd better not, he may be very busy like yesterday; besides, he may think I'm a little pushy."

The afternoon dragged on, but eventually the evening arrived and she could feel herself getting all excited at the prospect of seeing him again. She dressed herself up in a pretty blue dress and cream-coloured shoes, and went to great lengths to make herself look pretty, brushing her hair till it shone like silk. On checking herself in the mirror, she had to admit that she looked very presentable and she was especially proud of her beautiful hair.

All the same, she felt extremely nervous and couldn't stop shaking. "Come now, Winifred, stop this nonsense and pull yourself together, it's only a date." Then she became a little flustered as her imagination flared up again, "Oh I hope he turns up, I don't know what I'll do if he doesn't. Stop it, Winifred, have a bit more confidence in yourself; even if he doesn't, it won't be the end of the world."

After regaining her composure, she shrugged her shoulders and set off to meet him with her head held high. He had arranged to meet her at nine o'clock outside the Palatine Club near to the monumental clock. As she neared her rendezvous, she realised all her fears were unfounded when she spotted him in the doorway. He was very smartly dressed in a light brown suit with matching shoes and sporting a white shirt and tie. As she approached him, her heart seemed to skip a beat as she felt it beating faster and faster.

On seeing her, his eyes lit up. "Ah, Win, I'm so glad you've come; I've been really looking forward to this moment all day, and at times I kept getting funny feelings that you wouldn't turn up at all." He kissed her on the cheek and then complimented her, "My, Winifred, I think you look gorgeous, and your hair is absolutely beautiful; it's so black it has a blue tint in it."

This made her feel good and boosted her confidence, but all the same, she blushed a little as she answered, "Thank you, John, I think you look gorgeous as well."

"Righto, Win; I've got to tell you that I really missed you today, and I mean to make up for it tonight by taking you dancing, as promised, to the Winter Gardens. Have you ever been there before?"

"No I haven't, but I have walked past it a few times and wondered what it was like inside."

"Oh it's great! It has many facilities such as variety shows, an aquarium, a cafe and built on to it is the splendid Victoria Pavilion; it's magnificent inside and can hold up to four thousand people and attracts visitors from all over the place." He took hold of her hand. "Anyway, so much for that, Winifred, tonight belongs to you and we're going to the ballroom where, without any doubt, you will be the belle of the ball; so come on, Win ... let's go!"

On reaching their destination a live band was playing, the atmosphere was electrifying, pulsating with the energy of the happy young folk. It turned out that he was very popular with almost everybody, including the young ladies. This didn't surprise her too much, but what did was that many people kept calling him Jack. On seeing the puzzled look on her face he pointed out that it was his nickname back in Burnley, and somehow it had followed him here too.

As promised he took her on to the floor and introduced her to many different dances such as the Quick-step, the Waltz and the Slow

Fox-trot; she really struggled at first and felt rather awkward and clumsy but he kept reassuring her, "Don't worry about it, Win; you're doing fine. Keep coming here with me and within a few weeks, you'll be able to compete with the best of them."

Throughout the evening, he coached her and taught her many different steps. There was no doubt about it, he really was a fine dancer and so light on his feet; it transpired that he was a competitive dancer and had won many medals. It also so happened that his regular partner in most events was Sally, the good-looking blonde girl. He introduced Winifred to many different people, including some from the group that he met up with on the promenade. He was so popular that many of the gorgeous young ladies kept asking him for a dance!

He always declined saying that he was with Winifred, but on a couple of occasions, she turned to him and said, "Oh, it's all right, John, I don't mind, honest! Besides, it will give me an opportunity to watch you on the floor." She watched in wonderment as he glided around the ballroom as though he was floating on air.

It was during one of these times that she felt a tap on her shoulder; on turning she was standing face to face with Sally, the blonde girl, and she was fuming, "What do you think you're playing at, girl! John Cowell is my boyfriend and I've been going out with him for the last six months."

"Excuse me," replied Winifred, "I don't know anything about that, all I know is that he asked me out, and told me he wasn't involved with anyone."

"Don't come the innocent with me, I've met your type before, and I'm telling you now that John and I are thinking of getting engaged; so keep your flaming hands off him!"

Winifred was obviously taken aback and felt very hurt at this news and for a moment was stuck for words.

Before she had time to reply she heard John's voice from behind her as he rapped, "What's going on here then?"

Winifred turned to him with tears welling up in her eyes. "Is it true then? Is Sally your girlfriend and are you planning to get engaged?"

He didn't answer Winifred directly, but instead, turned to Sally, and this time it was John who was fuming. "What the flaming éck do you think you're playing at? What makes you think you're my girl, and even more so, where did you get the idea that we were getting engaged? I'm telling you now, there's not a cat in hell's chance!"

"But, John, we have been going out together now for quite a while and I always thought that ..."

He interrupted her, "Well you shouldn't have thought, should you? What you really mean is you took certain things for granted. Well I'm telling you now, just to set the record straight, you're not my girl and never have been. The only relationship there has ever been between us, has been as dancing partners." He paused for a moment then said in a very slow, deliberate voice, "Oh finally, I'd just like to say that if I have my way, Winifred will be coming out with me for a long time to come. So if you still want us to be friends, then you'd better not insult her again ... understand?"

At that moment the band started to play the Last Waltz; John turned to Winifred and smiled, offering her his hand. "All right, Win, please could I have the last dance?" On the floor he looked straight into her eyes. "I'm awfully sorry about that, Win, I hope it hasn't spoilt such a wonderful evening."

"No it hasn't, John, although I've got to admit that there was one awful moment when I thought it might."

At this point, he put his arms around her and whispered sweet nothings in her ear; the lights were low and the band was playing soft romantic music. The thought did pass briefly through her mind that he had spoken rather sharply to Sally, but then she quickly dismissed it. Even though she was quite capable of looking after herself, it felt wonderful to have this charming young man come to her aid; he was her knight in shining armour.

To complete the evening, he took her into the restaurant and they had a lovely supper during which he talked heartily, "I've had a great night, Win, and I'd love to see you again. If you're agreeable I'd like to take you to the Alhambra Picture House tomorrow night; it's a magnificent building which was originally used for variety shows, films and dancing alike, but it died a death when the cinema started to come into its own."

She agreed with enthusiasm, and that is how they completed their first marvellous weekend together. The following day was Easter Monday and it passed similarly to their first working day together. Taking everything into account, Winifred was in ecstasy and felt happier and more relaxed than she'd ever done in her life before.

"I can't believe it," she kept saying to herself, "he's so kind and considerate, such a gentleman, he could have any girl of his choice and yet he chooses me."

This was the start of their relationship and things went on in much the same way for the next three months; she was genuinely besotted with him and had fallen deeply in love.

On their days off, they spent many happy hours together on Happy Mount Park Boating Lake; sometimes they would take boat trips around the bay or visit Lakes Windermere and Coniston in the Lake District. One day they watched a special event, which was a local custom in Morecambe that took place annually; it was "The Challenge Of The Cross Bay Swim". In the event, competitors from many different places swam across the bay. John was quite knowledgeable about the local history and informed her that the custom first started in 1907 when the Victoria Swimming Club had approached a Professor Stearse, a professional swimmer, and asked him to swim across the bay and it had continued ever since.

John talked on as Winifred's interest grew. "On the first occasion, he did it in just over five hours but the present record stands at four hours forty-eight minutes."

Other places he took her to were Glasson Dock, Hest Bank, Grange over Sands, Bolton le Dale and Silverdale and, to make the trips more interesting, he always gave a running commentary. For example, when they visited Heysham Docks, he mentioned how they were built in 1904 by Irish navvies costing about £3,000,000, taking more than two thousand men seven years to complete.

They also enjoyed walking hand in hand along the promenade, which stretched as far as Bare and was laid out with beautiful rock gardens. Sometimes, they took a trip on one of the many horse-drawn carriages, although of late, a few cars were beginning to emerge on the scene.

"Oh, John!" exclaimed Winifred one day as they were walking

hand in hand along the front. "Look over there on the beach, there's a Punch and Judy show; do you mind if we watch it? I know it may seem childish, but I've never ever seen one before."

It turned out to be quite amusing; afterwards, they were given leaflets informing them that Punch and Judy dated back to the Italian theatre in the 16th/17th centuries. It was known then as the "Comedia del Arte". The puppet masters made their own puppets, creating many new characters and stories relating to the times.

After watching the belligerent puppets and reading the leaflet, John turned to Winifred. "You know something, Win? I quite enjoyed that, today it's been my turn to learn something," he said laughing a little.

By the West End Pier, the Black and White Minstrel Show and a medley of popular bands could be seen performing in the open-air on the sands, a custom from bygone days. One place that John and Winifred particularly liked was the Harbour Arena where the Harbour Band played. It was a rather large open-air circular stadium with accommodation for hundreds of deckchairs. It acted as a suntrap and on the whole created a splendid atmosphere and it turned out to be one of their favourite spots where they'd sit for hours on end just listening to the music and holding hands.

A weekly event they enjoyed watching was the beauty-contest "Fashion Parade of Windsor" for fashion belles.

John would always remark as the belles paraded before them, "You know something, Win? It's just as well that you're not competing; they wouldn't stand a chance."

Sometimes, they visited Blackpool, which was even busier than Morecambe; Winifred reflected on the time she almost chose to go there instead of Morecambe, and was so glad now that she hadn't.

It wasn't all fun and games though, especially as the season got into full swing and they had to work very long hours. No matter, they were so engrossed in each other that they enjoyed every minute; it appeared that John was just as smitten as she was.

Winifred wrote regularly to her parents and sister Katie telling them of her young man, how wonderful he was and of all the good times they spent together.

the *broken biscuit*

"You know, our Katie, how I couldn't dance a step?" she would write. "Well now, thanks to John, I'm quite a good dancer … not brilliant, mind, but good enough to really enjoy myself."

Before they knew it, it was mid-June and they both had two days free time on their hands and so decided to go to Blackpool. They spent a couple of hours on the Pleasure Beach, as it was much larger than Morecambe's and had a Big Dipper. After that, they went swimming at the Derby Baths, which was renowned internationally as an Olympic swimming pool for world-class swimmers and divers alike.

That evening, they danced in the magnificent Tower Ballroom, which was even more impressive than the one in Morecambe's Winter Gardens. It was a wonderfully romantic setting against a backdrop of beautiful music, the acoustics were magnificent and they danced the night away oblivious to their surroundings. The inevitable happened: they decided to stay overnight together. They spent the night in a small cosy hotel called The Bringewood just off the north promenade near to the cliffs.

After that, Winifred was even more besotted, if that was possible; she loved everything about him. But John seemed to cool down, just a little at first; then it became much more apparent as he became quite complacent towards her. In his way though, he still loved her but he couldn't handle the closeness and responsibility of a serious relationship. She started to notice that he appeared to be avoiding her at work; when he wasn't working on the Ghost Train, she wouldn't see him all day. The brews were no longer forthcoming, and when he did see her he was all apologetic, making lame excuses, which she always fell for. He still took her out now and again, and on these occasions, always treated her like a lady. Sadly though, there were many other times when he made arrangements to meet her, only to let her down and go on a drinking spree with his mates, leaving her lonesome and forlorn.

But one event brought things to a climax; it was a Saturday night, he'd arranged to meet her as usual outside the Palatine Club at nine o'clock to take her dancing. She was dressed up in all her finery and looked very pretty as she waited excitedly. After half an hour, she knew in her heart that he wasn't coming and felt quite despondent, but didn't want to think the worst; by ten o'clock, her fears were confirmed, so she decided to make her way home. She couldn't believe it; it seemed so out of character of the young man she had courted for three glorious months.

"Mind," she told herself, "it's been coming on for a while now, I've just been kidding myself and ignoring the warning signs." She then started to blame herself. "It's your own fault, Winifred, you've gone against all your beliefs, you shouldn't have given yourself to him; now he's lost all respect for you."

At first, the feelings troubled and tormented her, but as she walked along, she became more positive and her emotions turned to anger. "Hang on a minute!" she blurted out. "I'm not at fault here, and I certainly haven't given him cause to treat me this way; blow that for a tale! I don't see why I should go home so soon when I'm all dressed up to go dancing!" She suddenly realised she was talking out loud to herself and strove to regain her composure. "Right Winifred!" she reassured herself. "You can do without him," and on that note she decided to make her way to the ballroom.

On arrival at her destination, it was packed to capacity and everybody seemed to be thoroughly enjoying themselves. Once inside, she felt rather awkward and subdued but got over this by placing herself amidst other young ladies who were standing by the bar. She had just ordered her first drink when a young man tapped her on the shoulder and asked her for a dance. After it had finished, she was walking back to her place when she bumped into John, who was quite drunk and linking arms with Sally, the pretty blonde girl.

"Hello there, John, I thought you were supposed to be meeting me tonight."

At that, Sally sarcastically interrupted, "Oh, isn't that a shame, he was supposed to meet you, was he? Didn't I tell you once before, girl, that he was my boyfriend?"

"Excuse me, Sally, but I'm not speaking to you," Winifred replied indignantly, "so just keep your nose out of it … right!"

At this, he smugly intervened, "All right, ladies, I don't want you arguing on my behalf."

Winifred looked straight at him. "John, why are you being like this? I thought we had something really special between us."

Being drunk, he was a different person, revealing another side to his nature. "Oh don't give me that," he bleated arrogantly, "I'm a free agent and can do what I please and, besides, I like my own space!"

Winifred was furious but she remained calm, and assertive. It all came flooding back to her now, just how he'd talked so abruptly to Sally on their first date, and how the young girl had just stood there and took it.

First, she spoke to him, her voice determined and her manner deliberate. "Right John, if that's the way you want it … then so be it. You can have your freedom, but don't you dare speak to me ever again!" Then turning to Sally and making sure that he heard every word, "I should have listened to you the first time you told me about him, shouldn't I, Sally? All I can say now is he's yours and you're welcome to him!"

With that, she threw back her head and proudly walked back to her position at the bar. It wasn't long before she was getting plenty of attention from lots of admirers, not a dance went by when she wasn't asked on to the floor. John was watching and getting hotter under the collar by the minute; he'd always been accustomed to getting his own way with the ladies and Winifred's attitude was really affecting him; he was becoming jealous. It was even more apparent at the end of the night when he saw her being escorted out of the ballroom. A friend of John's had asked if he could walk her home, and although she wasn't interested, he'd insisted on walking her to the door. John didn't like it when he was on the receiving end; he became more and more frustrated and so followed them out.

On approaching the bloke, he angrily blurted out, "What do you think you're playing at, Eric? You know darned well that Winifred is my girl."

"Correction!" Winifred said quite calmly. "I was your girl, but that's in the past, there's no more to be said about it." She turned to Eric. "Right, Eric, did you say you'd like to see me home then?"

"I certainly would, Winifred, it would be my pleasure," he answered enthusiastically as he offered her his arm. She linked up with him and they walked off together, whilst John just stood there with his mouth open completely dumbfounded.

Eric turned out to be a really nice man, and he told Winifred that he'd liked her for a while and would feel honoured to take her out. He went on to say, "I know you may think I'm being disloyal to a friend but I think you deserve far better than John Cowell. I'm from Burnley myself and I've known him for many years and it's only fair to warn you that he's a wrong ún; he's forever getting drunk and creating chaos back in Burnley and consequently, he's better known around town as 'Barney'."

She took heed of what he said, but inside, she didn't want to know. He was a handsome young man and very smart but, all the same, she just wasn't interested in him and politely refused his invitation to court her.

That night, she was very unhappy and cried herself to sleep, but was determined never to have anything more to do with John. That's what she intended, but things didn't go according to plan. Next morning, after finishing work in the hotel, she smartened herself up and decided to go for a stroll. She was just leaving the hotel when who should be waiting outside? None other than John! He was holding a large bouquet of the most beautiful flowers, and looking rather embarrassed. First she just glared at him, then put her nose in the air and turned around to go back into the hotel.

"Winifred, please!" he implored. "Please hear me out I beg you, I didn't mean to hurt you, honest! And I promise it won't ever happen again!"

She looked at his forlorn face and wanted to forgive him there and then but didn't let him know that. "Too true it won't because I don't want to know you, I won't be going out with you ever again."

"But, Win, please give me another chance to make it up to you, you only said last night that we had something really special between us."

"Oh, is that so? I'm surprised you can remember anything that was said last night, the state you were in."

"Look, Win, I know I was drunk and treated you badly and I'm really sorry about that, but I can tell you now; I remember only too well everything that happened and it's made me realise just how much

I love you!" Then, hanging his head and putting on a little boy lost act, "Win, I beg you, please forgive me!"

She couldn't help but notice his sad puppy-like eyes, and she could feel herself weakening, but felt compelled to ask, "And what about Sally the pretty blonde girl?"

"Oh I promise you, Win, on that score I've been telling the truth. Like I said before, on my part there is nothing going on."

"All right, I'll go along with that, but I still don't hold with the way you spoke to me and how you've been treating me lately."

"Yes, you're right, Win, I have treated you badly but please believe me, it's not that I don't love you any more … in fact, it's just the opposite."

"How do you mean, I don't follow you?"

"Well like I told you once before, I've never been able to face up to responsibility; it just frightens me." He pondered for a moment, then really put her under pressure. "I could feel how close we were becoming and even though it was nice, it made me feel strange because no other girl has ever affected me like that before."

"Strange? What do you mean 'strange'?"

"Please don't get me wrong, Win, I mean strange in a really nice way; the plain truth is that I knew I was falling in love with you and I suppose I just panicked."

She couldn't hold out any longer and succumbed to his abject appeal. "Oh all right, John, I forgive you, but please promise me it won't ever happen again," and, after a little sniffle she added, "And I love you too!"

This was his cue, he walked up to her, took her into his arms and once more … she was in heaven. Everything returned to normal and, once again, they were inseparable; however, it was only short-lived, about a fortnight to be precise before Winifred discovered she was pregnant! At first, she was in a complete spin, as she reflected on the time when her sister Katie had been in the same predicament, and how she herself had responded to the news; also, how her father had reacted.

John responded by going out on the beer for a couple of days to drown his sorrows before gradually coming to terms with it.

Eventually, they discussed it together, and decided to get married as soon as possible. Although Winifred dearly wanted to marry him, she felt sad at the fact that their hand had been forced. She so wanted to marry in the Catholic Church, and, although he was a Protestant, he was quite willing to go along with this for her sake; however, it wasn't to be, as the Catholic Church refused them a dispensation. They were married instead at Lancaster Register Office, on August 27th, 1934.

6: finding a home

Only two guests attended the wedding service, both were casual friends of John and acted as witnesses. After the ceremony, the four of them went to a local bar to toast the wedding, after which John and Winifred made their way back to Morecambe. On arrival, they went for a meal, then John took her to the same bar close to the Pleasure Beach, where they'd had their first drink together. He was in quite high spirits and determined to enjoy the occasion no matter what the circumstances.

"And what would you like to drink, Mrs Cowell?" John asked mischievously.

She reacted like a little girl to these words, as it just hadn't sunk in yet that this was now actually her name. "Oh, John, please say that again, it sounds wonderful; please repeat it over and over, I really love it."

They were quietly enjoying themselves when the barman noticed the flowers in their buttonholes and asked what the occasion was.

"We've just got married today," John answered proudly, "and this is my lovely wife. We've come here purposely to celebrate in this little bar because it is very special to us; you see, it was in here that we had our first drink together, and made our first date."

"In that case ... you are my honoured guests; the next drinks are on the house," said the barman.

It hadn't exactly been the type of wedding day that every young girl dreams of, but it didn't matter one iota to Winifred, she couldn't have been happier; all that mattered to her was that she had married the man of her dreams. To complete the night, he took her back to their matrimonial home where he had been living at 61 West End Road, carried her over the threshold, and that is where they spent their first wedded night together.

He had already sent his mother some money and a letter telling her the news, asking her to prepare some sort of reception at her home for his bride. Within a couple of days he received a reply implying she wasn't happy at the way he had married unexpectedly without notice. Still, she said, she'd like him to bring his new bride home the following weekend to celebrate the occasion, and give the families a chance to meet.

Winifred informed her parents of the arrangements, saying how she was so looking forward to seeing them. But her high hopes were dashed when she received a letter saying her father refused to attend, as they had not been married in church, and he wouldn't condone the marriage. The good news was that her mother, sister Katie and Aunt Alice would be coming. Winifred was naturally disappointed at her dad's decision, but all the same, she tried to look on the bright side.

"Never mind, John," she remarked sadly, "at least it will give me a chance to meet your family."

John and Winifred arrived in Burnley on Saturday morning around twelve o'clock; she was a little apprehensive, wondering what sort of reception they would get. It wasn't good, in fact, it was just the opposite. John's home was a pretty terraced house, very neatly furnished; and in comparison to her parents' house it was a palace. Besides his mother, all his sisters were there being, in respective order of age, Annie, Evelyn, May, Beatie and Lily, and so too was his half brother Ted. One thing that struck Winifred was that they were all strikingly good-looking, especially Annie and May, who had both won beauty competitions. Another thing she noticed was that everyone, except his mother, kept calling John, 'Jack'.

The little party was set to start at two o'clock. Winifred had arranged to meet her family at the Cattle Market bus station where the bus from Bacup was due in at half past one, so, after making her apologies, she made her way to the rendezvous.

No sooner had she left the house than John's sisters reprimanded him for not inviting them to the actual wedding ceremony.

"Now come on, our Jack, what do you think you're playing at, getting married without inviting any of us to your wedding?" rapped Annie.

"No, it's not right," snapped Beatie. "The least you could have done was to let us know."

"Yes, and another thing," said Lily not to be outdone by her sisters, "you haven't given my mother much thought, have you?"

At that point, Ted intervened, "Now come on, girls, that'll do, I know you're annoyed, but what's done is done; after all, this is their day and we don't want to spoil it, do we?" Then, turning to Jack he said, "Congratulations, our Jack, I think your bride is gorgeous, and I wish you both the very best in the world."

The afternoon got under way, but although the buffet was excellent, the event was rather strained because of odd snide remarks from the sisters like, "Oh, you're expecting then, so that's why you decided to get married so quickly, is it?"

It was quite evident that theirs was a much better-off family than Winifred's, and this was made quite clear on more than one occasion. Winifred felt very uncomfortable, but was determined to keep her composure, and answered their queries as politely as possible. But despite remaining positive she couldn't help but feel frustrated. Although the party went reasonably well, the atmosphere was uncomfortable, there was a feeling of resentment on both sides, sadly, this was to last over the coming years.

The couple spent the next week of their honeymoon in his mother's house, before returning to Morecambe to finish the season. In the meantime, Winifred took Jack, as even she was beginning to call him, over to Bacup to meet her family. Being the likeable person he was, Jack was readily accepted, but Mat made it quite clear that he would like to see them both remarry in church.

In contrast, Winifred's stay in Jack's home was fraught with tension; his youngest sister Lily was still single and living at home, and she and Winifred didn't get on at all. What made things worse was that of all his sisters, Jack had a soft spot for Lily, and tended to take her side; the reason for this was that Lily had suffered a terrible childhood illness, which had left her stone-deaf and he felt protective towards her.

As the season drew to a close, Morecambe did everything in its power to lengthen it, especially in the last week, which was Carnival Week when many different events took place. One in particular that stuck out in Winifred's mind was "The Crowning Of The Carnival

Queen"; it was the most prestigious beauty contest of them all and the winner automatically became eligible to enter "The Miss Great Britain Competition".

The beauty contest was preceded by "The First World War Peace Celebration". Hundreds of children from outlying towns and villages paraded through the town in fancy dress to the sound of brass bands, followed by large floats. The atmosphere around the town was magnificent, as thousands of people attended the procession. Winifred enjoyed this all the more because it showed great respect for people like her dad, who had given so much during the war. On the last day of that special week, which coincided with the end of the season, the roasting of an ox took place in the centre of town, the first slice of which was always carved by the Carnival Queen. Afterwards, spectators could buy a sandwich for a nominal fee, which Jack and Winifred did, and they thoroughly enjoyed it too.

With the end of the season came the end of their jobs on the Pleasure Beach; now came the time to face up to reality. Winifred managed to keep her weekend job in the hotel, but even that was only guaranteed for another month at the most; Jack had to sign on the dole, which meant that money was tight.

At first, she wasn't too concerned as she was a great believer in the saying, "Two people pulling together can overcome any obstacle." Sadly, though, what she didn't take into account was that she would have to do all the pulling.

Jack didn't turn out to be the supportive husband she'd so often dreamed about; and it wasn't too long before his antics started to come to light. He'd set off in the morning on the pretence that he was looking for work and would arrive home late at night in a drunken and very argumentative state. The following morning, when sober, he'd always be apologetic, coming out with the most lame excuses which would win her over. This became a regular pattern of events, and hardly a day passed when he didn't go out on a drinking spree with his boozy friends. The demands for bills were not being met, which greatly concerned Winifred. What made matters worse was that money started to disappear from her purse; when questioned about it, he'd always swear blind it wasn't him. Being a practical woman, she was already beginning to realise he was a very unreliable person, who she wouldn't be able to depend upon, and that she'd made a bad mistake in marrying him.

In spite of this she still loved him; all he had to do to win her favour was to put his arms around her and show her a little affection, her heart would just melt and her better judgement would fly out of the window.

She wanted so much for him to settle down and be right, and so, in her mind, she made excuses for him and would convince herself by saying, "It will be all right, Winifred, we're still only very early into our marriage, I'm sure he'll change once the baby arrives."

Despite her high hopes, though, things didn't change for the better, and there were many confrontations.

During one of the rows, Jack mentioned something, "Look, Winifred, it's obvious we're not making ends meet here, so how about us moving to Burnley where I have quite a few good connections?"

"What do you mean by connections?" she queried.

"Well, back in Burnley, I've done a lot of wheeling and dealing in the scrap iron and rag trade."

"The rag trade," she blurted out nearly falling off her chair, "you mean like a rag man?"

He couldn't help but notice the shocked expression on her face. "Hey, hang on a minute, Winnie, don't knock something when you don't know anything about it! I can tell you now, it's a good business to be in, and can be very lucrative."

"Oh yes, if it's so lucrative, why did you come working over here in the first place then?"

"Don't be like that, Winnie, as I told you before, I used to be irresponsible, and I came here for a change and a bit of excitement; but that doesn't alter the fact that I could still make a good living at it now."

At that remark, she couldn't resist saying, "You used to be irresponsible! You're talking as if you're a changed man, what about the way you've been behaving lately?"

"Yeah, all right, I agree with you, I haven't treated you fairly up to now, but I promise that things will be different from now on, and especially if we do what I've just asked."

Once again, he won her over, so they went to live in his hometown of Burnley. Houses to rent were scarce, so to start with, they lodged in the house of his sister Beatie and her husband Joe Price, on Healey Wood Road. Winifred wasn't too keen on the idea, but at least she thought Jack would treat her properly in their presence. On the contrary, he actually went on the booze even more, and often didn't come home till the early hours. She felt so awkward and isolated but didn't like saying much being in his sister's home. What made it worse is that when she did, Beatie would always take Jack's side, and tell her to leave him alone. Being the person she was, Winifred didn't take things lying down and many cross words were exchanged, which consequently created friction and a tense atmosphere, so they moved out and went to stay with his sister May.

Things didn't change. The pattern of events repeated themselves; in fact, something happened there that added insult to injury. It was late January, just ten days before Winifred's twenty-second-birthday. She was seven months pregnant and the only thing that kept her going was the thought of the new life inside her. Like most evenings, she was sat in whilst Jack was out on the rant. She was extremely unhappy, and just happened to mention to May the unfairness of it all. If she was expecting sympathy, she didn't get it; May immediately leapt to Jack's defence and an argument ensued. During the heated debate, Jack's sister Lily entered the house and immediately sided with May; she actually struck Winifred quite hard across the face. Winifred was taken aback and quite shocked; her first impulse was to set into Lily and tear her hair out; however, she restrained herself because she feared for the baby's safety. Glaring at them with piercing eyes, she realised in that moment that they could see no wrong in their brother.

"To carry on would be futile, I might as well bang my head against a wall," she thought to herself before saying emphatically, "Right that's it, I've had enough of the lot of you; for the first time, I can see now what I'm really up against. Well, I'm telling you both, from now on you won't be seeing me again ... ever!" She then went straight to her room and started packing.

Neither of them took her seriously at first, and even made sneering remarks like, "Right, goodbye and good riddance!"

Nonetheless, their attitude changed when they realised she was in earnest and determined to go; they then tried to make her change her mind. But Winifred was unmoved because she knew they weren't too concerned about her personally, they were just being loyal to their brother, and a little wary of any repercussions from him.

"Come on, Winnie, you can't leave just like that, and especially in your condition," pleaded Lily, "Besides, it's freezing outside, where can you go on a cold night like this?"

Winifred was more in control now, and more determined than ever. "Leave it, Lily!" she growled. "You should have thought of that before you intervened and struck me across the face." She paused a little before stressing, "And just let me tell you now, you don't know just how lucky you are to get away with that; I give you fair warning, Lily, never ever do it again, or on your own head be it!" She then brushed past them and left the house. She hadn't made any plans, and the only place in the world where she could think of going was to her parents' already overcrowded home in Bacup.

As she sat on the bus, she started to reminisce over the past twelve months. "Life is really strange, this time last year I was returning home from London with such great expectations, and so looking forward to surprising my family with all my achievements; now look at me going back to them in this state." Her thoughts saddened her, as she didn't want to burden them with her troubles, knowing only too well that they already had plenty of their own; on reflection, though, what else could she do? She didn't expect the most glorious reception in the world, but on the other hand, she wasn't prepared for what happened; unlike the last time, the atmosphere on this occasion was cold to say the least.

On entering the house, Mat immediately made it obvious that she wasn't welcome. "There's no chance ó thi stoppin here, our Win," he grunted, "tha's med tha bed and tha can sleep onnit; this is what comes o not geddín wed in a proper church."

"Thank you very much, Dad, I love you too," she muttered holding back the tears.

"And it's no good thí geddín like that either, cós I'm not gonna change mí mind."

the *broken biscuit*

Her mum tried her best to win him over, but he was adamant. "It's no good thi tryín to ged around me either, no, I'm not wearin' it; there's nod enough room here to swing a cat round as it is!"

Winifred could see the position was hopeless. "Right then, Dad, that's it, is it? I should have known not to come here, shouldn't I? I'll go now but before I do, I've got to say that I know just how difficult it is for you here, but at least I expected a little more understanding from my own family." She looked him straight in the eye adding, "Then again, Dad, you always have been pig-headed, haven't you?" Then turning to her mum, "Thanks, Mum, I'm sorry if I've caused you any distress; that's the last thing in the world that I wanted."

Her sister Katie put her arms around her and started whimpering, "O-oh ... our Winnie, what are you going to do?"

"Don't worry, our Katie, God's good, I'll get by somehow, and like before, I'll keep in touch. Anyway, I don't want you fretting yourself, you've got enough on your plate looking after your little boy."

With that, she kissed her younger siblings and little Tony goodbye, then left. Proud as she was, she was heartbroken and all cut up inside, she felt so alone and rejected; not only had her husband cast her aside, but now, her own kinfolk as well. By this time it was getting quite late and the last bus had already left for Burnley. She had no idea what she was going to do, and for what seemed an age, just wandered aimlessly around Bacup town centre in a trance.

Finally, she sat on a form outside the Conservative Club, and placed her two hands together in prayer. "Oh dear God," she pleaded, "please help me in my plight, I feel that I have no one to turn to, and I'm so very lonely and afraid, and I just don't know what to do. Please, I beg You, shine Your holy guiding light around me and show me the way. Also shine it on to my dad, who I love very much because I know he didn't really mean what he said; he was only doing what he thought was best for the rest of the family. I know in my heart that he would put me up if I went back there now. I'm not too worried about myself but I am concerned about my unborn baby, I so much want everything to be right for its sake. I once made a covenant with You before that should I ever have children of my own, I would love them unconditionally; as from this moment I renew my vow to You."

At that moment, her thoughts were interrupted by a light from a torch and on looking up, it was the local bobby, who asked, "Excuse me, young lady, is everything all right?"

"Oh yes thank you," she replied wiping back the tears, "it's just that I've had a little setback."

He couldn't help but notice her condition and how distressed she was, so enquired in a very concerned voice, "Do you realise just how late it is, my dear? It isn't very wise to be out all alone at this time, and on such a cold night too. May I enquire as to what you are going to do?"

"To tell you the truth, sir, sniff, sniff, I don't really know … that's what I was just thinking about."

"Oh dear!" he exclaimed. "I can see we have a problem here, haven't we?" He was clasping his jaw in deep thought, when suddenly an expression of recognition came to his face. "Just a minute, my dear, don't I know you? Aren't you Winifred, the sister of young Jimmy Walsh, who used to sell the *Evening Telegraph* in the square before his terrible accident?"

"Yes, that's right, officer, and now I remember you because our Jimmy often talked of you and really looked up to you."

"Did he now? Well, all I can say is I'm flattered, he was the nicest, happiest lad I've ever had the honour to meet in my whole life; I know for sure that he wouldn't like to see you unhappy as you are right now."

With those kind words, a strange tingling feeling came over Winifred, all her fears seemed to vanish; she felt inspired as a wonderful thought came to her. "Winifred, you're no longer alone, Jimmy is looking down on you; you needn't be afraid any more."

The constable noticed the curious expression on her face, and asked, "Winifred, is everything all right?"

"Oh yes, sir, definitely, more than you'll ever know; and you'll be happy to know that thanks to you, I now know exactly what I'm going to do."

"Oh yes? And may I ask what that is then?"

"You may, I've decided to call a taxi and take myself off to Bank Hall Maternity Hospital in Burnley."

"Right, my dear, in that case, please permit me to make the travel arrangements for you, and while I'm at it, may I enquire as to whether you have enough money?"

"Oh yes thank you, I think so, thanks all the same for asking."

"Thanks all the same?" he repeated. "Winifred, I'd be honoured if you would accept this half a crown just to help you a little, and also as a small token to young Jimmy's memory."

She was overcome by his kind gesture and accepted it with humility in the spirit in which it was offered. As promised, he went to a police telephone box, arranged for a taxi, then courteously waited with her till it arrived, and that's the last she ever saw of him. As the taxi drove off she felt so humble; she couldn't help but think that her prayer had been answered, and the messenger had been her guardian angel in the guise of a policeman.

Although the episode made her feel a little better and more able to face the world again, she still felt quite upset. Upon reaching the maternity ward, her distress was apparent to all the nursing staff. She was allowed to stay overnight, but as the baby wasn't due for another eight weeks she was transferred to the Workhouse at Burnley General where there were a few spare maternity beds. She actually enjoyed it there because at least she had food and shelter, and she was well looked after.

Meanwhile, back in May's home, Jack had arrived home to find Winifred gone. In his intoxicated state, though, he couldn't care less one way or the other and just went to bed muttering obscenities to himself.

Next morning, he was still unrepentant and made it obvious. "Not to worry, our May; she'll be back with her tail between her legs cós the only place she can go is Bacup, and there's no room for her there. Anyway, I'm not going to mope about it, at least I can go for a drink without being nagged."

Consequently, for the next few days he went on the binge; however, when the drinking spree finished and he'd sobered up, his conscience began to prick him and he became quite concerned; he was also starting to miss her. On finally coming to his senses, he decided to make his way over to Bacup, only to find out what had happened; on seeing him, panic stations set in all round.

"Oh my God!" exclaimed Mat remorsefully. "What have I done, and what kind of a father am I anyroad to turn my lass away in the state she was in?"

"Don't worry, I'll find her," Jack muttered guiltily. "I'm more to blame than you, it's all my fault."

"It's too late now to start laying blame on anyone," replied Mat. "The time's come now to do somèt about it. Now you go and find my lass, and think on tha looks after her when tha does! Aye, and don't forget to let us know reight away."

Jack immediately set off back to Burnley, the first place he made for was the Casualty Department at Victoria Hospital. As they had no record of her there, he then went to the police station, where he was advised to go to the Maternity Hospital; that's when he discovered that she'd been sent to the Workhouse, he also learnt what a state she'd been in at the time.

On reaching the Workhouse, he was surprised to find her in high spirits; more so when she made it abundantly clear that she had no intention of going back to him ever again.

After a while, when he realised he wasn't getting anywhere, he started pleading with her, "Please, Win, please come back! I promise I'll change and treat you better, and I'll put you and the little one before anyone else."

"Oh, Jack, don't give me that either, it just doesn't wear any more, anyway, come back to what? If you think I'd go living back in any of your sisters' homes, there's no chance!"

"Oh come on, Win, I promise you, it will only be for a short time. I'll get the ball rolling right away and sort out a place of our own," he begged, and added, "And as from today, I'm going to stop boozing."

"No, Jack, that's no good either, you're full of empty promises, they always fall flat on the ground. You just don't impress me anymore; let's face it … you're just a weak character."

When that didn't work, he got down on one knee, and begged even more fervently, but to no avail. Finally, he had to eat his own words; it wasn't Winifred, but him, who had to walk away with his tail between his legs. As she watched him leave, she felt heavy-hearted yet strong, as she knew deep down she was doing the best thing for both herself and the baby; she had no doubts that it was definitely the end of her relationship with Jack. She felt strong and in control for something very touching had recently happened on the ward, which boosted her self-confidence and raised her self-esteem. She had met and befriended a lady called Maria Clark, who had just had a baby girl.

During one of their many talks together, she'd said to Winifred, "Do you know something, Winifred, I love the sound of your name, and that is what I've decided to call my little girl."

It gave Winifred a nice inner feeling and she was very moved. What she didn't know then was that the little girl would become almost part of her own family in years to come, and always be known as young Winnie Clark.

The following day, she was still pondering on the way Jack had left feeling so dejected. She still felt the same though, and was even more determined never to take him back again. Nevertheless, he was full of surprises and once more he came up with a bombshell that completely bowled her over. She was sat by her bed reading a book when he popped his head around the ward door, with his little boy lost look, and gave her a cheeky grin. As he entered the ward, she could see he was once again carrying the most beautiful bouquet of flowers, as he always did when trying to win her round.

She could never resist him when looking into his blue eyes and especially when they were sad; however, on this occasion, she was determined to stand her ground. "It's no good trying to get round me, Jack, what I said yesterday still stands and what's more ..."

He stopped her in mid-sentence as he muttered very humbly, "Happy Birthday, Win!" adding as he gave her a beautiful birthday card and a box of chocolates, "Our first one together." She was totally dumbfounded!

With the entire goings on, she'd completely forgotten all about it, and now it was her turn to feel humble. "U-um, thank you, how did you remember it then?"

"Oh that was easy because, when you first told me your birthday, I remember thinking that it was the day after mine."

"Oh that's right!" she exclaimed. "I remember now, it was the day when …" It suddenly struck her. "Oh no! That means it was your birthday yesterday when you came here, wasn't it? Oh flippín éck! You were so sad and I wouldn't wear you at all, would I?"

He was quick to seize the opportunity. "Oh that's all right, Win, I can't say as I blame you for that, I've been a right swine, haven't I?" Sensing that he was winning her over, he carried on, "Oh that reminds me, I've found us a place of our own, it's only small, but at least we can be together and ..."

This time she cut him short, "Hey hang on a minute, slow down! I haven't promised anything yet."

She hadn't, but he sensed that she only needed a little more gentle persuasion. "Oh come on, Win, you know we're made for one another; how about giving it another try?"

That was it, once again, he had won her round; as promised, he took her back to their own place. It was just a one-room bed-sit in the Forester's Arms Pub on Bridge Street, and was entered directly from the pavement. It was certainly very small for when you entered the front door, you were almost up to the fireplace. The furniture consisted of a table, a bed and two small wooden chairs. There was another door at the back of the room that led into the pub's hallway where Winifred could do her washing and attend to her personal hygiene. Not exactly what she wanted, but she didn't mind, as far as she was concerned she'd have lived in a tent with him so long as he treated her right.

Alas, that was not to be, he still kept up his antics and frequented many pubs around town, mainly the White Horse, the Dog and Duck and the Boot Inn. One of his favourite haunts though was The Salford, which was situated near to the Swift River and the Railway Viaduct.

One evening in mid March, whilst Winifred was doing a little shopping in the Mitre area, she felt twinges in the lower part of her back, then she started to have contractions. She panicked, the only thing she could think of was to make her way to The Salford pub where Jack might be. The most direct route was via Westgate and Ashfield Road, and it was on the latter part of the journey that an incident occurred. She was walking very slowly on the opposite side of the road to the archways and two young girls were walking on the other side of the road. She heard a train passing over the viaduct when suddenly a large coping stone fell from the top missing the two young girls by only a few feet. It smashed into fragments and some of these shot across the road towards Winifred; by the grace of God no one was hurt, but all the same, Winifred was quite shaken by it. A kindly lady who lived in one of the adjacent houses heard the crash and took Winifred in and made her a cup of tea before arranging for an ambulance to take her to the Maternity Hospital.

On March 18th, 1935, Maureen was born. She was to be a Godsend to her mum, just as Winifred's brother Jimmy had been to his. She was the most beautiful child with golden locks and rosy cheeks, with a temperament to match. Everyone made a fuss of her; even the nurses loved to pick her up and cuddle her. Jack also made a fuss of her and was very proud, and, for a short while, started to pull in his reins and act responsibly; he even went with Winifred a few times to arrange to be remarried at St Mary's Catholic Church. The remarriage took place when Maureen was three months old. Although dispensation had now been granted, they were not allowed on to the altar, and the ceremony took place in the vestry. Both Winifred and her parents were very happy about it; however, it stirred up a lot of animosity amongst Jack's family and they refused to attend the service; subsequently, the gulf between Winifred and her in-laws widened even more. There was further controversy two weeks later when Maureen was christened in the same church. Prior to the christening, Jack's sisters had unsuccessfully tried to persuade him to have Maureen baptised in their church. Winifred adamantly stood her ground, and wouldn't be swayed an inch; she reminded Jack of the promise he had made that should they have any children, they would be brought up in the Catholic faith. To give him his due, it was one time that he didn't renege, and actually stuck up for Winifred against his family and backed her up.

"No! It's only fair," he told them, "it's her child and it's only fitting that she does what she thinks is right. Anyway, it doesn't matter to me one way or the other where she's christened, whereas it means an awful lot to Winnie."

About fifteen months passed and Winifred was coping quite well in spite of Jack's boozing; at least she was near to the town centre and the marketplace, which was handy for shopping. He still spent most nights in the pubs leaving her to cope on her own, but she didn't feel quite so alone now, having little Maureen to care for. Still, she yearned for him to be there alongside her.

Things went on in much the same way, then she became pregnant again. She applied to the council for a council house but was informed there was a long waiting list.

When she pointed this out to Jack, he came up with a solution. "I know where there's a house going for rent in the Croft area; it's not much to look at; and is, in fact, condemned, but at least the rent's cheap."

"Oh come off it, Jack," she rapped, "I'm not going living down there near to your Lily's, you know very well we don't get on."

"Whoa, hang on a minute! Why don't you use your head for once?"

"Use my head, what on earth are you talking about?"

"Well you want a council house, don't you?"

"Yes," she replied still looking puzzled, "but what has that got to do with anything?"

"Aye, Winnie, you can't see the wood for the trees, can you? The house will be demolished quite shortly, which means that the council will have to rehouse us."

And so it came to pass, they did move into the place, which was near to Pickup Street in the middle of a block of terraced houses, some of which were already boarded up. There was a constant fishy smell about the place, as it was right next door to a fishmonger. They were to spend the next eighteen months there during which time Winifred had many rows with Jack's sisters, which tested her patience to the hilt.

In spite of everything, Jack was a clever businessman and he built up some good connections in the scrap iron trade; the irony of it was that they could have been quite well-off but for his drinking habits. Winifred pointed this out to him many times and tried to get him to change, but he couldn't or wouldn't see the error of his ways.

On June 2nd, 1937, Jimmy was born. (Named jointly after Jack's father and Winifred's brother.) Unlike Maureen, he was an extremely naughty child and very hard work, even in Bank Hall. Only hours after the birth, he had a distinct cry and he screamed incessantly. He was always very frail, yet hyperactive, and very clinging, and he wouldn't go to anyone except his mum, forever demanding her undivided attention. Still, Jack remained indifferent to his parental status and carried on with his wanton ways.

Winifred's fears that Lily might interfere were confirmed. Constant quarrelling accrued and, sadly, Jack always sided with Lily. Many insults were exchanged, but the most infuriating thing as far as Winifred was concerned were the times she endlessly toiled over the hot stove striving to have the tea ready.

Jack would come home late and say quite unconcerned, "Oh I'm not hungry – I've already had my tea at our Lily's."

When she reacted, he would turn nasty and throw out insulting remarks like, "Yeah, so what, she's a much better cook than you anyway."

She went to see Lily many times, and asked her not to make his meals but it didn't make a scrap of difference.

In fact, more insults were thrown at her including many hurtful ones like, "Get home to your scruffy kids. I don't think they're our Jack's anyway!"

Things didn't alter, and the gap between Winifred and Jack's family widened into a chasm.

All of them that is except his brother Ted, who always stuck up for her against Jack. "Nay, our Jack," he'd say, "I don't think tha beín fair to yon lass at all; she's a good wife and mother and deserves better."

It didn't alter things, especially when Lily was involved; she was his favourite sister and could do no wrong. Winifred tried to take Lily's affliction into account but to no avail as their temperaments were just too incompatible. Finally, Winifred's torment came to an end when she received a letter from the council stating that the house was to be demolished and that she would be re-housed.

Three days later they moved into the house of her dreams at number 36 Dalton Street on the Bleak House estate. She called it her sunshine house as it had a through lounge; what really pleased her most, though, was that it had a bathroom and also a nice garden for the children to play in. Another thing was that she got on very well with her next door neighbour, whose name was Alice King. Alice had two daughters called Ada and Jean; they were a little older than Maureen, but from the start they all got on fine together.

Jimmy was just fifteen months old when she realised she was pregnant again; she wasn't coping very well as it was, and this bombshell just floored her.

At one point, she thought she was going out of her mind and in her frantic state started to cry, "Oh God! What am I going to do, I can't cope with the two I have already?" Then, she became a little angry. "I don't want this baby, God, so please, take it away; I know I always wanted four children, but that was with a good loving partner to share them with, but certainly not under these conditions."

She got her reply all right; it was as if God had answered, "*Oh you don't want this child, do you not, Winifred? Well, we'll just have to see about that!*"

Consequently, when she went to the clinic for a check up there was some startling news awaiting her.

One of the nurses greeted her with a smile on her face. "Well well, Mrs Cowell, we've got some wonderful news for you … you're having twins!"

After recoiling from the initial shock she got back into some sort of routine and devoted all her time and energy to the little ones. Here she was with twins on the way, and Jack still indifferent; sadly, the only thing that interested him was a pint of bitter and a game of cards with the lads down at the pub. He could always find money to squander amongst them, and was well known for his generosity around the town's pubs; but when it came to giving his wife some housekeeping money, that was a different matter. It used to cause ructions in the home and he wasn't averse to hitting his wife either; it became quite commonplace to see her sporting a black eye, but he didn't get away with it scot free and often finished up with worse injuries than her. Really, though, it was quite pointless because, despite the ructions, he still had to cough up something. Her lot seemed a thankless task; she was constantly short of money and unable to pay the bills or afford a decent buying in. There was the time when she was eight months pregnant with the twins. She was, as they say, 'as big as a battleship.'

She had been to the hospital for a check-up and didn't have any money for the return fare home and had to scrounge tuppence from one of the nurses.

On April 11th,1939, John and Mary were born. The births were very difficult. John came into the world at seven o'clock in the morning presenting feet first; Mary didn't arrive till five hours later at noon and was breech, presenting buttocks first. Consequently, Winifred had to stay in hospital for a further three weeks. During her stay, all the nurses made a fuss of the twins and suggested that Winifred call them Bobby and Beryl or Jack and Jill; she wasn't swayed though, and finally settled for plain John and Mary. Right from the start, John was much bigger and stronger than Mary; be that as it may, she was always more dominant and soon became the boss.

In the next bed was a lady called Mrs Cheetham, who'd just given birth to a little boy whom she called Robert; fate is quite strange for John and Bobby were to become lifelong friends.

It was a happy time all round because even Jack was thrilled with the event, and behaved more responsibly; to be fair, he always did when Winifred wasn't there to care for the children. He was in good spirits for more reasons than one; it was the Easter period, and he'd recently acquired a horse. On Good Friday he hired a trap and went down Pendle Bottoms, also known as Jack Moore's Gardens, giving rides to children; consequently, he had a very profitable weekend. Usually when he was flush, the money just seemed to burn a hole in his pocket but on this occasion he stopped at home looking after Maureen and Jimmy ... things couldn't have been better. When sober, he had a vibrant personality and the kids absolutely adored him; he was spotless in the home too, and liked everything in its place. When he was washing up, Maureen loved to help him; he'd lift her on to a little wooden box so that she could stand by the sink. Maureen was only just turned four, yet she was already coming into her own as far as being a Godsend to her mum was concerned; she was much older than her years, and instinctively acted like a little mother to her younger brothers and sister.

She well remembers standing at the front door of Dalton Street waiting for the twins to be brought home, watching her mum step out of the ambulance, followed by her dad, who was carrying one on each arm. This memory was to stay with her all the days of her life; oh, how she'd wished that things could've remained as they were at that moment. Alas, Jack was now the father of four beautiful children, yet would not give up his selfish ways, frequently leaving Winifred short of money.

His sisters still remained argumentative and interfering towards Winifred, and continued to throw out their slanderous remarks like, "Aye, you're nothing but a trollop, and half o' them bloody kids are not our Jack's anyway!"

What made things worse was that he tended to take on board these scurrilous remarks, and sometimes in a drunken state, he'd also throw out the same insults.

By now, Winifred had long since lost all hope of him changing his ways and completely devoted her life to her children, even to the point of putting some kind of invisible protective cloak around them. As far as she was concerned they were her world and main purpose in life, she was their salvation and guiding light; no one would ever hurt them, and that included their dad. This was especially so when he was drunk and she had one strict house rule that even he had to abide by; he could never ever bring any of his boozing cronies into the home.

He tried it on a few times, but in spite of becoming aggressive and cantankerous shouting things like, "You bloody swine, the bleeding kids ... that's all you bloody well care about!" there was no chance.

Sometimes, though, his words would set her to thinking, "Maybe what he says is true ... u-um, perhaps I am shutting him out." Then, being a realist, she'd see things for what they really were. "No, it doesn't matter, it's his own fault, he brings it all upon himself." She still loved him though, and when he was sober and treating her right, her love for him was plain to see.

The twins were four months old when Hitler invaded Poland, and the Second World War was imminent. Everywhere you went, you could hear the voice of Winston Churchill over radios and see warnings on billboards alerting people to the impending danger and preparing them for war. Unlike the First World War, this one would be far different as civilians would be much more involved ... it would not be just a soldiers' war, it would be a people's war too ... every man, woman and child would be involved.

Gas masks and ration books were issued from specially selected government buildings; the gas masks for babies were in the form of a box, into which the child could be placed. Air-raid shelters were built in backyards, workplaces and near to schools. Stacked around everywhere were thousands of sandbags that were used to build stockades in designated places.

An ultimatum was given to Germany by the British Government to vacate Poland by eleven o'clock in the morning on September 3rd. It was ignored. Consequently, once again, the country was in a state of war! It seemed ironic that the last one finished at eleven o'clock, and this one started at eleven o'clock.

From the onset, much to the pleasure of most children, all schools in Burnley were closed, and no definite decision was made as to when they would re-open. Official letters were posted to every household laying down orders which everyone had to strictly adhere to; these involved things like curfews and putting blinds on to the windows so as not to show any light during the blackout. They were also given instructions about what to do in case of emergency, and people were urged not to talk loosely about their jobs, in the interest of National Security. Public notices were placed in local newspapers advising people where to go if their homes were destroyed; these were mainly the closed schools in different parts of the town, but the Salvation Army Citadel was also used. The future looked grim, but the government realised the importance of keeping the people's morale as high as possible; therefore, there were many broadcasts on the radio, and items were put in newspapers to that effect.

The following is a quote from the *Burnley Express*, Sept 39:

> Readers,
> In these times of stress and trouble, it is rather difficult to know what to say to be a comfort to all. Yet! If the cause is just – and our cause IS just, we cannot tremble.

finding a home

If our consciences are clear, we need not be afraid. If
our hearts are strong, we cannot fail. And if we have faith
in God, victory for the right is sure.

Therefore, to the citizens of Burnley I say: "Be
steadfast, strong and of good courage, and our cause must
prevail.

The war was to last for six years and cause much heartache, but one
aspect of it was positive: it brought the community together, for the
sense of shared danger made people much more caring towards each
other.

Notwithstanding, war or no war, Winifred had an ongoing battle
of her own, as normal everyday occurrences continued to blight her
life. One very testing and most distressing time for her was when the
twins were five months old, just a few days into the war. Maureen and
Jimmy were getting over a bout of whooping cough when the twins
contracted it. They were both affected quite badly but John being much
more sturdy and strong soon recovered, whereas Mary, being so frail,
became seriously ill and almost died, and certainly would have done
but for the constant vigil kept over her by Winifred. The cough
developed into Croup and poor Mary gasped for every breath.
Winifred's GP was Dr Bird, and he was very conscientious and
understanding and made visits to the home every single day for almost
five months. The little girl wouldn't take any feed whatsoever and
Winifred had to give her medicine and spoon-feed her at all times of
the day and night. In spite of having to cope on her own with all the
other children, she remained calm. However, she was quite exhausted,
and at one critical time during the crisis she approached the doctor and
made a request.

"Dr Bird, I feel that I can't cope any more, could you please take
little Mary into hospital so as to take some pressure off me and make
things a little easier?"

"I'm sorry, Mrs Cowell but I can't do that. You see, they won't be
able to look after as well as you can, and when she cries they won't
always have the time to pick her up and cuddle her. No, they can't do
any more for her than what you are doing right now."

So the constant vigilance and spoon-feeding carried on ... and on ... and on, for almost five months. Despite being very weary, Winifred never once lost her patience; as a matter of fact, she had a strange wonderful tranquillity about her throughout the whole period. During the first three months, Mary was forever nauseated; she retched at every spoonful, going almost down to her birth weight. Even so, during that wretched illness, the little girl seemed to have a cheeky look and a spark of mischief about her; she'd struggle to lift up her little hands in front of her face and stare in wonderment at her own tiny fingers. Winifred noticed this and it gave her hope and inspiration.

"Yes!" she thought hopefully. "She may not be progressing very well, but at least she's bright."

Then, one wonderful morning, Winifred's prayers were answered; little Mary actually took a couple of spoonfuls without being sick, and Winifred knew instinctively that her little girl was on the way to recovery. A few days later, Winifred had to pop out to the corner shop, which was about a hundred yards down the street; she didn't like leaving the children with Maureen, but didn't have much choice.

She was only away a few minutes, but when she returned, Dr Bird was inside the house, and on seeing him she panicked. "Oh, I'm sorry, Doctor, I ... I haven't been out for long, please believe me, it's just that I had to ..."

He stopped her there, "Whoa ... steady on Mrs Cowell, please don't upset yourself, everything's perfectly all right; now just sit yourself down for a moment please, I have something I'd like to say to you." His face became very serious, making Winifred feel rather anxious. "Right, Mrs Cowell, I can tell you now something that I didn't dare tell you before. That is," he stressed by snapping his fingers, "I didn't have that much hope for your little girl, and that is why I wouldn't send her to hospital; I knew she couldn't have been in better hands than she was right here with you." Then approaching her, he finished by saying, "Well done, Mrs Cowell, you have done a marvellous job, and I personally think you are a wonderful mother. I'd just like to add, though, your little girl is not out of the woods yet, and there's still a lot of hard work ahead; however, she is certainly on the way to recovery."

Nothing in the world could have given Winifred greater pleasure or satisfaction than hearing those words; they made everything seem worthwhile.

Little Mary did recover, and it wasn't long before she was pulling John's ears, nose and hair, and clonking him with anything she could lay her hands on, just to show him who was boss. Nothing ever seemed to bother him though for he quite naturally took everything in his stride and hardly ever retaliated. By now, he was much bigger than her and had a crop of thick dark curly hair, whereas hers was thin and wispy. However, Mary was back to her normal self and here to stay. Every day, Mrs King would take care of Maureen and Jimmy whilst Winifred took the twins in the pram to a clinic on Cog Lane for sunlight treatment.

People would stop her in the street and make remarks like, "Oh, the little girl is much bigger than the boy, isn't she?" Winifred would politely point out their mistake leaving them with egg on their face.

The children were Winifred's whole world: she felt they were her sole purpose in life. Without a doubt, she strove to be a good mother but even with the best intentions, she still made mistakes. With a little more foresight and guidance, perhaps, they could have been avoided. One particular thing that she regretted in later years was her lack of understanding at the time. It was during the above crisis that she hadn't fully realised that Jimmy was still only a child himself; she'd been very protective of the twins and, because of this, little Jimmy tended to have his nose shoved out.

If he went anywhere near the pram, she'd say things like, "Oh, keep away from the pram! Don't touch the babies! Mind their heads!" and so on.

Poor little Jimmy, he had only just turned two years old himself, and being the clinging child he was, he obviously felt rejected and a little resentment began to set in.

Hardly had Mary got over the critical part of her illness when Winifred was faced with another crisis that had dire consequences on her and the family. Being the home-loving husband and father didn't last long, and Jack was once again out on the rant leaving Winifred short of money; amongst other things she couldn't pay the rent and so got into arrears. The council, a very unforgiving landlord, served her with an eviction order, and it wasn't too long afterwards that the Bailiff's van arrived. On arrival, the twins were in a pram in the front garden and Maureen and Jimmy were stood on the front step. The Bailiff's men were used to this kind of situation, but even they were touched by the pathetic sight which confronted them. They didn't have the heart to carry out the grim task; nonetheless, the council did not relent and the order still stood. Finally, Jack did the job himself with his horse and cart and they moved to a very small terraced house on Short Street, just off Piccadilly Road. They only stayed in that house three weeks, as there was something eerie about it. From the beginning, Winifred felt uneasy and afraid to stay there; even with her children around her, she felt very lonely. There was a good reason for this because she had a very frightening experience during her short stay there.

She'd already had an extremely trying day and it was almost midnight; she was sat alone in the small dank living room when Mary started crying loudly upstairs. As Winifred climbed the stairs there was a strange chilly feel about the place and she became very frightened; when she reached Mary, she tried to comfort and console her, but to no avail.

Mary's bellowing became more intense and Winifred became quite agitated and started to cry herself, "Oh please, baby, please stop crying. Mummy's not very well herself, and you're making me feel frightened."

The pleading didn't help, and Mary seemed to scream even more, so Winifred decided to take her downstairs. It was when she reached the top of the stairs that she got a terrible feeling. The incessant crying was driving her to distraction, and she could hear voices in her head telling her to throw the child down the stairs; the most horrifying thing is that she got the hideous impulse to do just that! Then, by the grace of God, she came to her senses and realised the gravity of the situation; she just hugged Mary as tightly as she possibly could. On reaching downstairs, she immediately fell to her knees and begged God's forgiveness for having allowed such ghastly thoughts to enter her head.

Up until then, she'd never believed in ghosts or haunted houses, but at that moment she knew there was something very evil about that house. The very next morning she sent for the priest and had it exorcised; then, without any further delay, she pulled out all the stops to get away from it as soon as possible. She'd heard of a house on Whitaker Street, which was just off Trafalgar Street, and within a week the family moved into it. It was only later that she heard tales about the ghoulish house. It turned out that a man had lived there alone; one night after a boozing spree he'd offered to put a younger fellow, who had just missed the last bus to Rawtenstall, up for the night. As the tale went, the man made an indecent proposal to his young guest at the top of the stairs; this resulted in a fight during which the owner was thrown down the stairs, broke his neck and died!

The house on Whitaker St. was very small, and it was right next to the main railway line; still, she felt more settled. One thing happened during her stay there which stuck in her mind. It was the winter of 1940 in January. On Jack's birthday and her own the following day they stayed in together around the fireside with the kids; it wasn't out of choice though, just two days earlier it had snowed, snowed and snowed again. So much snow fell over those few days that every house in Burnley was covered up to the bedroom windowsills, it was nigh impossible to leave the house; it was estimated that three quarters of a million tons of snow had fallen on Burnley over the weekend. It wasn't just the snow either, as the freezing temperature was almost the lowest ever recorded, fifteen degrees below zero.

Also in the same month, food rationing was introduced on commodities like bacon, sugar, butter, meat and tea, and was later extended indefinitely. Ration books were issued according to the number in each family; in this respect, Winifred fared quite well, as extra rations were allocated to expectant mums and small children.

In July Jack got his calling-up papers, and had to report to Litchfield in the Midlands where he enrolled into the Catering Corps. Winifred didn't like him being away from home but at least she had a regular allowance from the Army. It wasn't much, but it was there every week without having to fight for it. Like her mother before her, she learned to get by any way she could, including going to the market near to closing time in order to buy produce at knockdown prices. One item she always bought in quantity was broken biscuits; these were the only kind her children ever got during their early years; no matter, they tasted just as good as full ones, and she never once had any complaints. Another method of getting by was to exchange one particular commodity for another. She was a great believer that sugar was good for sustaining the children's energy levels, and would often exchange a packet of tea for a two-pound bag of Tate & Lyle; hence, the kids were quite accustomed to drinking sweet, weak tea.

Soon after Jack got called up, Winifred realised that she was pregnant once again; Maureen was only five years and three months old and was already the eldest of four.

The little house was already too small for them, and when she was offered a bigger one in the same area, she eagerly took it. In early January 1941, when she was eight months pregnant, the family moved into 14 ALBION STREET.

It was to be their home for the next twenty years.

7: trafalgar

Burnley, like Bacup, was a busy industrial town only much more so, and the Trafalgar area of Burnley was a thriving community in its own right. Trafalgar Street was known to the local folk as simply TRAFALGAR; it was, and still is, a main thoroughfare for traffic, and a main route for local and out of town buses. It ran from the Mitre, which was the main junction of Accrington Road, Padiham Road and Westgate, for a distance of half a mile passing through Sandygate Junction and on as far as Manchester Road.

The Leeds & Liverpool Canal ran parallel to this main thoroughfare, being overlooked on each side by numerous cotton mills and weaving sheds. One in particular that stood out was the Clocktower Mill, for standing proudly on top of it and dominating the skyline was a large clock; it was a distinctive landmark, and known to all the local people as Watt's Clock. Burnley had more cotton mills than any other town of comparable size in the world, and the most congested industrial district was Trafalgar. In the heart of Trafalgar a cluster of tall chimneys punctuated the skyline, polluting the air with thick, dense smoke; this locality was known as THE WEAVER'S TRIANGLE.

Wager

In the days of the tall chimneys, many a wager was won and lost, and one went something like this:

"Which is the longest chimney in Burnley?"

"Oh, that's easy, it's the one in the Corporation Yard."

The first fellow then quipped, "I'll bet thi it's not."

After careful deliberation, the other said, "Go on then, you're on, I'll bet thi a couple ó bob," then, after shaking hands on it, "Right, which one then?"

"The one on the Clifton pit site," replied the first.

"Whattaya talking about? That's rubbish! It's nowhere near as tall as the one in the Corporation Yard."

"Ah yes, that's true, but I didn't say tallest, I said longest, and although Clifton Chimney only stands about fifty feet above the ground, it goes way deep down into it, right to the bottom of the mine."

The second reluctantly agreed, and handed over the money, and was wiser albeit poorer.

Built in close proximity to the dreary mills on the opposite side of Trafalgar was a labyrinth of cobbled streets. Many of these branched directly off the main road running uphill as far as the main railway line finishing against a stone embankment. Albion Street was the exception being situated in the centre of Trafalgar. It continued beyond the railway line, via a stone bridge, progressing for another half mile as far as the gates of Scott's Park. It was also much steeper than the adjacent streets and the back, being elevated, overlooked the rooftops of the other houses. At the bottom of Albion Street, directly opposite on the other side of Trafalgar, an iron footbridge stretched in between large cotton mills and over the canal, and was a popular shortcut to town. Number fourteen was situated in the middle of the block; it was bigger than the normal terraced house, having two upstairs bedrooms, two ground-floor rooms and two large cellars.

On entering the front door a passageway led into a tiny parlour with no lighting except for the dim glow cast by an old Victorian gas-lamp, which stood on the pavement outside. The living room in Albion Street was small with a flagged floor. It was the only room in the house with lighting – an antiquated gas-lamp that hung from the centre of the ceiling. It dangled very low down and the mantle was forever being broken by someone's head. The focal point of the room was a large cast-iron fireplace with a mantelpiece similar to the one in Winifred's mother's home in Bacup. In the alcove were wooden cupboards from floor to ceiling with bulky drawers underneath. Cast-iron legs supported a pot sink beneath the window; small curtains were draped around the legs concealing cleaning rags and bundles of firewood. Above the sink was a gas geyser, and next to the cupboards a gas boiler to heat up the greater volume of water required for clothes, washing and bathing. A dolly tub and mangle stood alongside the boiler.

Furniture consisted of a large wooden table with extending flaps, and placed around the table in the centre of the room stood four standchairs. A huge ornamental sideboard occupied most of the space against the back wall, and the reflection from the enormous mirror added depth to the room making it feel much cosier. Around the fireplace stood a comfy old sofa and two sagging armchairs; the only piece of floor covering was a peg-rug made from old coats. A much-used wooden rack above the fireplace ensured that the kiddies' clothes were always crisp, dry and well aired.

The back door opened on to a steep flight of stone steps, which led down to the backyard. Most of the yard space was taken up by the air-raid shelter, which housed the lavatory.

The front bedroom looked out on to the houses across the street and Watt's clock was clearly visible over the rooftops of the houses lower down. The back bedroom was bare, but it had a magnificent view from the window on a clear day. In the distance the green rolling hills above Cliviger were clearly visible. Beyond in the far distance, the barren Lancashire hills provided a welcome contrast to the grimy mills and clustered rooftops of Trafalgar. The Town Hall Clock loomed large in the foreground and alerted everyone to its presence as it chimed simultaneously on the hour with Watt's clock.

Soon after moving into her new home Winifred took stock of her life. It had just turned eight o'clock, and she had settled all the younger kids down for the night. She was sat in front of the fire pondering on what might have been, but still had high hopes for the future.

"Married for six years," she thought, "u-um, and already, I've moved seven times. Still, another home, another beginning; yes, this is our chance to start afresh, and try to make our marriage work. Four beautiful healthy children, and another baby almost ready to be born;

surely that's enough to make Jack happy." It was a far cry from her dreams as a young girl but still, she had a good feeling about it, and that's all that seemed important to her.

Her thoughts were interrupted by Maureen tugging at her sleeve. "Are these all right, Mummy?" she asked.

Winifred looked down at young Maureen, who had just finished darning some of little Jimmy's socks. "Ah, our Maureen, aren't you a real little love? Now why don't you just sit yourself down and Mummy will make you a cup of cocoa before you go to bed?"

"All right, Mummy, thank you ... but can I please stay up a little bit longer, and help you do some ironing?"

"No, that's all right, love, you've already done enough for one night."

"Oh please, Mummy, I don't mind, honest! I love helping you with my little brothers and sisters."

"Come here and give me a big hug ... you're a right little angel, what would I do without you?"

Later that evening, after Maureen had gone to bed, Winifred reflected on her blessings. "Well, God, I haven't much money, and my husband may be unreliable, but at least You've given me the four children I asked for, and another one for good measure by the looks of things. There is one thing, however, that I must sincerely thank You for ... in Your infinite wisdom, my firstborn was my Maureen. Without her I just don't know what I would have done; she's my right arm and inspiration, not only to me, but the young ones as well."

As yet she didn't know any of the neighbours, but at least she knew where all the shops on Trafalgar were, which were close to hand. She did most of her shopping at the Co-op Building, on the corner of Patten Street, where it was slightly cheaper and one got a dividend or "divi" as it was commonly known. She received the divi number 12842, which was registered after each buying in. It was a way of saving up, and enabled her to draw a small amount of cash from time to time. Every little helped along with her other schemes; she had to be thrifty, and scrimp and save, as inflation was really taking off. Fish and chips had recently gone up to fourpence-ha'penny, and no longer could one buy just a pennyworth of chips unless they had a fish as well; steak pudding, chips and peas had actually risen from fivepence to a staggering eightpence.

The war brought the people much closer together; they helped each other in many different ways and this made the hard times bearable. Garden allotments sprang up all over the place and some people started to grow their own produce. There was a gentleman called Mr Shackleton, who had a pen behind Christ the King Church, where he kept hens; he lived right across the street, therefore Winifred was almost guaranteed a steady supply of new-laid free-range eggs.

Like many other towns, Burnley was classed as a 'Neutral Evacuation Receptive Area' and designated to accommodate evacuees from London and other places. In June 1940 more than eight hundred arrived from the Channel Islands. Some were dispersed to Nelson, Brierfield and Colne but most of them remained in Burnley. Advertisements were displayed throughout the town asking for families to foster these unfortunate people, as most of them were children. A small payment was allocated to any household which took on this obligation; the going rate was twenty-one shillings for an adult and about nine shillings for a child, depending on age. Winifred would have liked to help, but her home was already far too overcrowded.

Every town in Britain pulled its weight to help the nation's plight. Burnley was no exception; each town used to have a special war effort week, and during the week 18th/25th of January, Burnley did something exceptional. During these specially allotted times, each person in the town would do their bit to raise money for the war effort; all monies collected went towards buying arms to fend off the German invasion, a Spitfire, a tank, etc. The feeling of patriotism and unity was fantastic; every single person pulled together as one.

People saved waste paper, scrap iron, rags and whatever else the authorities asked for. Individual streets collected bucketfuls of keys or any small metal objects they could lay their hands on; they also made small donations out of the little money they had. Children's competitions were organised, and one of these involved designing a poster illustrating the war effort.

Large firms, such as Building Societies, Banks and Assurance Companies, donated substantial amounts of money, as did well-known local firms. Everywhere you went, there were advertisements on billboards and factory walls and on the gable ends of houses. One in particular was a large mural that took up the whole of a massive gable end on Yorkshire Street. It depicted a tall factory chimney that symbolised a large barometer. It was divided into seven sections representing degrees; from the bottom upwards, each section was in turn named days of the week from Saturday to Saturday, excluding Sunday. The aim was to raise £600,000 in the week; this figure was written right at the top of the chimney. It seemed an impossible task, given that the average wage was only about £4 per week. Impossible or not, something phenomenal happened; by Monday, the total had already reached an amazing £410,060, and by Tuesday the Burnley people had donated a further £126,940 to top it up to £540,000.

The *Burnley Express* congratulated the extraordinary effort and their headline was 'Let's make it a million!' A tough challenge but nevertheless … that's exactly what the people of Burnley did; by the end of that outstanding week, the total figure had reached a staggering … £1,000,570!

Ordinary working folk like Winifred had contributed what they could out of their meagre wages or allowances. Everyone anticipated a good response to the appeal, but the amount raised was far beyond anyone's expectations.

There was a local joke at the time:

It was the wedding anniversary of a collier and he wanted to give his wife a special treat. "Get thasel ready, mi luv, I'm tekkin thi out tonite."

They started to change and he was ready first, and just nipped to the corner shop for some fags. On returning, his wife was ready and carrying an umbrella.

"Tha'll not need that, lass, it's not gonna rain."

"And how do you know that?" she asked looking rather puzzled.

"Ah well!" he replied feeling quite pleased with himself. "I've just passed that barometer thing, and there was a bloke lookín up at it, and I heard him say Fine."

That particular mural stuck out in people's minds for obvious reasons but even more so in Winifred's. There were various photographs of it in the *Burnley Express* and other newspapers, therefore, it was the topic of conversation on many people's lips. It happened to be Jack's birthday, and Winifred was down town with Maureen; she had just bought a present for him.

They were just passing the gable end when Maureen spotted it. "Oh look, Mummy, there's that big painting that's in all the papers."

"Oh yes, you're right, my love."

"Bloomin éck, Mum, it's a lot bigger than I thought it was."

"It is, isn't it, love? I only thought that ..." She didn't manage to finish her sentence because of a sharp stabbing pain in her abdomen, accompanied by other well-known symptoms.

Little Maureen was keenly aware of her mum's condition, and instinctively became concerned. "Oh, Mummy, are you all right ... is it the baby?"

Winifred recognised the signs only too well, and knew the baby would soon be born, but she struggled to keep her composure for Maureen's sake. "Don't fret yourself so, my love, things are going to be all right. Now just hold Mummy's hand, and we'll go to that café on the corner and call for an ambulance."

Luckily, everything went quite well, she was taken to Bank Hall, and the next morning on January 29th 1941, her birthday child, Barry was born.

It was a normal birth and Winifred was soon transferred to the ward amongst all the other young mothers and their babies. For most, it was obviously a happy event and especially so at visiting time when all their husbands came to celebrate their joyous occasion. As for Winifred, she felt rather sad as she gazed round the ward. She could plainly see the happiness and closeness of all the other couples with their new babies; yet, here she was, having just had the most gorgeous little boy, but sadly, no husband by her side to share in the joy.

"Mind," she kept telling herself, "this is one time when it's not his fault, as he can't help being away in the forces."

To be fair though she was also fretting about her other young ones. Maureen and Jimmy had gone to stay at her mum's house in Bacup, whereas the twins were being cared for on one of the hospital wards. Her thoughts were interrupted as two nurses approached her bed; one was holding little Barry and the other was carrying a cake with candles on it.

One leaned over the bed and very politely said, "Mrs Cowell, from all the nursing staff, we wish you Happy Birthday!" Then as she handed over the newborn child. "And here is the best present that anyone could ever give you."

Winifred was quite taken aback by the event, and had to hold back the tears as she held her new tiny son in her arms.

She was touched even more when the young mothers surrounded her bed and started to sing, "Happy Birthday".

To make things even better she was later informed that Jack had rung to say he'd got a few days compassionate leave, and he'd be home the next day. She was much happier now, and as always at times like this, she started to reminisce. She couldn't help but think how uncanny it was that the important events always seemed to happen on, or around, her birthday. She reflected on the time she had returned from London, then when she had been in the Workhouse, and now this.

The following day Jack came to the ward, and little Maureen was with him. As on previous occasions, he picked up his newborn son and made a great fuss, appearing to be highly delighted.

As always he was full of false assurances. "This is great, three sons and two daughters, this is what life is really about." Then turning to Winifred, "Right, Win, I swear to you that when this war's over, I'm going to be a changed man. We're going to be a proper family, all cosy and nice together."

She'd heard all the empty promises many times before, but still she wanted to believe them. "Anyway who knows?" she thought to herself. "This war has brought lots of people together, so why not us ... u-um, why not indeed? Perhaps being away from his home and family has brought him to his senses."

On coming back to reality, she pointed out her concerns. "How's our little Jimmy going on then in Bacup? I hope he's not fretting; I'm a bit worried that he's too hard work for my mum, she's got enough on her plate as it is."

"Don't you worry your head about it, Win, it's all sorted. Whilst I'm home, Maureen and Jimmy are stopping with me, and when I go back to the barracks, our Beatie said she'll look after them."

Winifred wasn't too keen on the idea, but at least she realised that Beatie was trying to be friendly, and so went along with it.

Two days later Jack came to visit her. Once again Maureen was with him.

"Well, love," he said, "I don't like telling you, but my leave is almost at an end, I have to return to my billet this evening." He then added, "I'm sorry, Win, but I've run out of money, and there's not much food in the house, if you give me the family allowance books, I'll go down town and do a good buying in for when you get home."

She rummaged through her bag and handed them over, then, after kissing her, they both reluctantly left.

Winifred had to stay in hospital a little longer than normal, but it wasn't so much for her sake, as for the child's. Barry was very delicate; his chest was quite wheezy, which was the first sign that he was in future years to suffer from asthma.

Finally, though, the time came for them to go home, she was feeling quite elated, as she was looking forward to seeing her little ones again; however it was quite daunting, as it was a cold blustery, wintry day, and the snow was thick on the ground. Besides that, she didn't have enough money to order a taxi, and she knew she'd need to catch two buses in order to get home. She wrapped Barry in a woollen shawl ensuring that he was snug and warm; then, after giving all her thanks to the nursing staff, she left carrying him in her arms. By now it was late afternoon, and she had to wait about ten minutes before a bus came; unluckily she missed her connection in Burnley Town Centre, and had to wait another ten minutes in the cold shelter near to the Boot Inn. By the time she got off the bus she was absolutely frozen to the bone, and so scurried up Albion Street, thinking that she'd be all right once she reached home. Things didn't turn out that way … there was a shock in store for her.

Her sister Katie was waiting for her in the house, and as soon as Winifred saw her she knew something was amiss. "All right, our Katie, you look a little worried … is anything wrong?"

"Yes, I'm afraid there is, our Winnie," she uttered in a rather concerned voice. "I only arrived about twenty minutes ago, and I'm sorry to be the bearer of bad news, but someone has broken in and smashed your cellar windows, and they've been through all your cupboards."

"Oh no, please don't say that! I haven't got a penny piece, and the family allowance isn't due for another two days."

Sure enough her fears were confirmed, there wasn't a crumb left. To make matters worse, when she went down the cellar, she discovered that the gas meter had been robbed as well; not content with that, most of the coal had been pinched.

At that moment she had an appalling thought, and turning to Katie asked, "Our Katie, you don't think that Jack would stoop so low as to do something like this do you? I know it's an awful thing to say, but what else am I supposed to think?"

After serious deliberation Katie replied, "No, our Winnie, I don't, I know at times he's a wrong un, and he can be a right swine, but this just doesn't seem to be his style at all. No, he wouldn't stoop to anything as low as this."

Winifred calmed herself down, then looked at little Barry, who was laid on the small sofa, still wrapped in the shawl which was now quite wet. "Righto, our Katie, first things first, let me get my priorities right. The most important thing right now is that I tend to my baby's needs, so let's get the fire going and get some heat into the house."

Luckily there was sufficient coal left to do this, also none of the baby's clothes had been taken, which meant that she was able to change him.

After that, Katie turned to her in a concerned manner. "Right, our Winnie, now it's your turn to be looked after, just sit yourself down and relax while I go out and get some food, then we can have something to eat."

"I hope you have some money, our Katie, because I haven't even a penny."

"No I haven't," Katie replied quite calmly, "but don't worry about it, our kid, surely they have strap shops here in Burnley, the same as Bacup, don't they?"

"I'm sure they do our Katie, but don't forget, I'm not too well known to most of the shopkeepers around here as yet."

"Never mind about that, just point me to the nearest selling out shop, and I'll tell 'em what the situation is .... yeah, I'm sure I'll get round 'em."

"Just let me think a bit ... the only one that will be open at this time is the one up the street, just over the bridge on the right-hand side."

"Right now, just you leave it with me and put kettle on, and I'll be back in two minutes."

True to her word, she returned shortly after with enough food to get by on for a couple of days. "There what did I tell you?" she laughed with a cheeky glint in her eye. "It was like taking candy from a baby. No, joking aside, our Winnie, he was quite an understanding kind man, and very sympathetic to your plight, and also very trusting. I promised him faithfully though that we'd straighten up with him before weekend."

They both laughed heartily, and that night went to bed quite contented with full stomachs. Katie stayed another week till Winifred found her feet and got into some sort of routine.

The kids had all returned home now, and were soon into everything. The house began to take on a definite feeling of being lived in. Winifred also felt happier when Maureen confirmed that her dad had definitely done a good buying in, and stocked up all the cupboards full of food. Then came the sad day when Katie had to return to Bacup.

Winifred gave her a peck on the cheek, "Eh, our Katie, thanks a million, I don't know what I would have done without you."

"Don't be so daft, our Winnie, you'd have done exactly the same for me if shoe had been on t'other foot ... anyroad, I've quite enjoyed myself." Her tone changed becoming a little more serious. "You know something our Winnie? You've got a lovely family here, and it's plain to see just how much you love 'em, but I'm a little concerned about you. I want you to promise me that you'll look after yourself as well. Aye, and that means giving yourself a little treat now and again."

"Oh thanks a lot, our Katie, that means an awful lot to me; I love you too, and I promise that I'll do as you ask." She gave Katie a final hug, adding, "Don't forget to give Mum and Dad and everybody my love, and a special hug to your little lad Tony from his Auntie Winnie."

With that they both hugged each other for the last time, then Katie left the house to catch the one o'clock bus to town at the bottom of Albion Street. The house felt rather empty after she'd gone, but then Winifred had to settle down to the serious business of raising her young ones.

8: trials & tribulations

Winifred never had much money, but was more than compensated for this by all the love that she got from her children. As for leisure time, she never missed that at all, as there was never a dull moment, or enough time in the day; no sooner had she finished one job than she had another to start. Never a day went by that she didn't get out the mangle, dolly tub and posser, the traditional Monday morning washday was out of the question. One daunting task that she did quite naturally, without giving it a second thought, was hanging out the washing on a line that was strung above the air-raid shelter. To achieve this, she had to straddle over a steel handrail, then stride across a ten-foot drop from the stone steps, onto the air-raid shelter...not so easy with a bundle of washing in one arm. Regardless of this, there was always some clothing on the line blowing in the wind, and the inside rack was forever full of nappies and other clothing.

Barry was just nine months old when Jack was discharged from the army on medical grounds, suffering from bronchitis and emphysema; he was only thirty-three, but already, his fast living lifestyle was beginning to catch up with him. On first arriving home, he was very poorly and had lost a lot of weight that he could ill afford to, as even in a fit state, he only weighed around nine stone at the most. Consequently, he needed a lot of care and attention, which meant even more work for Winifred. Still, she took everything in her stride, and if the truth be known, she actually enjoyed it because for the first time in their married life, Jack actually stayed in; they were all one big happy family. It was during this time that something happened that they were to remember for a long time. In the Burnley, Nelson and Colne area it was widely publicised on billboards and in public newspapers, that the police and army were looking for a deserter, who they described as bald, very well built, with mad staring eyes; he had been nicknamed "The Mad Eyed Vicar".

One particular evening, about five weeks after Jack had been discharged, he was still quite poorly, and was sat downstairs in the living room. At around nine o'clock, Winifred and Maureen were upstairs putting the younger children to bed, when there was a knock on the back door . This was very unusual, as no one ever came to the back door at that time of night because of the steep steps; also it was pitch black on the back street, and especially so during the blackout. On opening the door, there, stood at the top of the steps was a strange looking man wearing a scruffy army greatcoat, and looking rather dishevelled. Jack didn't know the bloke, but let him in on the pretext that he was looking for an army mate.

"I'm sorry mate," answered Jack, "I don't know the bloke, I haven't a clue where he lives."

"That's funny, I was sure he lived around here somewhere." muttered the stranger, who then changed the subject, "Are you in the army then?"

"No I'm not; I was up until just recently, but then I got discharged on medical grounds."

"Oh, tha'll have some discharge papers then?"

"Yes, of course I have, why do you ask?"

"Well it's just that I've ne'er seen any afore, and I'm curious as to what they look like … is there any chance o' me looking at 'em?"

Jack wasn't usually so gullible, but on this occasion he was, "Yes I don't see why not," he replied naively.

Without further ado, he rummaged through the built-in drawers, dug the papers out from underneath some of the children's clothes, and handed them over to the man.

Meanwhile Winifred had heard voices and wondered whom Jack was talking to. She went downstairs to find out with Maureen following close behind. Upon entering the living room, just shortly after Jack had handed over the papers, she was taken aback to see the stranger stood by the sink.

The bloke turned his head and looked at her, and she immediately noticed his big staring glaring eyes, and thought to herself, "Oh my

God! It's that deserter chap who the police are looking for." She began to feel panicky, and the hairs stood up on the back of her neck, but her immediate fears were for her kiddies in bed.

Maureen was clinging tightly to her dress, and Winifred instinctively shoved her behind her as she asked Jack, in an annoyed yet perturbed voice, "Who's this then, and what is he doing in my house at this time of night?"

Before Jack replied, she noticed the papers that the stranger was clutching tightly, and realising just what they were, she reacted angrily, "What do you think you're doing with those papers? Put them down now!"

He started laughing, then replied mockingly, as he made his way to the back door, "You're joking ... I'm keeping these!"

She approached him but Jack intervened, managing to get in between them both; turning to the stranger he said, "Right that's it, things have gone far enough ... now hand them over to me now!"

The chap became very aggressive, and without any warning, he savagely hit Jack in the face knocking him to the floor shouting, "You bloody little wimp ... I'll kill thi as soon as look at thi!"

Jack, still being very ill, was gasping for his breath and couldn't get up; the stranger who by now was standing over him, laughed scornfully.

He drew his right foot back with intent to kick Jack, but Winifred knelt in front of him and started to plead, "Oh please ... please don't hurt my husband! He's only just come out of hospital and he's still very poorly."

"Argh! Still very poorly is he," sniggered the stranger sarcastically. "Well I couldn't care less, and I still think he's a wimp!"

He was enjoying the moment, but it was only short-lived because, unbeknown to him, Winifred reached for an axe that was kept underneath the sink. With it firmly grasped in her hand, she stood up directly in front of him and confronted him with her arm raised in a threatening manner.

Deadly serious now, she made her request once more, "Now I'm asking you for the last time ... drop those papers!"

"And what will you do if I don't?" he mocked all the more.

Never taking her eyes off him for a second, and quite calm, she replied in earnest, "So help me ... I'll put this axe right through your skull!"

He glared at her for what seemed an age weighing up the situation, he could see she meant every word; then, in a very slow serious voice replied, "Yes ... I really believe you would!" He dropped the papers, and after mouthing a few obscenities, started to open the back door.

Still with the axe in her hand, she snarled, "Now get out of here!" and as he was stepping over the threshold she kicked him in the back and gave him one almighty shove, sending him sprawling head over heels down the fourteen stone steps. Unconcerned as to his condition, she then slammed the door shut and bolted it.

The following morning the incident was reported to the police. No more was ever heard about the "Mad Eyed Vicar". He certainly never returned to 14, Albion Street!

It was shortly after this incident that old Rosette arrived on the scene. She was to become a much-loved member of the family. She didn't actually live in the house, but was there most of the time; as far as the twins and Barry were concerned, they'd never known a time when she wasn't there.

She was a typical old lady of the times, with short straight hair that was as white as snow. She always wore a black shawl, an apron, and clogs with rubber soles. She must have been in her seventies then, but in spite of her age was quite sprightly, and like Maureen, she was a Godsend to Winifred. She helped with all the chores and just like Winifred's mother, she had a fad for donkey-stoning the front doorstep, and polishing the black cast-iron fireplace. Rosette had always been a kind of housemaid and nursemaid in Jack's home ever since he'd been a young boy and was therefore very fond of him. But she didn't go along with his wayward ways, and used to let him know in no uncertain terms.

She was quite strict with the kids, but all the same they grew to love and respect her. If Winifred happened to be out somewhere, and Rosette had just mopped the flag floor, she wouldn't let them in the house, come rain or come shine, till it dried. She had a quaint sense of humour, and used to have everyone in stitches with her comical ways.

Rosette talked in a very broad Lancashire accent, and would come out with the most amusing comments such as, "I'm just gonna go petty," or "Dusta wanna a cuppa tay?" and it was forever, "By gum" this, or "By gum" that. Another thing that amused Jack and Winifred alike was that she was constantly saying, "I'm just gonna tek misén off to labour exchange, to see if there's any jobs a goín."

Winifred didn't take her for granted she was eternally grateful, and would make her meals and give her whatever little money she could afford.

As time passed Jack began to feel much better, and despite Rosette getting on to him, he predictably drifted back into his wily ways. Five young ones now, but they hardly ever saw him, as he stayed in bed late every morning and they were always in bed by the time he got home late at night. Hence, Winifred took on the role of Dad as well as Mum, and although she loved them dearly, she knew she had to be strict; there were times though, when she felt really bad about this.

She was convinced that she was over-reacting to their mischievous behaviour. Consequently, she decided to see her G.P. about it, Dr. Kerr, a very regimental man, who had served many years as a medical officer in the Forces.

In the surgery, she confided in him just how she felt, then asked, "Is there something wrong with me Doctor? I'm always shouting at my kids, and I feel as though I'm not fit to have them."

"Mrs Cowell, try not to fret yourself about it too much, I can assure you that lots of young mothers feel the same way as you. Allow me to put you at ease by saying, I think you are doing a marvellous job under very difficult circumstances. All your children are in obvious good health, and if I thought otherwise, I would be the first to let you know." His tone changed, and he became a little more serious, "But I have to say you are walking on a tightrope, and you could tip either way; the balance is very delicate. The only thing I can suggest is that you foster some of your children out for a short while to give yourself a bit of a break."

Her heart sank, as she knew that she could never do that, for she wanted them all to grow up together knowing one another. Besides, she felt that she could never leave Jimmy in the care of anyone with him being so hyperactive and possessive; as for the twins, they'd never ever been separated. So, she had no alternative but to cope with her lot in the best way she could; however, her consultation with the doctor wasn't a total loss, because at least she felt a little better about herself.

She soon got to know most of the neighbours and on the whole, she got on with them quite well despite her reputation for being very protective towards her children. All the same, she tried her utmost to be fair and if anyone came to the house complaining about any of them she would look into the matter and sort it out accordingly.

In the early days, the main source of complaint was about Jimmy. Even as a child, he was a bit of a loner and he would sit on the stone flags outside the house routing in between the nicks with his fingers, and woe betide any other child who intervened. He was only slender, yet very strong and wiry with a quick temper and got into trouble at the drop of a hat. A favourite trick of his was to dig up worms, then put them down the necks of unsuspecting kids ... especially the girls.

It so happened that one of the neighbours called Bella Whittam lived just across the street. She had a little boy named Terry, who was a similar age to Jimmy, but very spoilt, he would run home crying if anybody so much as looked at him. She also had another boy called Peter who was two years older than Jimmy.

Bella was forever at Winifred's door complaining about Jimmy for one thing or another, and Winifred did her best to ease the situation, but then something happened that caused a right ruction. It was a typical day for Winifred and as usual she was up to her eyeballs in work and actually wasn't feeling at her best.

She was just about to hang out some washing when Bella came ranting and raving at the front door, "Right Winnie Cowell! I've come about that little brat of yours ... he's gone and thumped our Terry again, and this time he's busted his nose!"

"Oh come on Bella, things can't carry on like this ... I'm forever checking my little lad for yours, it's not really on because they're both the same age. No, I'm sorry but your Terry is just going to have to learn to stick up for himself."

"Right ... we'll see about that," rapped Bella as she angrily stomped off.

Winifred didn't give it a second thought but then Bella's husband Walter came knocking at the door in an irate manner; the front door was ajar and as Winifred approached him it was plain to see that he was very angry.

"Yes, Walter, what can I do for you?"

"You know darned well what you can do," he retorted, "it's that little brat of yours!"

"Hey, now just hang on a minute Walter, I've already had this out with your wife."

"Aye, you can sod that for a tale as well! I want to know what tha gonna do about it?"

"Walter ... what you've got to realise is that I can't keep chastising my little lad for yours, he's only three and a half years old, and already the eldest of four."

"Right, so that's your answer is it?" he growled angrily, "Well, I'm telling thí now ... if it happens again, I'll get our Peter to hit him!"

"Yes, and if he does ... so help me, I'll hit your wife!"

"Arrgh! It's a waste of time arguing with the likes ó thee," he snarled, then walked away muttering under his breath.

A week or two passed by, Winifred was putting some clothes through the wringer when little Jimmy came running in really heartbroken; he kept pulling at her apron string spluttering, "B-be-e-wa! ... Be-ewa!"

At first, she couldn't make out what he was trying to say, and asked a little edgily, "O-oh, what's to do again?"

No matter, he wasn't to be put off, in between sobs he kept spluttering, "B-e-e-wa! ... Be-e -wa!" Then, she noticed he was holding his cheek, and realised he was trying to say Bella; on kneeling down in front of him, she could actually see finger marks on his face.

At that moment, he finally managed to blurt out the words, "Bewwa ... hit me Mummy!"

That was it! The adrenaline started flowing and every hair on her body seemed to stand on end as the blood boiled in her veins. She dropped everything there and then and ran out of the house.

As usual, Bella was stood on the front doorstep but on seeing Winifred she flew into the lobby and bolted the door.

Winifred's first impulse was to smash her windows but thought better of it, so she crouched down and started to shout through the letterbox, "Bella ... open this flaming door or so help me, I'll break it down!"

"Go away," shouted Bella, "I don't want anything to do with you!"

"You don't do you not? Well you should have thought of that before you struck my little lad across the face."

Bella more or less repeated the same, "Go away I tell you ... I don't want any truck with you."

"Right! That's your answer is it? Well listen to me Bella and listen good, cós I want something to do with you ... you've just hit my child and I want to feel the same imprints on my face."

There was no response, Winifred became quite frustrated and started banging and kicking on the door, which resulted in Bella screeching, "O-oh, go away from my front door or I mean it ... I'll have the police on you."

"You will, will you? Well you can have the whole bloody police force on me for all I care ... I'm telling you now Bella I won't rest till it's sorted." Winifred could see she wasn't getting anywhere, and resorted to other measures, "Right Bella, I'm going now but take heed; if I've to wait a month ... a year ... or a lifetime, I won't rest until I feel the weight of your hand across my face."

She could do no more so she went back to her own house and carried on with her daily routine. The incident happened in March and during the next few months she never saw hide or hair of Bella; even as summer approached, Bella never stood on the doorstep.

During this time a neighbour, Mrs. Higgins, stopped Winifred in the street, "Hello Winnie, I've just bin talkín to Bella about that incident wí tha little lad ó thine, and she were tellín me that things should a blown o'er by now."

"Oh, she did, did she? Well that's what she thinks ... and what did you say to that?"

"Oh, I telt her straight Winnie; I shrugged mí shoulders and telt her, I wouldn't like to be in your shoes Bella. I also telt her, no matter what anybody thinks ó Winnie Cowell, she doesn't need a regiment o soldiers behind her to fight her battles ... tha's done worse thing tha cudda done hittín' one of her kids. As far as Winnie Cowell's kids are concerned, I said, they are her life, she's like a cat with kittens and would gladly die to protect ém."

"Umph!" shrugged Winifred, "And how did she react to that?"

"Well, she's still living in hopes that tha'll forget all about it. Anyroad, I telt her straight, 'I don't think so, cós in my opinion tha's done worst thing tha cudda done ... no,' I said, 'Winnie Cowell wont forget about it till its bin sorted good and proper.' "

A little time passed then one day in August Winifred was shopping on Trafalgar and happened to be in Tom Howarth's chemist shop. She was just being served when she heard voices outside the shop, and felt sure that one of them was Bella's.

"Excuse me Tom," she said politely, "I won't be a minute."

Sure enough, there, on the pavement outside Dick Smith's grocers, was Bella, chatting away to a lady called Bertha Sutcliffe.

As Winifred left the shop, Bella saw her and the colour of her face turned distinctively paler; her first instinct was to take flight, but she couldn't, as she had a basket full of groceries on her arm.

Winifred slowly approached her and very calmly said, "Hello Bella ... nice to see you after all this time."

"Look, just go away Winnie Cowell, I don't want any truck with you."

Still calm but with her eyes fixed on Bella, Winifred repeated what she'd spoken through the letterbox, "Oh, you don't do you not? Well, I'm telling you now Bella, like I said before, you've hit my child and I want to feel those same imprints on my face."

At this point, the other lady intervened, "Now come on Winnie, leave her be ... she hasn't done anything."

Turning to the woman, Winifred replied politely but firmly, "Bertha, just keep out of this ... this is strictly between me and Bella." Turning to Bella again, she repeated, "Right Bella, I'll say it just one more time ... you hit my child, so now you have to hit me."

"Just let me be Winnie Cowell," insisted Bella becoming rather agitated, "I just want to go home."

"Oh, you want to go home do you? Well take this with you!"

retorted Winifred as she gave her one hell of a smack across her left cheek ... then just for good measure, followed that up with a solid back hander to the other.

Rightly or wrongly, she then wrenched the basket of groceries from Bella's grasp and threw it right into the middle of the road into the path of an oncoming bus. Onlookers, their curiosity aroused by the skirmish, looked on in surprise as Bella stood there squirming.

Winifred was happy now, turning to Bella once more, she added, "Right Bella, as far as I'm concerned, that's the end of it, but I give you fair warning, don't you ever lay your hands on any of my kids again or so help me, I'll swing for you." She then calmly collected her things from the Chemist's, and went on her way.

She was satisfied with the outcome, but unbeknown to her, the matter was by no means finished. Lizzie Arkwright, Bella's mother-in-law, lived just a few doors higher up and was renowned for fighting around town. She was about forty-eight years old but quite a fit looking, big rawboned lady. On a summer day, one could fair see her muscles rippling in the sun. She was also notorious for having one too many at the pub, which in turn, made her rather quarrelsome.

It was always easy to tell when she was coming home from the pub, as she always sang the same line from her favourite song, "Don't sweetheart me ... if you don't mean it."

A few days after the Bella incident, Winifred was on the front street as Lizzie was coming home with some of her boozy friends.

As they approached her, Lizzie snarled belligerently, "Right Winnie Cowell, what's this I hear about thee thumping our Bella?"

"Leave it be Lizzie, it's got nothing to do with you, it was between me and Bella, and now it's finished."

"O-oh, is that reight then ... it's now't to do wí me is it not? Well now, I'm mekkín it my business and I'm gonna githee same good hidín as what tha's given her."

Winifred didn't want to get involved, so tried to play down the situation, "Please Lizzie, let it go, I've got no truck with you."

"Tha doesn't want any truck wí me dusta not? I believe that's what our Bella said to thee, but it didn't mék much difference did it?"

"Lizzie," replied Winifred placatingly, "that was a different matter altogether, and like I said, it was between me and Bella."

"Eh, just arken at her," mocked Lizzie to her drunken friends, who in turn encouraged her all the more.

"Go on Lizzie, give her a good hiding same as she gave Bella … she's asking forrít."

By now, Lizzie was all primed up for a fight and without any further warning, she gave Winifred such an almighty smack across the face, that she saw stars.

"Right!" she gloated, "A ta ready to feight now, cós there's plenty more where that came from?"

Winifred was fuming but still kept her cool and once again tried to diffuse the situation, "Lizzie, I'll tell you one more time, I don't want to fight you. Number one, you're much older than me, and number two … you're drunk."

By now, Lizzie was really psyched up, "O-oh. I'm drunk am I? Well, whether I am or not, I'm still gonna githee a reight good hidín."

"Lizzie," implored Winifred, "Please don't hit me again, I'm warning you for your own sake"

Alas, the warning went unheeded Lizzie landed another smack right across Winifred's face.

That was it! No more niceties. Winifred tore into her and they both rolled about the street thumping and scratching each other. Lizzie was very strong, but it soon became apparent that she was no match for Winifred. As soon as Winifred had the better of her though, that was the end of it. When Lizzie's, so-called friends saw how Winifred could handle herself, there were no more sneering remarks from any of them.

Winifred helped Lizzie to her feet and even apologised to her, "Look I'm sorry Lizzie, I didn't want it to come to this." Winifred then dusted herself down and walked briskly into her house.

However, just half an hour later, Walter came knocking at the door and started to threaten her, "What's this about thee hittin mí mother Winnie Cowell, are you goin' mad woman? It's bad enough you beltín mi wife but now this."

Winifred tried to explain what had happened but he wouldn't listen to reason, and actually pinned her up against the wall.

"Get your flamín' hands off me," she yelled defiantly, "or so help me, I'll put a knife right through your heart!"

He sensed her deadly serious mood, so took heed of the warning, "Yes, you would wouldn't you?" he snarled before letting her loose and skulking off.

He hadn't hurt her physically, but be that as it may, she was shaken up and felt deeply hurt to think that a fellow had confronted her. She told Jack when he got home and to be fair, he erupted; he stormed across the road to Walter's house where a fight would have been imminent but for Winifred's intervention, asking him to leave it alone. At least he had taken her side and she felt good about that. Now all Winifred wanted to do was to get on with everyday things but a couple of days later she discovered that the issue was still not quite finished.

It came to light when an old lady, who had a second-hand shop in the town centre near to the White Horse Pub, paid her a visit, "Winnie" she said quite concerned, "I just had to come and see you because I think you are in terrible danger."

"Why Emily, what makes you think that?" queried Winifred.

"Well, it's just that Lizzie Arkwright has been out on the town all day boozing with her friends in the Dog and Duck and the White Horse."

"That may be so Emily, but what's that got to do with me?"

"Ah well, it's all over town about you giving Bella a good hiding and having a go at Lizzie. What makes it worse is that all her mates have been egging her on and getting her all riled up. The frightening thing though, is that she kept saying that she's going to bottle you today."

"Oh thank you for telling me and for your concern, but I think I will be all right, Lizzie often says things like that when she's drunk, but she doesn't really mean it."

"Oh no Winifred, it's different this time, she's all fired up, I've never seen her like this before." The old lady was genuinely concerned and made a request, "Please Winifred, will you promise me that you'll lock your doors tonight?" Winifred thanked her for her concern and promised that she would do as asked.

Nevertheless, after careful consideration and despite being a little afraid, she decided against it, "No," she thought to herself, "I have to bring my kids up on this street and there's no way I'm going to do that behind locked doors."

Consequently rather than hide, she actually did the opposite and decided to face the problem head on. At teatime, she stood on the front doorstep waiting for Lizzie to return. It wasn't long before she could hear Lizzie singing her favourite song as she staggered over the footbridge. It was obvious that her boozing buddies were with her, as they were bellowing loudly alongside her. Winifred was on tenterhooks and felt all her body trembling, but was determined to stand her ground; she was prepared for the worst, but thankfully, it didn't come to that.

Lizzie and her friends tramped up on the other side of the street and on drawing level with Winifred, Lizzie stopped and shouted across, "All reight Winnie? There's some onions goín down town; if tha wants any, tha'd best get thasél down there now cós there's loads queuing up forém."

"That's it," thought Winifred thankfully, "she's peaceful ... I'm all for that."

Not too long after Lizzie fell and broke her arm and was confined to the house for quite a while. A week passed before Winifred got to know about it, then she went to see how she was coping; much to her dismay, Lizzie was in a right state. Winifred immediately set to and made her something to eat, she even helped her to wash and dress. Lizzie was most grateful and kept repeating how sorry she was for the fallout. Winifred reassured her that it didn't matter, as she understood why.

"Yeah Winnie, that's all reight, but where's Bella now that I needs her ... dusta know, she's not so much as méd me a cuppa tay."

"Well never you mind about that either Lizzie," answered Winifred compassionately, "until you get back on your feet again, you're coming across to my house for your meals."

"Eh Winnie, I couldn't put thi to that cós ...."

"There's no more to be said about it Lizzie, I'd like you to come, and also, I'd like to add that I'll be popping across to help you till you can fend for yourself again." She kept to her promise, Lizzie did come across until she could tend to herself again, and the two of them became firm friends forever after.

A year passed and nothing much changed, then the house next door at number sixteen became vacant. Mrs Alice King, the lady who had been her next door neighbour on Dalton Street came to live there with her two daughters, Ada and Jean. Winifred was happy about this, as they had always hit it off well in the past; things appeared to be looking up.

All the children were in good health, but then something happened which gave both Winifred and Jack a real nasty fright.

One afternoon about two o'clock, little John came crawling up the lobby crying, "Bellyache Mummy ... bellyache."

It was really unusual for him, as he was normally robust and running all over the place and was a handful. At first, she thought he was constipated and so tried him on the potty, but nothing happened; still he carried on whinging. Then, due to inexperience, she gave him some working medicine, which made matters worse; his condition deteriorated and it soon became evident that something was very wrong. She rushed next door and asked Mrs King to keep an eye on him whilst she went down to the Trafalgar Pub to look for Jack, where luckily, she found him. At first, he was reluctant to come but on reaching home he soon changed his tune, as it was obvious that there was something terribly amiss. By now, the little lad's temperature was soaring, he was soaking with sweat and having convulsions, and his little eyes were rolling about in his head.

"Oh my God!" exclaimed Jack as he picked him up, "He's dying ... he's just like a rag doll!"

He immediately ran carrying little John in his arms, with Winifred following hot on his heels to the doctor's surgery on Manchester Road. After a brief examination, an ambulance was ordered and John was taken to hospital.

On arrival, the surgeon was pessimistic about the outcome, he spoke to Jack and Winifred in a very serious tone of voice, "I'm afraid your little boy's condition is critical, I suspect that he has a perforated appendix, and I have no alternative but to operate. However, before I do, I must tell you that I think it's been left too long, and his chances of survival are now very slim indeed."

They were both very distraught, Jack stayed there all night, but Winifred had to go home to tend to the other children. She was understandably very anxious and never slept a wink that night. Next morning after seeing to all the kids, she made her way to the children's ward where, to her surprise, John was stood up in his cot clinging to the rails as sprightly as ever.

As soon as he saw her, he started bouncing up and down, then gleefully held out his arms shouting, "Mummy! Mummy!"

Her eyes filled to the brim as she started muttering to herself, "Oh thank you God! Thank You ... I couldn't have wished for anything better."

He wasn't in hospital very long but whilst there, it so happened that his Uncle Ted had been admitted to Ward Three. John was only very young but even so, it was one of those times that lingered in his memory. He plainly remembers waking up with steel clips in his tummy, then being visited by his brothers and sisters and being made a fuss of. But most of all, he remembers the day when Jack came to take him home. It was so special because prior to going home, Jack took him to Ward Three to visit Ted. It turned out to be the one and only time that John ever saw his Uncle Ted, it was a very special and memorable occasion for him. Ted was in bed and very poorly, but all the same, he made a fuss of the little lad. He handed John a cloth cap and got one of the more able patients to escort him around the ward. To John's delight they all started to fill the cap with pennies and sweets. Uncle Ted created a great impression on John and the little lad asked about him many times after that, but sadly, Ted had died whilst on the ward.

Life settled back to normal for a short time then came the darkest period of Winifred's life. Jack had been caught red-handed handling stolen goods and was sentenced to fifteen months in Wakefield Prison. It was also confirmed that Winifred was expecting again, she became completely distraught not knowing which way to turn. She remembered just how she'd felt when she was pregnant with the twins but this was worse ... much worse!

She was devastated and depressed and as always in times of crisis, she started to talk to herself, "Oh, dear God ... what am I going to do?

I have no money, no one to talk to and not even a decent place to live. Bare-stone floors, no form of heating and just a tin bath to wash my children's bodies. My husband is so unreliable and thinks more of his boozing friends than his own little ones ... and when he is here, his constant drinking causes nothing but violent scenes that upset all our lives. I have nowhere to lay this new life ... I can't even offer the baby peace."

Subsequently, she became even more depressed and took a dose of Quinine that almost killed both her and the baby. She was admitted to hospital where she had her stomach drained. Throughout the first night, it was touch and go, and, at one point, she was almost given up for dead but somehow survived.

As she was slowly recovering, a doctor and the ward sister came to her bed, the doctor asked, "Mrs Cowell, why did you try to take your own life?"

She was still feeling very ill but was well aware of the question and explained quite openly, "I didn't take the awful stuff to kill myself, but to free me of the baby."

They were very kind and understanding, but she needed more than just words to ease her plight. Eventually, she was allowed home, but no sooner had she left hospital than thoughts of abortion were once more going through her head. These thoughts made her feel ashamed, but she kept reassuring herself that she couldn't help her feelings; by some strange chance or divine intervention, the little baby lived on. Sadly though, Winifred never did look forward to the birth and she carried the child with deep resentment.

The months passed and the baby was almost due when Winifred had a bad accident. She was going down the cellar for some coal when she fell, hurting her back. She was admitted to hospital where she remained until the baby was born three weeks later. Once on the Maternity Ward, she was informed that complications had set in, and that the baby was placenta previa. They explained that the afterbirth was blocking the birth canal, and that the baby would die without a Caesarian Section operation.

Winifred suddenly realised just how much she wanted the baby to live and prayed for it to be so, "Oh dear God ... please forgive me for being so selfish and foolish and please be with me for my baby's sake. This little one wants to live so much in spite of all the terrible things that have been done to the contrary and against nature."

Just then, she felt the baby kick as though it was telling her it was definitely alive and ready to face the world. She was later taken to theatre, and when she came to, she had given birth to a beautiful little girl.

On September 18th, 1943, Barbara was born. Winifred was in Intensive Care for quite a long while and baby Barbara was in Baby Care for over two weeks.

The nurses were very kind to Winifred; as she started to recover, they took Barbara to her saying, "Eh, just look at her ... and to think we nearly lost her."

Winifred smiled to herself as she thought, "Yes, but by the grace of God, we didn't." She then made a solemn promise to make it up to the little girl once they were home.

Meanwhile at home, Maureen and Jimmy went to stay at Aunt Beatie's house, but little Barry and the twins had to be put in the Workhouse. Barry wasn't old enough to remember the event but the twins could recall it forevermore because to say the least, they weren't treated very kindly. The first thing that happened was that they were shepherded along with lots of other children into a large barrack type room where some matronly type women in uniforms started to lay down strict ground rules. They were then frog-marched and shown a dark cubbyhole with stone steps that led down into the darkness.

One of the women rapped in a very regimental voice, "Right, now listen you lot and listen good, this is the Bogey Hole, and if you're naughty, that's where you'll go and the Bogey Man'll get you!"

The three children were very close and clung to each other for comfort. John was never a cheeky lad but he was always very protective towards his sister and younger brother and this tended to land him in trouble. They'd been there just a few days when one of the nurses grabbed him by the scruff of his neck and dragged him to the Bogey Hole. He wasn't an unruly lad, but he wasn't having any of that; when he saw the darkness, he started kicking and screaming at the top of his voice. But it was to no avail and he was eventually locked in there. It was pitch black and his imagination took over ... he became very frightened and imagined all kinds of creaky noises, and started kicking at the door screaming for all his worth. Mary had witnessed the whole event and came out in sympathy with him, she screamed even louder than he did, this in turn triggered off little Barry.

They dragged Mary upstairs but found her to be more of a handful than they bargained for as she screamed at them, "You leave my brother alone you big bullies and let him out of that Bogey-hole. Anyroad, I'm gonna tell mi mummy over you lot, and she'll get you!"

Eventually they let John out, but afterwards, he wouldn't tolerate any of them or calm down no matter how they tried to placate him; even at his young age, he knew something was sadly wrong and that he'd been done an injustice. Nevertheless, in spite of being very unhappy during their stay in the Workhouse, they had to remain there for two months. But the staff realised they couldn't treat them just as they pleased and none of them were ever put in the Bogey Hole again. The whole episode was relayed to Winifred, but at the time, she was just too ill and alone to do anything about it.

Then one happy day, Jack, who had been released from prison early on good behaviour, arrived to take them home. They were highly delighted, but on reaching the house their delight changed to perplexity. It seemed so strange to the twins, as their mum was in bed in the living room, and she was cradling a little baby in her arms.

9: barbara

Barbara was just eight months old, and Winifred was still quite weak and not feeling well; Jack was still on the booze and couldn't care less one way or the other. The children were involved in all sorts of scrapes and were a handful. They needed lots of care and attention and Winifred wasn't coping very well. Little Maureen was her life-saviour; without her, anything could have happened. All the same, Winifred was constantly concerned about this, as she felt that Maureen was only a child herself and missing out on her childhood. Rosette was also a Godsend, helping in many ways, but with the best intentions in the world, she was now very old and limited to what she could do. Winifred counted her blessings and thanked God every night for Rosette and Maureen, but she was very despondent, as nothing could make up for the support of a good loving husband and father.

About this time, she became acquainted with a well-to-do lady called Mrs Smith, who lived in a beautiful house in Nelson. The lady had been married for seven years to a doctor but they had no children of their own. She used to make regular visits to Winifred's home and could plainly see how she was struggling, so she offered to take baby Barbara off her hands for a couple of weeks or so until she got back on her feet. Under normal circumstances, Winifred wouldn't have even considered it but because of her present predicament, she gave it a lot of thought.

One thing that cut her deeply, though, was that when she asked Jack about it, he just answered nonchalantly, "Yeah, why not? It seems like a good idea to me."

So, the lady took Barbara into care on a temporary basis much to the distress of Winifred and also Barbara's brothers and sisters. From the start, Maureen made it abundantly clear that she wasn't pleased and let both her mum and dad know in no uncertain terms.

"Listen, my love," Winifred tried to explain, "it's not for good; it's just till Mummy gets better and strong again." She said much more but it was fruitless.

"I don't love you any more Mummy," Maureen said petulantly. "I want my baby sister back."

It wasn't just Maureen either, because each of the twins, who didn't really understand what was going on, kept asking in turn, "Mummy, where's baby Barbara gone? I miss her?"

Even Jimmy kept asking, "Mummy, why is our Barbara not with us any more?"

After a week of this, Winifred couldn't take any more; she was also feeling quite fretful herself, so she decided to catch a bus to Nelson. It was nine o'clock at night when she arrived at the house.

Mr Smith answered the door, but on seeing her, he was a little taken aback. All the same, he gave her a warm reception, "Oh hello, Winifred, this is a surprise, we didn't expect to see you; do come in."

On entering the lounge, Winifred looked around in awe; she couldn't help but admire the beautiful room with thick wall to wall luxurious carpets, and the most gorgeous matching furniture and curtains.

Little Barbara was crawling about on the carpet and put her arms out as soon as she saw her mummy. Although Winifred was very impressed with all the finery, she was certainly not pleased that Barbara was still up at that time of night.

Her displeasure increased when she noticed that there was no fireguard. "Excuse me!" she asked quite sternly. "Why is little Barbara not in bed at this time of night?"

"It's all right, Winifred, we don't take her to bed till we go," replied Mrs Smith. "You see, that way we can keep an eye on her."

"Oh that's no good," responded Winifred, "she's only a baby and needs to go to bed much earlier than this. Besides, I've only just got her into a sleeping pattern, which is going to be all upset."

"I can understand your concern, Winifred," replied Mrs Smith, "but I do think you're worrying unnecessarily, I can assure you, she'll be all right."

"No I'm sorry, but that's not good enough!" stressed Winifred. "Besides, another thing that concerns me is that you haven't got a fireguard … my child could hurt herself."

At this point, Mr Smith intervened. "Now come on, Winifred!" he emphasised. "I think you're overreacting a bit; give us a little more credit than that."

"Credit be blowed!" rapped Winifred. "With a child, you've got to have eyes in the back of your head. No, I'm telling you straight … I'm not happy about it, not one little bit."

The couple could see she meant every word and tried to pacify her. "All right, Winifred, we agree with you, I promise you personally we'll buy a fireguard first thing tomorrow."

"What about the other thing, keeping her up till this time?"

"Yes righto, I promise we'll do that as well; from now on, she'll go to bed much sooner."

"Oh, it's not just that either," stressed Winifred, "you see, I've been fretting for her and so have all her brothers and sisters. Look, I'm sorry, I only came here to see how she was getting on but now … well it's made me realise just how much I miss her; yes, I want her back amongst the other children."

Mrs Smith became quite agitated. "Oh, Winifred please! You can't do that, you promised we could have her for at least a fortnight or longer, and you even signed a paper to that effect."

"Yes, I know I did, and please don't think that I'm not grateful for what you've done because I am, and I'm awfully sorry if I have caused you any distress. But what you've got to understand is that she's my baby, and I want her back with me; there's nothing more to it than that."

They could both see that she wasn't about to change her mind and Mr Smith intervened again, but this time in a more formal tone. "Right Mrs Cowell, we both understand how you feel and we'll go along with that but, as you will appreciate, it isn't very practical to take little Barbara with you tonight. So, how about you going home and returning tomorrow at noon, and we'll have her ready with all her clothes and things for you to pick up?"

Winifred could see the sense in this, so agreed to return the following day; still, she was quite distressed about the whole thing. That night, she only slept fitfully and when she did she kept dreaming of little Barbara crawling near to the unprotected fire.

Next morning, even though she hadn't much money, she ordered a taxi to ensure that she got there on time. She arrived with ample time to spare, only to find something quite unexpected and unpleasant awaiting her. The couple were there all right, but so too were two rather official-looking ladies, who turned out to be social workers. On this occasion, Winifred was shown into another room at the front of the house.

After introductions, one of the ladies addressed her. "Mrs Cowell," she said haughtily, "we have been discussing the situation about Barbara, and I'm very sorry to inform you but you can't take her back just like that. You see, it's not quite so straightforward as you may think."

"What are you talking about?" queried Winifred. "I can't see any complications whatsoever, she's my child, and I'm taking her with me."

"I'm sorry but you can't do that," the lady said, her tone unsympathetic. She then produced an official-looking paper, and showed it to Winifred. "You see, we have a restriction order here, as you signed a legal document putting the child into the care of Mr and Mrs Smith."

"Surely that means nothing!" stated Winifred. "I'm her mother, and that must override everything."

Remaining very detached, the social worker answered firmly, "I'm afraid it doesn't, Mrs Cowell, if you want her back then you'll have to attend an official hearing."

Suddenly, Winifred saw Mr and Mrs Smith in a different light as the consequences began to dawn upon her. "Oh my God in heaven! What have I done?" she thought. Then glaring at Mr Smith she silently cursed him, "You swine! You've used your position of authority to undermine me, so as to take my child from me."

"Right, Winifred, keep calm whatever you do … come on, think … think!" She was absolutely fuming inside, her natural instinct was to tear into them, but she had the presence of mind to keep calm, as she knew it wouldn't help her cause to lose her temper. After a pause she swallowed and took a deep breath, then asked in a controlled voice, "It is all right to see my child I take it?"

One of the ladies answered that she could see no reason why she shouldn't.

Turning to the couple, she asked, "Is that all right then?"

Mr Smith very smugly replied, "Umph, well actually, I don't think it's a very good idea myself, as we don't want the child upsetting, do we? Mind, I suppose we can allow it for just a little while."

Winifred gritted her teeth as she felt her hackles rising; she just calmly sat there though, saying nothing till they brought little Barbara to her. On seeing her mummy, the little girl showed her obvious delight; Winifred took advantage of the moment.

She picked Barbara up and cuddled her saying in a slow deliberate voice, just loud enough for all to hear, "Righto, my love, Mummy's here now. I'm going to have to leave you for a short time with these people but don't fret, my darling; Mummy's coming back very soon to take you home to your big brothers and sisters." She knew only too well that little Barbara didn't understand what was being said or going on; but all the same, it gave the couple plenty to think about, making it quite clear that they had a fight on their hands. Then turning to the social workers, she said, "Oh yes, whilst we're at it, there is something very important that needs sorting out. There's no fireguard in the living room where they allow my child to play, and I'm frightened she may get hurt. I insist that they get one right now and I'm not leaving this house till I see one in place."

"Right, I've got to agree with you Mrs Cowell," replied one of the ladies, who then advised the couple, "Mrs Cowell has made a valid point, so I suggest that you go and get one right away."

"Yes righto," replied Mr Smith. "I'll sort it, I'll nip to the shop."

Whilst he was gone, the atmosphere in the room was rather cool. Mrs Smith tried to break the ice by offering Winifred a cup of tea but she politely refused. Winifred felt rather uncomfortable and fidgety; she didn't know what to do so she just looked around the room. Then ... something unusual at the back of the room caught her eye and aroused her suspicions; what she saw were about eight tea chests filled with crockery and other oddments.

"That's strange," she thought to herself and felt compelled to satisfy her curiosity. "Excuse me, Mrs Smith, are you thinking of flitting?"

Mrs Smith blushed and was obviously embarrassed. "We-ell … u-um, yes Winifred, didn't you know?"

Still trying to keep her calm, Winifred affirmed, "Now now, Mrs Smith, you know darned well I didn't know. And now would you like to tell me where you're planning to move to?" There was a long pause with a few ums and ahs, but no answer was forthcoming.

Winifred, becoming more and more impatient, prompted her further, "Well, come on then … what's your answer?"

Mrs Smith, who by now was feeling very uneasy, replied, "I … I u-um, think it best, Winifred, that you wait till my husband gets back."

"You what? Blow that for a tale, you can tell me right now!" Winifred growled. "Where are you going?"

"We-ell … you see," she stammered, "my husband has been offered a job in Kent."

That was it, there was no more diplomacy, all the pretence was now at an end. Winifred couldn't believe what she'd just heard and let out a shriek, "Kent! Do you mean the south of England Kent?"

Mrs Smith didn't answer; she just bowed her head in embarrassment.

"Well, you bloody conniving, scheming bitch, you're nowt else! You must have planned this right from the start knowing only too well that it would have been nigh impossible for me to get in touch with you once you'd gone. What kind of a woman are you anyway? You came into my home and gained the confidence and respect of my family, and pretended to be my friend. Well, if you think you're getting away with it, you're well mistaken, I'll go through hell and high water before I'll let you take my child from me!"

"Just a minute, Mrs Cowell," interceded the same social worker who had done most of the talking, "losing your temper isn't going to help the situation."

Winifred just turned on her and snarled, "Yes, and you can rap up as well; you ought to be ashamed of yourself! You come here waving your little piece of paper asserting your authority; you make me sick! Yes, everything by the book, but not one sign of human compassion or consideration as to how I felt."

"Mrs Cowell, this is not about you," she replied quite unconcerned, "what you've got to understand is that we have to weigh up everything, and take into consideration what's best for the child."

"Oh have you now?" retorted Winifred. "Well we'll soon find out what's best for her because right now I'm going straight to the Citizen's Advice Bureau, and then to my solicitor. And whilst I'm at it, I'm going to report you to your superiors because you're definitely out of order. Yes, without a doubt, there's something very underhand going on around here."

She waited in the house until Mr Smith returned, and after giving him a good dressing down, she then informed the couple she would be coming every day to visit Barbara until the date of the hearing.

"Another thing!" she warned. "Before I go, I'm telling you now, don't even think of absconding with my child because I'll have the law on you quicker than you can blink."

"Oh please, Winifred … don't be like that!" implored Mrs Smith. "We're friends."

"Hey don't Winifred me! We were never friends … I just thought we were; but that's all over, because now I see you for what you really are."

On arriving back home, Winifred told Jack what had gone on in the hope that he would want to bring little Barbara home but, as always, he was quite unconcerned.

"I don't know what all the fuss is about," he said apathetically, "she'd probably be better off with them anyway, and she'd certainly have a better chance in life than staying here with us."

Winifred was really deflated by his uncaring attitude and responded accordingly, "With us! You don't know the meaning of the word *us*; all you care about is the pub and your so-called friends. If you cared half as much about your own family as you do about them, she'd have every chance in life. Yes, and that goes for all your other kids as well." It was quite pointless going on at him though, as he really didn't care and was not interested.

Over the next few days, she was on tenterhooks but, nevertheless, she never missed going to see Barbara. The day of the hearing finally arrived. She made herself presentable in order to create a good impression. All the same, she couldn't help but feel nervous.

Mr and Mrs Smith were well represented, and their case was presented along with the social worker's report.

Winifred's representative showed letters to the tribunal from her doctor, teacher and welfare officer all stating that her children were always well fed, clean, well clothed and they all appeared to be very happy.

"Under very difficult and trying circumstances, Mrs Cowell is a very good and caring mother," stated her counsel. "Yes indeed! It is obvious that the best place for the child is in her own home amongst her own brothers and sisters."

After taking everything into consideration, the chairman turned to Winifred and asked in a very sympathetic voice, "In spite of all your hardship, you really do want your child back, don't you, Mrs Cowell?"

"With all my heart, sir," she replied in a determined yet humble voice, "and not just for my sake but for hers as well."

He smiled at her reassuringly, then spoke the words she'd been praying to hear, "Then, Mrs Cowell, you shall have her back."

At this point, Winifred broke down and sobbed, muttering repeatedly, "Oh thank God. Thank God!"

Thankfully, Barbara went home with her mother and was to grow up amongst her older brothers and sisters in that humble terraced house on Albion Street.

10: cut fruit & broken biscuits

The war years lingered on and times remained hard, but in spite of everything all was not quite so grim; there were many happy moments that were to remain forevermore in people's minds. Perhaps it was because Winifred's children knew little of the world beyond Trafalgar that they were so happy and contented; whatever the reason, there was no doubt that they were.

In the event of a German air raid the sirens sounded loudly, and people would scurry down the steep stone steps to the air-raid shelters; however, Winifred refused to do this. She'd weighed the situation up from every angle and, rightly or wrongly, had decided that if her children were going to die, then it was to be in the warmth and comfort of their own beds, not in a cold, dark, dank air-raid shelter. She hadn't reached the decision lightly; in fact, she'd pondered on it for hours on end.

"Besides," she thought to herself, "if there was to be a direct hit on the air-raid shelter, then no one could possibly survive anyway." She was also concerned that should a bomb land on the house, the rubble would bury the air-raid shelter, trapping her family only to face a horrible death. "No, I certainly don't want that for my children," she assured herself.

Despite this, she was always on tenterhooks during an air raid, especially when she could hear the sound of German planes droning overhead. They'd all cuddle up together in one big double bed comforting each other. It was a very trying time for all and everyone was relieved when the sirens finally sounded the all clear.

Every evening as darkness loomed, it was the responsibility of each household to make sure that all curtains were drawn tightly, not even the smallest chink of light was permitted to show on the outside.

The regulations concerning this were very strict, heavy fines and even imprisonment were imposed on anyone infringing the rules. Many broadcasts were made over the wireless, and newspapers regularly displayed government warnings, encouraging people to be diligent. They did however make clear the rationale behind the strict blackout rules pointing out that a sitting-room light could be seen from a height of ten thousand feet or more.

Cars were only allowed on the roads at night in special circumstances, even then they could only display one dipped headlight, which had a special cover to dim the beam; this led to many accidents, but it was, regrettably, unavoidable. Curfews were implemented, and everyone had to carry identification cards. Curfew or not, lots of people used to stay out longer than the permitted hour, but at times, it was purely unintentional; they just couldn't find their way home.

There was one incident when an elderly gentleman, who happened to be the mayor's brother, fell into the canal after mistakenly taking a wrong turning into a factory yard that led down to the water.

But the blackout wasn't all doom and gloom; like anything else, it had its funny side. Many a cryptic line was written about it and the following is one from the *Burnley Express*:

> Policemen, when investigating cases of offences against the blackout hear many and varied excuses – "Oversight" – "Lapses of memory" and so on. But the answer of the Burnley old age pensioner to the officer who told him he would be reporting him for showing a light was original – and obscure, "I have nowt and thá can't get nowt where there is nowt."

Besides the anecdotes, there were also many jokes and cartoon drawings about it. Indeed, everything was done to keep public morale as high as possible.

A local joke at the time:

> A woman had just bought some fish and chips at the chip shop, and she had a very strong aroma about her.

As she was trying to find her way home by groping her way along the walls of buildings, a man knocked her down.

On picking her up, he apologised, "I'm awfully sorry luv ... I thought tha were t' door to chippy."

At the outbreak of war, everyone carried their gasmasks slung over their shoulder like a handbag, but as time progressed, many people became complacent and left them at home. The government encouraged everyone to carry them on their person at all times in case of attack, and constantly advertised in newspapers and on billboards to that effect. Also, there were many gas-mask checks when people were asked to attend designated schools with their respirators. Many parents had problems because their children didn't like wearing them, but to help overcome this, lots of Mickey Mouse gasmasks were made. Another regular occurrence was the gas test; each district had a designated spot; the one for Trafalgar was the Mitre area.

The following is a quote from the *Burnley Express*:

REMEMBER GAS TEST TOMORROW

A tear-gas exercise will be held in the Mitre district and in the section of Church St, near to Gunsmith Lane tomorrow. It is timed to begin at 3 o'clock. The alarm will be indicated by the sounding of rattles by wardens, and the "ALL CLEAR" will be given by the sounding of hand bells.

The people, who live in these areas and those whose business takes them there tomorrow should wear their gasmasks. The gas will cause their eyes to water if they don't. Residents in the districts should cover up all food, for it may have an unpleasant taste if the gas gets to it.

The community spirit remained close knit and everything possible was done for the war effort and the collection of pots and pans was relentless. Housewives offered their aluminium kettles and pans to help towards making fighter planes and the like, and were proud of it.

They got a big kick out of it, often the topic of conversation would be, "Hey, tha never knows, the spitfire that shot down that Jerry Plane might well a bín my old kettle."

The Town Council was now taking scrap from everywhere and all garden railings and gates were removed from every house in the town. Even two memorial canons, souvenirs from the Crimean War, which stood near to Bank Hall Hospital, were removed and melted down in order to help the war effort. But throughout it all, people still went about their everyday lives.

Winifred could never give her kids much as far as luxuries and material things were concerned, but they never went short of love and affection. One thing that she did teach them, though, was how to use their imaginations. There was always a good supply of broken biscuits and cut fruit from the late market shopping trips, but certain commodities such as cream buns and other delicacies were very scarce. To compensate for this, she would bake bread, then spread slices with margarine and cut them into small segments.

"Now, children," she would say, "what you must do is pretend that these are little magic soldiers, and when you eat them, they turn into cream buns or anything else that you want them to be."

Cream buns or not, one thing was certain … they always ate the lot and really enjoyed them. Mind you, so did lots of other kids, as the house was always full with one friend or another. One of these happened to be young Winnie Clark, the girl who was born in the Workhouse, and now lived just two doors higher up. Young Winnie was a very sprightly young girl, and fitted in really well, and was treated like one of the family; in fact, she looked a lot like her namesake and lots of folk actually thought that Winifred was her mother.

The hardship continued but Winifred struggled on. Consequently she fell into the clutches of Blakey, a notorious moneylender, to the amount of £20, despite being forewarned of the pitfalls of this by her mother. She'd also heard many tales of how, once in their clutches, it was nigh impossible to be free of them. However, like many before her, she didn't have much choice and had taken the plunge. The interest rate was twenty-five shillings for every pound borrowed, and the repayment rate was one shilling a week for every pound owing, which meant that she had to repay twenty-five shillings a week for twenty weeks. But ... there was an added clause that should anyone default on a payment at any time, then compound interest was added.

The inevitable happened, she got behind with her payments, subsequently the unscrupulous businessman put her under a lot of pressure; penalties were added, hence the debt increased and seemed everlasting. She struggled on taking in washing, and doing other little tasks, but despite this, after paying off more than originally borrowed, the outstanding amount was still £14. She was at her wits' end, but then one day by an act of providence or whatever, the debt was cleared. She was looking through the drawers where she kept the family allowance books, but couldn't find them anywhere. She was already overdue with her payment, so decided to go and see Blakey to ask for leeway. He owned a children's clothes-shop in the town centre and on reaching there she explained the situation to him.

She got the shock of her life when he answered smugly, "Now come on, Mrs Cowell, don't give me that, you know darn well where the family allowance books are."

She was rather puzzled and asked, "Sorry, am I missing something here, I haven't a clue what you're talking about?"

"Oh come off it, don't play the little Miss Innocent with me; are you trying to say that Barney hasn't told you that he's borrowed another £20, and that he's used the family allowance books as collateral?"

Winifred was absolutely fuming and she screeched, "You what! You mean to say, you've got my kiddies' books in your bloody custody?"

"That's right," he sniggered, "and that's where they're staying until every penny's been paid in full."

"Give me them back right now," she demanded, "they're my little ones' lifeline!"

He just scoffed all the more, "You're joking ... they're my safeguard to make sure the debt is paid in full. Yes and that includes the extra £20 plus interest."

"I'm asking you just one more time," she shouted, "give me back my kids' family allowance books! If you think for one second that I'd let you profit off their backs, then you're sadly mistaken."

"Listen here, I'm not interested, and I don't want to know; I couldn't give two hoots about your kids, all I'm concerned about is the money you owe me."

"Blakey, I'm warning you for the last time," she growled, "give me back those books now!"

"And what will you do if I don't?" he smirked.

What he didn't realise was that he was now treading on dangerous ground; the way she saw it, he was attempting to take food out of her children's mouths.

"Right then, Blakey, if that's the way you want to play it, these will do for starters," she said, and calmly started to stuff a load of clothes into a carrier bag.

It was now his turn to lose his cool. "What the bloody hell do you think you're playing at? Put those down right now, and get out of this shop or I'll …"

"Or you'll what … call the police happen?" she hissed. "If you try and take these off me, I'll call ém myself; I don't think they'd take too kindly to you having my children's family allowance books under false pretences, do you?"

"What do you mean by that … I've just told you that Barney gave them to me?"

"Now look who's coming the innocent; you know Jack from old, and you also know that he's been in prison and that he's still on parole."

"Hey, hang on a minute! I agree with you that I knew he'd been in prison, but how am I supposed to know he's on parole?"

"Well, let's put it this way, shall we; you should have known, shouldn't you? Anyway, let me tell you now, I'll be back again tomorrow for some more clothes, yes, and every day after that until you give me back my kids' books. Also, I give you fair warning, Blakey, not to cash in one penny or, so help me, I'll inform the police quicker than you can blink."

He could see that his back was up against the wall and his attitude became much more placatory. "All right, Winifred, I agree with you, there's obviously been a misunderstanding here; but surely you can see my side of it, can't you?"

"No, no I can't, and like you said to me, I'm not interested, and I don't want to know."

"That's all very well, Mrs Cowell, but what about the outstanding balance?"

"What about it? Right, I'll tell you! I was quite willing to repay you everything that I owed you, in spite of the fact that I thought it was daylight robbery; but now because of your greed and deviousness, you're not getting another penny."

It was now Blakey's turn to be frustrated. "But what about the £20 that Barney has just borrowed?"

Winifred just sneered at him, "I'm afraid that's your problem, I couldn't care less; as far as I'm concerned, you can whistle for it."

He reluctantly handed over the books, and that's the last she heard of the matter. Wisely, she never had any more dealings with him. Whether Jack ever repaid the £20 or not is still a mystery, but it's extremely doubtful.

Things didn't change much and Winifred was forever short of money. There were times when she didn't even have a penny piece to put in the gas meter and the house was in darkness except for the eerie light emitted by the fire in the grate. On these occasions she was left with little alternative but to go to bed early along with the children. At times like this she would tell them stories, not only fairy tales but true ones about her own life as a child. The children loved her story telling and became quite adept at telling a tale themselves. Maureen and Jimmy were also good at telling stories and would hold the younger family members spellbound. Maureen used to tell fairy tales such as Cinderella and Snow White, but she also made up many more similar ones. On the other hand, Jimmy's tales were more bizarre, ghost stories about dragons, demons, vampires, spiders and such things. His imagination used to run away with him, scaring everybody half to death so that Mary and Barbara always finished up in Maureen's bed. The same thing happened in the lads' bedroom; in fact, Jimmy's tales were so explicit that he too was frightened.

the *broken biscuit*

Winifred never had much to give but when it was one of the children's birthdays she always put on a little party for them. It was invariably quite meagre, but the children always enjoyed and appreciated it. She also gave the birthday child a shilling, which was enough to go to the pictures and treat a friend.

Maureen was the first one to learn the awful truth that there wasn't a Father Christmas. Still, she strove to keep this a secret from her younger siblings for as long as she could, knowing how they loved the idea. Despite having accepted the fact herself, she used to love Christmas, especially Christmas Eve. She'd help the younger ones to get ready for bed telling them to go to sleep so that Father Christmas could come.

"Now you must go to sleep as quick as you can," she would say to the over-excited youngsters, "or Father Christmas won't come; he doesn't want anyone watching him coming down the chimney."

"Oh I'd like to see him," said John one time. "I'm going to try and stay awake and have a peep."

"Oh you mustn't do that, our John," responded Maureen tutting a little. "Father Christmas can tell if anyone's peeping because of his magic powers. If you do that, then he won't leave you any toys at all, just a bag full of cinders."

Little John furrowed his eyebrows not being too sure whether to believe her or not. Nevertheless, little Barry believed her and he became quite alarmed as John told him he was going to try and stay awake anyway.

"Oh no, go to sleep, our John!" he pleaded. "I want Father Christmas to come; I don't just want a bag of cinders."

All the same, not to be beaten, John tried his best to keep his eyes open; he was determined to see this mysterious figure.

Meanwhile, downstairs, Maureen, along with her mother, was excitedly preparing all the goodies for her younger brothers and sisters. She was well aware of John's little game and had told her mother all about it. John did manage to stay awake till about eleven o'clock but eventually drifted off to sleep. Winifred and Maureen then crept stealthily up to the children's beds, removed the pillowcases, which the children had hung up in preference to stockings, and, without a sound, crept back downstairs. After filling them, they then had the precarious task of putting them back in position at the top of the children's beds without disturbing them. Both Winifred and Maureen became quite skilful at this; never once in all the years did one of the children wake up during the venture.

On this particular Christmas morning, Barry was the first to wake, gleefully shouting and waking the others, "Oh look what Father Christmas has brought me ... a car and some books and crayons and loads of sweets," he bellowed excitedly.

"Oh great, look what I've got!" yelled Jimmy heartily as he rummaged through his pillowcase.

John eagerly opened his pillowcase only to discover, to his horror, there was nothing inside it except a few cinders. Unlike Jimmy and Barry's shouts of delight, he let out an anguished yell, "Oh no," he cried out in despair, "look what Father Christmas has left me!"

"Well it serves you right, our John," said little Barry solemnly, "our Maureen told you what would happen if you peeped at Father Christmas."

At that moment, Maureen entered the room; she'd played the little prank on John but wasn't so cruel as to spoil his Christmas morning. "Merry Christmas everybody!" she greeted them. "Have you all got some nice toys?"

Jimmy and Barry were really excited but John just sat there with his bottom lip quivering.

"It's not fair," he complained. "Father Christmas has only left me a few cinders."

"Oh yes I know, that's what I've come to see you about." Immediately little John's ears pricked up. Maureen continued, "Well, just before Father Christmas left last night, he had a word with Mum saying that he thought you'd been peeping."

"But I wasn't peeping our Maureen, honest! It's not fair, I was only ..."

"Whoa, hang on a bit, our John! It's all right, don't get upset cós he did tell Mum that he'd left you some cinders but he also said that he'd left you some toys as well, seeing that he wasn't too sure whether you'd been peeping or not."

"But he hasn't," protested John as he peered into the bag, "all he's left me are these cinders."

"Oh yeah, I remember now … he mentioned something about hiding them under the bed."

Immediately, John peered underneath the sagging bedsprings where, sure enough, right up against the wall, was another pillowcase. He eagerly dived under to drag it out, discovering to his delight that he'd got his fair share of presents like everybody else. Maureen then quietly turned away with a smile on her face and went back to bed to catch up on her sleep. John played merrily away with his brothers but he never tried staying awake on Christmas Eve again.

Five years into the war and still no signs of peace, by now, everything from food and clothing to petrol was on ration. People survived because of the close-knit community spirit and like their predecessors in the First World War, neighbours exchanged commodities with each other, and got by on their wits.

Maureen and Jimmy were now attending St Thomas's RC Junior School; the twins were in the infants' class. The headmistress was Miss Gordon, who was renowned for being strict, but also fair. Winifred's children were no more or less boisterous than the other kids; sometimes, though, Miss Gordon would send for her, as one or other of her children got into a fracas, but it was usually sorted out quite amicably.

There were also plenty of out-of-school skirmishes between neighbouring kids, but Winifred soon learned that she couldn't be falling out with the neighbours all the time over these childhood feuds. On occasions, she'd done just this, only to find that, shortly afterwards, the two children who had quarrelled were now happily playing together.

She got on very well with her next door neighbours on both sides. Like Alice King, who lived higher up at number sixteen, the lady who lived on the lower side was also called Alice. Alice at number twelve, had a girl called Marian, who was the same age as Maureen; the two youngsters got on really well and were best friends. Winifred and Alice both had very similar natures as far as being protective towards their kids was concerned; however, they both acknowledged the situation and respected each other's views. They made a pact between themselves to always sort out things amicably, should the need arise.

Winifred was never one for camping or idle gossip in other people's houses, but she did tend to swap little confidences with Alice. Alice's husband was called Chris; he was a very hard working man, who never went out boozing, and he put every penny he earned into the home.

One day, Winifred was rather surprised to hear Alice say wistfully, "Do you know something, Winnie? Your Jack may be a sod-pot and a swine in many ways, but I'll tell you what it is, I'd swap him for Chris any day of the week."

"Oh, I don't know how you can say that, Alice, Chris is a really good breadwinner and he just lives for the home. And besides, we never hear any rows in your house but you certainly must hear them in ours."

"That's all very true, Winnie, and I understand what you're saying, but what you don't know is that he never talks to me. All I ever get is a little gesture when he's leaving for work in the morning and another when he arrives home at night, but in between ... absolutely nothing!"

"But surely, Alice, that's far better than living from hand to mouth, as you would have to if you were married to someone like Jack."

"It might seem strange, Winnie, but at least Jack shows you some affection. I'd give the world if only Chris would take me into his arms now and again and tell me that he loved me."

Winifred was quite taken aback, and she struggled in her mind for just what to say. "I'm really surprised to hear that, Alice, it makes me feel a little sad; Chris appears to be such a gentleman when he's outside."

"Oh don't get me wrong, Winnie, he is kind and gentle; it's just that he's so quiet, and all he wants to do is sit in the chair and read the newspaper. Nobody knows, I ... I feel so very lonely." It became the most frequent topic of her conversation, Winifred felt at a loss, but tried her best to console her.

They remained good friends, but then one day they did have an argument, in spite of their pact, after young Maureen and Marian had been fighting. Winifred and Alice usually sorted out their differences quickly, but on this occasion, they weren't on speaking terms for a few weeks. It wasn't so much that they didn't want to make up as the fact that they never saw each other during this period. The irony of it, though, was that the two young girls were now best friends again and merrily playing together. Then one day Maureen came home at dinnertime with Marian, and Winifred heard the young girl mention something about her mother being ill.

"And what's the matter with your mum then?" she asked the little girl.

"I don't know, Mrs Cowell, it's just that she's in bed in the living-room."

"That's strange," thought Winifred, "she must be quite poorly to have the bed downstairs." Then after careful deliberation, "Right, that's it, I'm going in to see her whether she orders me to leave or not; she might need me."

Little did she know how true this was; on seeing Alice, she was quite shocked and realised that her friend was seriously ill. Alice looked woefully frail and delicate, and she had lost a lot of weight; she also had a rather large swelling on her neck, which turned out to be a goitre.

On seeing Winifred, Alice put her arms out in greeting and quietly muttered, "Eh, Winnie, I'm glad you've come, I thought you'd fell out with me for good."

The warm greeting made Winifred feel good, yet very humble. "Oh come now, Alice, how could I ever do that? You know we've always been such good friends, it's just that I didn't know you were ill."

Alice's mother was in the house, and she turned to Alice saying, "See, our Alice, didn't I tell thi? I knew darn well that Winnie didn't know thá were poorly." Then turning to Winifred, "Oh, Winnie, I'm so glad tha's come, she's bín frettín her heart out about thi ever since thá both fell out."

This humbled Winifred even more as she thought to herself, "Oh dear, I'm just going to have to stop being so proud." Alice's mother smiled as Winifred replied, "Well you needn't worry yourself about it, because she's not going to fret any more; I'm going to pop in every day to help out till she gets better and regains her strength."

True to her word, never a day went by that she didn't go in and make meals and do other little chores for Alice. Unfortunately, though, Alice was not to get better; she had a morbid fear of hospitals, and had refused point blank to go there, against the doctor's wishes. Then one morning whilst Winifred was making her a cup of tea, Alice's condition suddenly deteriorated. Winifred immediately went to the police telephone box, and was put in touch with the doctor; afterwards she was connected to Chris's workplace. Chris and the doctor arrived at the same time and after a brief examination the doctor gave his diagnosis. He made it quite clear that Alice's condition was critical, and that she needed to go into hospital immediately; accordingly he ordered an ambulance.

Chris was visibly upset and yet he still couldn't bring himself to open up his heart to his wife. She held out her arms beckoning him to come to her, then she asked him to adjust her pillows to make her more comfortable. What she really wanted was for him to put his arms around her and give her a cuddle and some loving assurance. Sadly, though, this didn't happen, and although he did go to her, he merely arranged the pillows as requested. He did mutter a little something under his breath, but appeared to be fidgety and on edge; she sensed his feelings and became quite agitated, shoving him away.

"Oh go away, Chris, just leave me alone!" she cried with tears rolling down her cheeks.

Winifred knew the reason for this, and went to the bedside to comfort her. At that moment, another neighbour, Mrs Bacon, entered the house followed by two ambulance men.

On seeing them, Alice started to cry out, "Oh, Winnie, don't let them take me into hospital, please! I'll never come home to see mi kids again!"

She must have had a premonition, because no sooner had she spoken these words than she started to stiffen and the colour drained from her face. She desperately clung to Winifred and barely managed to utter "Oh, Winnie! I'm going, I ... I'm goi ..."

Winifred had seen all the signs before, and knew only too well that her friend was dying in front of her very eyes. The doctor and the ambulance men did everything in their power to revive her, but to no avail ... within minutes, she was dead.

There was a painful silence in the room for a few moments, which was suddenly broken by the loud wailing of her husband Chris as he knelt by her side taking her hand, "Oh no, Alice, please don't leave me! You know how much I love you ... how much I've always loved you! Oh, Alice, you can't go, I can't ... I can't live without you!"

His crying was momentarily checked as Mrs Bacon gently put her hand on his shoulder. "Come on, Chris; she's gone ... she can't hear you any more."

No matter ... there was no consoling him, his sobbing continued and he wailed uncontrollably, "No! No, she can't have gone ... I love her so much! O-oh ... what am I going to do without her?"

Winifred was overcome with emotion, but couldn't help thinking how strange life can be. It was obvious to everyone that Chris had loved Alice all along and yet he hadn't been able to express it to her whilst she was alive.

He never fully recovered from his sad loss; he couldn't face the prospect of living in the house without Alice. Within a few months, he uprooted and moved with his family to another part of town.

11: *the* cellar top

It happened one evening in April 1945, a few days before the twins' sixth birthday. It was nearly nine o'clock and, like any other evening, Winifred was getting the children ready for bed. Maureen wasn't there, as she'd gone to stay at her grandparents' house in Bacup. Jimmy, John and Mary had just been bathed and were sat around the fireside; Barbara, who was now nineteen months old, was sat on Mary's knee. Winifred had just lifted Barry out of the dolly tub, and was drying him as he stood on the wooden table. He only had a towel wrapped around his waist, and she was about to put his nightshirt on when Jack walked in. All were surprised to see him, as he was never usually home at that time of night; they were also taken aback, as it was obvious that he was drunk. His hair was disorderly, he was unshaven, his speech was slurred and he was unsteady on his feet. Barry was never Jack's favourite by any means and he made no attempt to disguise the fact.

"Eh-h, who's a bonny little boy then?" he drawled as he approached Barry reaching out towards him beckoning, "Come on then, give your daddy a kiss!"

Little Barry shuddered and then turned to his mum clutching at her dress.

"Come on then," he repeated drunkenly, "give your daddy a kiss!"

"Leave him alone," rapped Winifred, "you're drunk!"

Jack retaliated and sniggered at her, "O-oh! ... I'm drunk am I? You and your bloody kids, that's all you flamín well care about! Well, I'm telling you now, that bloody kid's gonna gimme a kiss right now, or I'll turn this flamín house upside down." He staggered closer to Barry, who clung still tighter to Winifred ... she in turn put her arms around him.

"Let go of the little brat!" Jack snarled.

- 173 -

the *broken biscuit*

Winifred adamantly refused and repeated angrily, "Leave him alone, Jack! He doesn't want to kiss you whilst you're in that state." She kept hold of Barry with one arm, whilst trying to fend Jack off with the other.

This riled him even further, making him more aggressive. "You bloody swine, you're nówt else!" he growled, then, without further provocation, he punched her in the face with his fist!

Immediately, all the kids started screeching simultaneously, "Oh no, Daddy, please! Please leave mí mummy alone! Please don't hurt her!" He looked at their appealing faces and appeared to calm down a little.

But he was still in an obstreperous mood and, turning once more to little Barry, he asked mockingly, "You don't love your daddy, do you?"

Barry was only a frail little lad, but even at that young age he had a mind of his own, and he answered, "No I don't!" adding sobbingly, "You're always hitting mí mummy you are."

Jack sniggered, then turned to Mary, who also always spoke her mind and asked her the same question.

She replied defiantly, "No I don't love you either … you're awful and I hate you when you're drunk!"

The same question was asked of Jimmy who replied in a distressed but determined voice, "No I don't … I love mi mum better than you!"

"Arrgh!" grunted Jack getting more despondent by the minute, as his ego deflated.

Barbara was whimpering but he couldn't ask her, as she was too young to understand what was going on.

Finally, he turned to John, but this time, he changed the question just a little, "And who do you love then, your mummy or your daddy?"

The little lad pondered as he looked straight into his daddy's sad eyes, he could see the hurt there, and actually felt sorry for him.

There were so many different thoughts running through his head all jumbled up together: How much he loved his daddy when he was sober and how he wished he would never be as he was at this moment. He was very confused for even at his young age, he felt that should he say he didn't love him, then his daddy would stand all alone and sorrowful in his own home ... should he say he did love him, then that would hurt his mum's feelings. Besides that ... he knew only too well that all his brothers and sisters really did love their dad, but felt that his daddy didn't know that.

He glanced at his mum knowing that she had done no wrong, then back at his dad. To everyone's surprise, he murmured warily through tight lips, "I love you, Daddy!"

Winifred looked rather bewildered and little John put his head down in embarrassment. Immediately, as though synchronised, his sister and brothers showed their obvious disapproval by tutting and blowing at him.

Jack intervened by roaring at them, "That'll do, you lot, we'll have less of that! Anyway, whilst we're at it, you can get the three of you up the dancers right now!"

"Leave them alone!" retorted Winifred. "They haven't had a drink yet."

Jack growled sarcastically, "O-oh, what a shame, your poor little kids haven't had a drink yet; well, this is one night when they're gonna go to bed without one."

Winifred stood defiantly in front of him stating, "Jack, I'm telling you now, my kids are going to have a warm drink before they go to bed ... and that's final!"

"O-oh, that's final, is it?" he growled becoming angrier still. "I'll show you what's bloody well final!" He approached the fireside where the three offending children were now huddled together and Mary was now holding baby Barbara in her arms. As he approached them, they all shuffled to the alcove close to the cellar top door. To prevent him herding them towards the stairs, Winifred placed herself between the children and the lobby. Then, he caught Winifred completely off guard as he suddenly opened the cellar top door and pushed each one of the children, including little Barbara, into the darkness.

After shutting the door, he stood with his back placed firmly against it mocking Winifred, "Right then, if they won't go to bed, then they can bloody well stop in there for a while."

He hadn't achieved this easily, for the moment Winifred realised what he was doing, she'd thumped, scratched and kicked him but to no avail, he'd finally succeeded. The four children were screaming at the top of their voices inside the cellar top, whilst little John was quivering with fear in the living room as thoughts of the Bogey-hole in the Workhouse immediately sprang to his mind.

Winifred was frantic for the safety of her children and she became quite hysterical screaming, "Jack, get away from that door, it's pitch black in there! If one of the kids fall down those steep steps, they could be killed stone dead."

He knew that little Mary was holding baby Barbara in her arms, and that there wasn't enough room at the top of the cellar for two let alone four, and yet ... he just replied by grinning and mocking her, "You silly woman! Now whatta you gonna do?"

She carried on biting, scratching, thumping and kicking him, but it was useless, he just wouldn't budge.

She then resorted to getting down on one knee and pleading with him, "Please, Jack! Please I beg you ... let my kids out of there!"

"There you go again," he snorted, "your bloody kids! Always your kids, never mine ... oh no."

But even as he was speaking, he realised that she was attempting to pick up the steel poker, which stood in the heavy poker stand on the hearthstone. He immediately bent down grabbing it before she could, then rammed his back once more firmly against the door. During this brief scuffle, the kids tried unsuccessfully to get out and now they were bawling all the louder.

Now, with the poker in his hand, he teased Winifred even more, "Ye-es! Wouldn't you just love to do it?" he mocked looking at the poker.

The taunting went on for a little longer and then, for some reason unknown to this day, he did a very strange thing; he turned the poker around in his hand so that he was holding the point, then handed her the handle.

"There you've got it ... are you happy now?"

Instinctively, she raised the poker ready to strike replying, "Right, Jack, that's it, this has gone far enough; now let my kids out of that cellar top or God forbid ... I will kill you!"

Jack remembered similar words directed to the deserter chap all those years ago, and yet he still chose to mock her, "You silly woman you're nówt else! Whatta you gonna do now?"

She was more in control now, and in deadly earnest. "Jack, I mean it!" she said calmly. "I don't want to do it, but for the last time I'm asking you to let my kids out of the cellar top, or so help me I'll ..."

He unwisely interrupted her at this point and unbelievably, he still carried on taunting her, "Go on then ... do it! Cós I'm telling you now ... they're not coming out."

Without further ado Winifred struck him as hard as she could, and the poker caught him right smack in the middle of his forehead. He was quite stunned by the blow and tottered forward a little as though he was going to fall, then he managed to straighten up, remaining on his feet with his back still propped against the door. There was only a little blood trickling down his face but he looked very dazed.

By now, Winifred had become more frantic than ever and, more in desperation than anything else, she repeated her warning.

He didn't respond, whether or not he could hear her didn't seem to matter any more; all that mattered to her was the safety of her kids. So when there was no reply, she let him have another blow, the poker landed in the exact same spot as before! This time, the blood gushed out flowing all down his face, downwards on to his clothes. His forehead had been split wide open, and there was a deep gash that ran from the top of his head right down to the bridge of his nose. He automatically put his hands to his head, then started staggering towards the staircase; his hands were crawling along the wall leaving smudges of blood everywhere. On reaching the space at the bottom of the stairs, he stumbled and fell into the passageway on to his back. He was motionless, but his eyes were open, and he was staring up at the ceiling with his head lying in a pool of blood.

John had witnessed the whole episode; he was shaking in his shoes and his jaw was quivering; strangely though, his fear was not for himself but for his dad. Arguments in the home always affected him this way, but usually it was his mum whom he feared for.

On seeing his dad fall into the lobby, he ran to him and knelt by his side pleading, "Oh, Daddy, please don't die! Please! Please! I love you, Daddy!"

He knew his dad wasn't dead because he could hear him murmuring; also his arms and fingers were moving a little as though he was trying to say, "I hear you, son."

Meanwhile, the children had emerged from the dark cellar top and were crying. On seeing all the smudges of blood on the wall and his dad lying in a pool of blood in the lobby, Jimmy became hysterical yelling, "O-oh mí daddy's dead ... mí mummy's killed him!"

After consoling him and the others, Winifred went to the lobby to see to her husband.

She could see how badly hurt he was and after giving little John a cuddle, she reassured him, "Don't fret yourself, our John, Mummy's going now to get some help for Daddy."

She then passed by him, and hurried next door to Mrs King's. Alice, who had heard the rumpus through the wall, came at once to take care of the young ones. Afterwards, Winifred went down Albion Street and across Trafalgar to the police telephone box. She first called for an ambulance, then the police, stating that she thought she'd killed her husband. Within minutes, there was a police squad car at the door with two uniformed policemen and two plain-clothed detectives.

On seeing Jack lying there amongst all the blood, one of the detectives asked, "Right ... what's happened here then?"

Without hesitation, Winifred blurted out, "It's my husband ... I meant to kill him!"

The detective in charge knew Winifred from old and tried to correct her, "Now, Mrs Cowell, please don't say that, you don't know what you're saying."

"I meant to kill him!" she stressed adamantly. "My children were in danger, and I thought they were going to be harmed."

"Mrs Cowell, I don't think you realise how serious this is; you've got to realise that anything you say will be taken down, and used in evidence against you. Up to now, I have heard nothing, but now I have to ask you again, what happened?"

For the third time, she replied, "I meant to kill him! I know he's my husband, but he was going to harm my kids," and that's all she would say.

The detective felt sorry for her and begged her to tell him more,

"Please, Mrs Cowell, I implore you … tell us more!" After a pause, he turned very serious and stressed, "There's a lot more to this than meets the eye, isn't there?"

Despite his coaxing, she refused to change her statement, leaving him rather despondent.

He said, "I'm so sorry, Mrs Cowell, but under the circumstances, you leave me no alternative but to place you under arrest."

"Yes, I understand that," she replied, "but first, can you please let me make arrangements for my children? I don't want them put into care."

In the meantime, the ambulance arrived and after administering first aid to Jack they placed him on a stretcher and took him to hospital. Winifred made arrangements for the twins and baby Barbara to stay with Mrs King, whilst the other two were left in the care of Mrs Bacon.

As the police were leading Winifred away, all the children were sobbing and pleading with them, "Please don't take Mummy away … she didn't mean to hurt Daddy!"

The expressions on the policemen's faces said it all; it was quite evident they didn't like their job at that very moment.

As Winifred passed by John, he grabbed hold of her dress and tugged hard till she bent down towards him. "I'm sorry, Mummy," he sobbed. "I love you as well!"

She embraced him giving him a little peck on his cheek, "Yes, I know you do, my love … now don't you fret yourself so! It's not your fault and Mummy does understand why you said what you did."

The curiosity of the neighbours had been aroused and they were all stood on their doorsteps as Winifred was driven away. She was remanded in custody overnight at Burnley Police Station, which was situated at the back of and underneath the Mechanic's Institute Building near to the Town Hall.

The following morning, she was released on bail on the condition that she appeared in court the very next day. Just before leaving the station, she was given the good news that Jack's condition was stable, and that he was going to be all right; nevertheless, the charge against her still stood. The first thing she did on being released was to go to the market to buy some cakes and other luxuries for her kids. On reaching home, she gathered the children together telling them the good news about their dad.

They were all highly delighted to hear that he was all right, and their delight increased still more when she announced, "Right, kids, tonight, we're going to celebrate and have a little party."

Winifred also savoured the moment as all her children responded spontaneously with cheers of "Hooray! Hooray!"

By the time evening arrived, Maureen had returned from Bacup and she helped her mum to organise things. The two wings were pulled out on the wooden table enlarging it, then all the kids sat around just staring in awe at all the goodies.

"Wow, we've no need to use our imaginations this time," they thought, "this is the real thing." After the little feast, they all sat around the fireside listening to Maureen and Jimmy telling stories, and that night went to bed feeling much happier.

The next morning before leaving to attend the court hearing, Winifred again had to make arrangements with the neighbours to look after the children.

On arrival at court, the detective in charge approached her and again made a request, "Mrs Cowell, I beg you once again to change your statement, and tell us exactly what happened. I'm almost certain that if you do, then all charges against you will be dropped."

She politely refrained and strolled quietly into the dock.

The proceedings started and were not going in her favour, until her husband Jack, who had discharged himself from hospital, was brought into court. His head was swathed in bandages and he was acting as a witness for the prosecution. He was quite sober now and full of remorse and guilt, once again becoming the nice person who everybody loved.

On seeing Winifred in the dock, he immediately started shouting, "Get my wife out of there! She's done nothing wrong … it was all my fault!"

"You mean to say you don't want to prosecute your wife, sir?" asked the prosecutor.

"No, I don't … it should be me in the dock, not her!"

Whereupon, the case was dismissed, but Winifred was placed on probation for a year.

The following is a quote from the *Burnley Express* dated April 11th, 1945, which incidentally was the twins' sixth birthday:

WIFE'S ALLEGED ATTACK ON HUSBAND

When Winifred Cowell (31), of 14 Albion Street, was placed in the dock at Burnley Magistrates Court yesterday to answer a charge of inflicting grievous bodily harm on her husband John William Cowell by striking him on the head with an iron bar, the husband, whose head was swathed in bandages immediately rose in court and said, "Excuse me but I am not prosecuting my wife."

The Clerk: "You don't want to take action against your wife?"

"No! It was my fault."

"You have no desire to give evidence against her?"

"No."

Following a conversation with the Chief Constable, the Clerk told the bench he would have to ask them to remand the accused in order that he could communicate the information laid on the charge, and the husband's desire not to give evidence to the Director of Public Prosecutions.

The presiding magistrate then informed Mrs Cowell that she would be remanded on bail for 14 days in order that the Clerk could communicate in the meantime with the Director of Public Prosecutions with a view to obtaining his consent to the withdrawal of the proceedings if necessary.

Ironically, there was an article in the same newspaper about ways of celebrating the forthcoming peace and the heading was as follows:

A 'PEACE' FESTIVITY OF 1814.
BURNLEY' CELEBRATIONS WERE
THE COUNTRY'S BEST.

The article was about how our ancestors celebrated the end of the

Napoleonic Wars. It went on to say how Burnley was preparing to commemorate the end of the present hostilities in Europe.

It was ironic because although the end was in sight in Europe, it still seemed to be ongoing at 14 Albion Street.

12: post war days

It was just about a month after the cellar top incident when the most joyous occasion happened ... The end of the war. One evening in May, all the family, including Jack and Winifred, were sat around the fire when they became aware of a commotion outside.

Jack was halfway through telling a tale, but like everyone else he was curious. "What's all that noise going on outside then?" he asked. "Go and have a look, our Maureen."

"Right, Dad, I was just going to go and see anyway cós I wondered what it was myself."

She'd no sooner gone than she was back again all excited blurting out, "Mum! Dad! Everybody come quickly; there's loads of people coming down Albion Street from above the railway, and all the neighbours are stood at their doors. I don't know what's happening, but there's something different going on for sure."

They all jumped to their feet and scuttled to the front door to witness the event; sure enough there were hordes of people coming down the street.

As they passed by the house, each one raised their arms and waved, they were all laughing heartily, and the chanting of, "The war's over," resounded through the air.

"Oh great! Fantastic! That's marvellous!" and other exclamations punctuated the constant cheering.

"But where's everybody going to, Dad?" asked Jimmy inquisitively.

"I don't know, cock, but I'll find out for thí."

"Where dusta think we're goín?" was the reply given by all. "We're goín down to Town Hall to have a réight good celebration."

The clamour was contagious; all the children in the house became very excited with the goings on and eagerly begged their mum to take them along with the crowd.

She didn't need a lot of persuading and, after briefly considering the matter, replied, "Yes, why not? This is certainly a one-off situation, and definitely one to celebrate."

They were all ecstatic, as they quickly got ready to set off behind the crowd. It was a very special occasion for more reasons than one, for it was the one and only time that all the family went out together with both parents. The atmosphere was incredible; there was a feeling of euphoria amongst the people and it was infectious. Jack carried little Barbara on his shoulders, whilst the others followed holding each other's hands. On reaching Trafalgar, the sight was unbelievable as hundreds of people joined in from neighbouring streets, all making their way to the Town Centre. By the time they reached Manchester Road, the crowd had swollen to thousands as more people swelled in from other areas, all making for the Town Hall. It was a wonderful sight to behold; it seemed like magic to see the Town Hall Clock lit up for the first time in six years; it was, in fact, the first time ever for most of the children.

They managed to get as close as the fire station at Finsley Gate, but didn't dare go any nearer for fear of the two youngest getting crushed. Despite the high spirits and everything that was going on, Winifred was really concerned about Barry and Barbara, so decided to take them home about eleven o'clock; but under the circumstances, she let the others stay in the care of Jack. The remaining four were highly delighted and completely mesmerised by the hullabaloo around them; it was as though they were in Wonderland. There was not a single place to be had anywhere in St James's Street, or in any of the adjacent streets. The largest section of the crowd gathered outside the Town Hall awaiting the mayor's speech, while thousands more thronged around Brunswick Church, which stood facing on the opposite side of Manchester Road. There were many local kids there and being sprightly they were able to obtain a good view by climbing on to window ledges, gas-lamps, tops of bus shelters or anything else to hand. Shortly after the mayor's speech, the Town Hall Clock started to strike midnight; at that moment a strange wonderful silence descended over the place. Hardly had the last chime struck when there was loud cheering and the festive mood filled the air once again. The celebrations were more spontaneous than planned, which made it even better.

It was like New Year's Eve only more so, as everyone began to sing "Auld Lang Syne" and other sentimental songs; and everyone was hugging and kissing each other. Brass bands appeared out of thin air, playing lots of wartime songs that Vera Lynn had made famous; then just like the celebrations that marked the end of the First World War, they started to dance. People formed up in lines and danced the Conga throughout Manchester Road, Elizabeth Street, Hargreaves Street, Parker Lane, St James's Street and all the other adjoining streets; it was certainly a sight to remember. There were many people in their nightclothes, but no one seemed to mind or take the least bit of notice. Lots of women formed their own type of bands playing kitchen utensils and ringing bells; men backed them up by playing mouth organs and clashing dustbin lids together. Never had such a public expression of joy been witnessed before; it was a magical event in every sense of the word. One just had to be there to experience it, as no amount of words could describe the feelings of every single person on that most wonderful of all nights. To make things better still, it was a warm night, which added to the occasion. All four children intermingled amongst the crowd; they thought it was enchanting, as never in their life had they been allowed up till this bewitching hour before.

Unfortunately, the time passed very quickly and before they knew it, it was one o'clock; Jack gathered them together outside the Canal Tavern telling them it was time to go home. He didn't feel like going home himself, as the festivities were still in full swing, and would obviously go on well into the early hours.

The atmosphere was electrifying and the inducement to stay was intensified when everyone merrily began to sing, "Hang out your washing on the Siegfried Line."

Still, Jack didn't give in to temptation, as he knew it was getting rather late for the kids.

They obviously didn't want to go either, so pleaded with him, "Oh please, Dad. Please let us stay a bit longer … please, we'll be good, honest!"

"Oh come on, kids, I'm in bother as it is, you know what your mum's like; she'll kill me when we get home now, cós I promised I'd have you all home before twelve."

"A-ah come on, Dad, please! We'll tell her it wasn't your fault cós we got lost in the crowd and you couldn't find us."

"Hey, that'll do! I don't want any of thí tellín your mum fibs. Anyroad, don't forget that I want to stay as much as you do, but if we did, your mum would have my guts for garters. Now come on the lot of you, let's go!"

They were a little disappointed but still, they'd all thoroughly enjoyed themselves; but little did they know that there was yet more excitement to come, for, when they reached Albion Street, there were still crowds of people celebrating in the street. Neighbours were sat on their doorsteps, and as the children passed by the open doors, the Good News was still being broadcast over various wirelesses. Winifred was waiting up for them, but she wasn't angry in the least, for she understood only too well just what had happened; in fact, she'd done some baking as a surprise. As always at moments like this, she'd been reminiscing, reflecting on the time her father had returned from the First World War, and how they'd all had a little party then. The children were allowed to stay up a little longer, as they all chatted about the goings on; it was a time they were to remember and savour for the rest of their lives.

In spite of going to bed very late, most people rose early the following morning in the knowledge that, at last, the country was at peace. Buntings and Union Jacks were once again dug out from the drawers; every street along Trafalgar was festooned with decorations. Everyone was in high spirits and the rejoicing went on throughout the next three months prior to V J Day, and welcome celebrations were organised for the homecoming soldiers. Also, much to the delight of the local children, street parties were arranged; each street did its own organising, which meant that every street held its party on a different day. This was good news for the local kids, because they soon got wind of when and where a party was taking place; accordingly they made their way there in the hope of getting an invite. For example: Rowley Street held its party one Saturday afternoon in August after the children's matinee; and children from Albion Street crowded at the bottom of Rowley Street till the residents took pity on them, inviting them to join in. The following week was the Albion Street party; on this occasion, it was the Rowley Street kids who eagerly waited to be invited to the festivities.

Every street did itself proud, each in turn putting on a good show for the children; but the Albion Street party outshone the rest by far. The street was blocked off to traffic, and the lines of tables stretched down from the railway bridge to the Trafalgar pub. It was a wonderful time for everyone concerned and the whole street echoed to the happy sound of children whooping it up, and the fervent gossiping of parents as they happily waited upon the tables. It hadn't been an easy task by any means, due to the steepness of the street, but it went down a treat because all the neighbours joined in and pulled together. To round off the event, each child was given a silver shilling.

VJ Day was celebrated on August 15th, and the sense of euphoria was once again revived; talk about the pub with no beer … every single pub in Burnley ran dry. Free matinees were put on for the children, and in places like the Mechanics Institute, old age pensioners were each given half a crown.

It was wonderful now that the threat of impending danger had gone from their lives. At first, people found it strange to be able to do ordinary things like putting the light on without first having to draw the curtains, or to be able to go out at night without question. It was also marvellous to go out after dark to see all the streets lit up by gas-lamps, or the lighting from official buildings and shop windows.

The gas masks were all routed out from the closets and other places and now used mainly as children's toys. In Winifred's home, they'd always been kept in the cubbyhole in the back bedroom, now the kids spent many a happy hour playing with them.

The war was over, but the times were still hard and rationing was to remain on certain commodities for a few years yet. One of these was clothes, but this turned out to be one of the ways in which Winifred made ends meet, as she obtained lots of clothes from jumble sales and the like, then traded the coupons for other things. Bedding was hard to come by, but she ensured that her children were always snug and warm by using surplus army greatcoats on the beds.

As time passed, things like bananas and other tropical fruits began to appear on the market. Sugar was still on ration, but, as before, she would exchange other items for this. The late-night market shopping for produce at knock-down prices continued and cut fruit and broken biscuits remained high on the agenda.

By now, the twins were at St Thomas's Junior School, which was situated on the other side of the canal on King Street. They made their way there every morning hand in hand with their older sister Maureen and brother Jimmy. To get there, they had to cross over Trafalgar and use the footbridge, which took them in between the high looming factory chimneys. Like many other local children, Winifred's were on free school meals, which helped towards the family budget. It also ensured that many local children got at least one good meal a day. Other commodities supplied by the local authorities were milk, orange juice, malt and cod liver oil, which were always given during the morning playtime; the first three were always relished but the latter ...u-ugh!

Winifred always made sure her children got a good meal, especially that they had a good breakfast in their bellies before leaving for school, with a warm drink and biscuits before bedtime. Teatime was often fish and chips from 'the chippy', but one meal which was always special was Sunday lunch. Without fail, she always ordered a leg of lamb from the butcher's; with it, she made the most delicious roast potatoes, cabbage, carrots, and peas, followed by fruit pudding and custard.

It was about this time that some new neighbours moved into next door, at number twelve, and it turned out to be quite catastrophic. Most of the evacuees had long since returned to their own towns, but there were some people who had decided to stay on in Burnley. These new residents were some of those who were evacuated from the Channel Islands in 1940 and they had been living rough in unsanitary conditions ever since. When they moved next door, they brought with them all their furniture and other belongings, which proved disastrous, for soon afterwards a pestilence of bugs swept through many of the houses in the terraced block. Although these houses were poor and run down, Winifred had never experienced vermin except for the odd mouse. However, this soon changed as the bugs created havoc infecting everything, the walls, furniture and the beds; indeed nothing was spared. Many a night the children would wake and find bugs crawling over their faces or bodies. Winifred responded by cleaning the house throughout, then she bought a special DDT spray gun with which to spray all the walls throughout the house; this was done on a daily basis. The three lads did the spraying, finding it quite amusing, as they said it was the first time that the walls had ever been decorated apart from the distemper.

Little did they realise just how unhealthy this task was; none of them wore any protective clothes, masks or gloves. It only came to light many decades later that this particular toxic pesticide should never have been used in this way. Be that as it may, it was used, but by the grace of God, none of the family suffered any serious consequences. Jimmy especially enjoyed this particular task; he would strike a match and put it against one of the many holes in the wall and the bugs could easily be seen scurrying all over the place.

Another thing that Winifred did was to untie the ends of the flock ticks, which were used as mattresses, filling them with soap powder. The flock ticks were large covers filled with cotton and woollen waste. She was very persistent, and finally, after months of effort, she succeeded and the house was clean once again.

Jack kept up his bad ways and, inevitably, landed up in trouble with the law again. Being his second offence, he was sentenced to eighteen months in Strangeways Prison, Manchester. It was yet another trying time for the family, but in spite of his antics, he was still loved by all. Every fortnight, it became a ritual for Winifred to make her way to the Cattle Market Bus Station with one or other of the children, where she caught the bus to Manchester. She always set off on a Saturday morning and it would be turned five o'clock before she got back home.

Jack only served one year, with six months off for good behaviour, and was released on probation one week in February 1947. It was an unforgettable time for more reasons than one, as there was the worst snowstorm since the big one in January 1940. Just like then, the temperature was sub-zero; also like then, all traffic came to a complete standstill. It had started off as quite a mild day, but as it drew to a close, it got colder and colder. Everyone was in the house eagerly awaiting Jack's return, and there was a warm cosy fire blazing away in the fire-grate. Winifred had been informed that he was due to be released about two o'clock, so they all expected him home around teatime. Then about four o'clock, it started to snow, the flakes were as big as leaves, sticking as soon as they hit the ground. The wind quickly began to stir up and they could all hear it blowing and whistling down the chimney; just the thought of having to go outside made one shiver. By five o'clock it was quite dark and everyone was becoming concerned.

"Oh bloomin éck, Mum!" muttered Maureen as she looked out of the window. "Just look at all that snow, I hope mi dad's going to be all right." She was rather anxious, and kept going to the front door to see if she could see him but he was nowhere in sight; by now, Albion Street was knee-deep in snow.

The kids bombarded Winifred with questions. "Are you sure it was today he was being released, Mum?"

"Do you think they might have kept him in a bit longer, Mummy?"

"Do you think he might be buried in snow somewhere, Mum, and can't get out?"

Even little Barry asked, "You don't think he'll be freezing to death somewhere, do you, Mummy?"

"Yes, I'm certain that he's been released today and no, they won't have kept him there any longer, he'd have made sure of that. As for the other questions … I just don't know. And anyway it's no good worrying about it, because there's nothing we can do except wait; mind, we could happen say a little prayer."

"Is he coming home on the bus, Mum, or the train?" asked Jimmy.

"Most probably on the bus because it's a straight run from Manchester to here … why do you ask?"

"Well, our Barry could be right when he said mí dad might be stuck in the snow cós buses are always getting stuck over them tops when it snows a lot."

"Oh thank you, Jimmy, thank you very much, that's all we need. Now listen, everybody! Try not to fret yourselves so because your dad is a lot more resilient than you think, and even if he is stuck somewhere, he'll be able to take care of himself."

"What does resilient mean, Mummy?" interrupted Barry.

Maureen had to smile to herself as she gave him a little hug. "It just means that Daddy can look after himself, our Barry."

"Oh right!" he responded, then after a little study, "I'm still gonna say a little prayer for him anyroad, cós God'll help him then as well, won't he?"

Another hour passed, the mood in the house became quite despondent with everyone becoming fidgety. Then, at half past seven, they heard the front door open followed by the sound of footsteps trudging up the lobby. All eyes were fixed on the living-room door; then, to their delight, he was really there. On seeing him the reception was rather mixed, as everyone was taken aback by his appearance for he was indeed a sight to behold. He was like a snowman with long white bushy eyebrows, his teeth were chattering, and he looked absolutely frozen to the bone.

At first, he didn't say anything; he just crouched forward resting his hands on his knees, puffing and panting. What shocked everyone, was that it was obvious that prison had taken its toll; he appeared drawn, and looked every bit of his thirty-nine years. Mother Nature was really catching up on his fast-living lifestyle.

After regaining some of his breath he grunted, "Oh, thank goodness for that, I'm absolutely frozen t'marrow, I thought I was never gonna make it. It started snowing when we were on the other side of Rawtenstall, and when we were coming up towards Dunnockshaw, the flamín bus got bogged down in a snowdrift, and I've had to flamín well walk all rest ó flippín way from there."

"See, Mum, what did I tell you?" blurted Jimmy excitedly. "I knew bloomín well that bus wudda got stuck."

Everybody then gave him a rapturous welcome and made a great big fuss. "Oh come on, Dad, get yourself out of them wet clothes and dry yourself down, and then get into this warm jacket," said Maureen handing him an army greatcoat. All the others gathered around him wanting a hug and a squeeze.

Winifred had to take her turn before getting her chance to embrace him. After giving him a peck on the cheek, she said, "Right, love, as soon as you've got yourself sorted, there's some hot broth and dumplings to get you all warmed up and feeling somewhat human again."

After tea, they all camped around the fire, he just slouched in the armchair, uttering in sheer contentment, "Cór blimey! I'll tell you what it is, it's great to be home again." Little Barbara sat on his knee, whilst the others sprawled all around him making a big fuss; Maureen and Mary brushed his hair, whilst the lads kept tugging at his trouser legs.

"Tell us a story, Dad, and make us laugh like you used to, please!" pleaded John.

"I'm sorry, cock, not tonight, your dad's not quite feeling up to it."

They were allowed to stay up a little later than normal, but before going to bed, they had a little treat in store for him; they'd all been rehearsing a short song especially for the occasion.

"Right, everybody," ordered Maureen, "get into your positions."

To Jack's surprise, Jimmy, John, Mary and Barry lined up in front of the fire, then started marching on the spot in their nightclothes. Maureen began to conduct them using a twelve-inch wooden ruler as a baton, leading them as they all started to sing in harmony:

> "We're a happy little family,
> Yes we are, yes we are!
> We're a happy little family,
> Yes we are.
> The reason for the fuss,
> Is cós Dad is back with us,
> We're a happy little family,
> Yes we are."

At the end of the first chorus, Barry broke rank, and went up to his dad, giving him a hug and a kiss saying, "I love you, Daddy, and I'm glad you're back home with us."

He then went and stood near to the living-room door, and each of the other three did exactly the same in turn. They formed a single rank file once again, then started to march up stairs to the second chorus.

"We're a happy little family,
Yes we are, yes we are!
We're a happy little family,
Yes we are.
All our sins are all forgiven,
And we're marching up to heaven.
We're a happy little family,
Yes we are, yes we are!"

Jack was very touched by their little gesture and tears welled up in his eyes.

It didn't go unnoticed and Maureen made a comment, "Eh Dad ... you're nothing but a big softy at heart aren't you?"

"Umm, I suppose you could be right there love, that was really nice and touching and quite unexpected." He wiped a tear from his eye adding, "Your dad really appreciated that our Maureen, and don't think I'm not grateful cós I am ... you must have all worked hours on it."

"Yes we did Dad, but it was worth it just to see the look on your face. Anyroad, I love you too Dad and it's great to have you back with us."

He knew in his heart that his family was truly his real purpose in life, and that he had gold at his fingertips. Whether or not he made a vow to himself to start leading a new life from then on is not clear, but one thing is certain, he tried. For the next couple of years, he pulled in his reins; although he didn't give up boozing altogether, he certainly curbed it quite a lot.

The following morning, it was impossible for anyone to get out of the front door, as the snow had drifted up to the bedroom windowsills and was about four feet deep on the other side of the street. They had to leave the house via the back door, by negotiating the treacherous stone steps and trudging through deep snow on the backstreet. First Jimmy and John set to clearing the steps, whilst Mary sprinkled them with salt to prevent ice forming. Afterwards, to their delight, Jack escorted them all to school hand in hand.

He didn't talk much about his time in prison but on odd occasions, he would make comments like, "Never again, never! I just couldn't face another spell inside; if they sent me down again ... I know I'd just die there for sure."

Much to the enjoyment of all the local kids, the snow lingered on for about a week; Albion Street became like a ski-resort. On account of it being so steep and long, it was ideal for sledging; consequently it was invaded by all the other kids in the district. Lots of fun was had by the younger children as they used shovels, fenders, tin trays or anything else they could use as make do sledges. Parents kept a wary eye on them as they sledged down from the railway bridge. The air was filled with laughter as they skidded down the street; some built snowmen, others had snowball fights, some even tried to build igloos. The more boisterous bigger boys, who used to start their sleigh run from as far up Albion Street as St. Mathew Street, then race one another, used to spoil the pleasure of the smaller children. They'd gather quite a speed on the less inclined gradient prior to Piccadily Road and then, they'd all come thundering down the lower part of Albion Street at breakneck speed. How nobody was killed is unbelievable, as they would go shooting straight across Trafalgar and down through the factory yard as far as the canal. The nearest anyone came to being hurt was when a bus happened to stop at the bottom of Albion Street and one lad had to skid to a halt, hitting the bus sideways on. It wasn't just dangerous for them though, it also created a hazard for the younger ones. The kiddies weren't so much concerned about the danger as the fact that they couldn't sledge properly themselves, for fear of being run over by the bigger boys, as they came roaring down the street laughing and shouting. The big lads were spoiling their fun, so the youngsters decided to do something about it. After each sleigh run, it took the big lads approximately half an hour or so to drag their sledges, trudging all the way back to St Mathew Street. This gave all the youngsters ample time to gather up the snow to make a ramp about a foot high, which stretched right across the street. The ramp was level with number fourteen. After constructing the barrier the kiddies just sat around and awaited the outcome; sure enough, it wasn't long before they could hear the bellowing of the bigger lads. The first boy came roaring over the bridge before he saw the hump, but it was too late to stop, leaving him no option but to go over it. It worked like a treat; the effect was just like taking off from a ski-jump as the sledge went hurtling through the air with the lad tumbling along behind it. The others suffered the same fate, all ending up in scattered heaps, as their sledges went careering on down the street. Nobody was badly hurt, but a few were shaken up and limped off home nursing their bruises much to the delight of the youngsters.

Sunday was a very special day, it always started with the children going to Christ the King Catholic Church, which was just above the railway at the far end of Piccadily Road. Jack was never one for going to church, but all the same he used to love helping them to get ready, then waving them off as they tramped up Albion Street. He openly admitted that he got a big kick out of this. Before taking Holy Communion, one had to fast from midnight the previous day and as the first Mass didn't finish till nearly ten o'clock, they were always starving. As soon as they got out of church, they'd run home as fast as their legs would carry them, where Jack always had a hearty breakfast awaiting them.

Sunday was also special because pubs were opened for fewer hours; Jack still went for a drink, but he only went to the Trafalgar or the Malakof. He was usually home just after two o'clock, and would spend the rest of the day listening to the wireless with the family or playing games with them. All the kids loved this for when he was good, he was very good and fun to be around. He never took them out for the day or walking for that matter, but when he stayed in, he'd tell them many fascinating, interesting tales of his own childhood and other events. He also had a great sense of humour and would laugh heartily and openly at silly little things. One thing that made everyone laugh was when he danced in front of the fire. He'd roll up his trouser legs to above the knees, which in itself had them all in stitches because his thin scrawny legs were like spindles.

The kids would make remarks, "Bloomín éck Dad, they're like picking sticks, there's more meat on a Ginnyspinner's."

the *broken biscuit*

He'd then do some kind of Irish Jig and to everyone's amusement he'd move really intricately across the floor. He was also a dab hand at card tricks and other things that needed sleight of hand; throughout his performances, he'd have all of them enthralled. He wasn't all footloose and fancy free though, as he had a very serious side to his nature too. He wasn't the best singer in the world but he would sing his favourite song with such feeling that it brought tears to everyone's eyes:

"T'is the ring, your mother wore,
On the day she took my name.
Just a plain gold band,
That I placed on her hand,
When partners in life, we became.
T'is a simple gift, I know,
But my fondest wish shall be,
That it bring the joy,
To you, and your boy,
That it brought to your mother and me."

During all the antics and goings on, Winifred would be busy preparing the leg of lamb with all the trimmings. Maureen always helped by baking apple pie or whatever; even Mary liked to dabble. It was usually dished up about three to four o'clock, and served as a dinner-cum-tea. Afterwards, it was a kind of ritual to listen to comedy programmes on the radio such as 'Wakey Wakey' with Billy Cotton, and others like 'Jimmy Clitheroe' and 'Educating Archie'. There was a kind of festive atmosphere as all the kids would sit around with a cup of tea, tucking into the broken biscuits, or anything else that their mum could muster up. One programme that created lots of amusement and was a particular favourite had a character in it, a little girl known as Jennifer.

Every week at the same point during the performance, this character would come into the act, one of the other actors would ask, "And what's your name little girl?"

To which she always replied in the most high pitched squeaky voice, "My na-me's Jen-ni-fer."

At this point, Jack would always break out into a fit of uncontrollable laughter, which was so infectious that it triggered off everyone else in the room. What made it all the funnier was that at the time, he would always be slouched in his favourite armchair, whilst everyone waited expectantly knowing exactly when Jennifer would make her appearance; their eyes would be fixed on their dad. Just before the moment, he'd chuckle and giggle a little to himself, then when she uttered her name he just broke out into a fit of the most contagious laughter. Every time, the kids knew exactly what to expect, they even tried to keep their faces straight, but no matter … as soon as he started laughing, it just set them off as well and they'd all roll about in stitches.

It wasn't so much Jennifer who made them laugh … it was the antics of their dad.

Another thing they loved was that on occasions he would take a couple of them to the pictures and treat them to some toffees. But afterwards on the way home, he'd always leave them at the bottom of Albion Street, before making his way to the Trafalgar Pub.

Even at her young age, Mary was quite high spirited, she'd say something like, "Now think on Dad, don't be late home and no getting drunk!" to which he would reply with a grin on his face, "Go on you cheeky young monkey!"

If only he'd been like this all the time, things would have been great. Alas this was not to be and despite his many blessings, he still unwisely preferred the company of his boozing cronies to that of his family and gradually slipped back into his wily ways. It really was a shame, he was quite clever and astute in many ways, yet so foolish in others; he had a real flair for making money, but an even greater one for spending it. When he was flush, he always had many so-called friends around him, he didn't think twice about buying drinks around the pub. Nonetheless, it was a different tale when it came to finding some housekeeping money; this was the main cause of the household rows.

His boozing continued and sadly, the kids never saw much of him, when they did it was often after being woken up by him shouting from the bottom of the stairs in a drunken state, "Winnie! Whe-er-e's my supper?"

This would cause ructions, but all the same, it was a regular occurrence. Many a time, he'd just fall asleep in the chair, remaining there till the early hours, awakening shivering as daylight dawned.

During many of the rows, he often threw out slanderous remarks, "Aye, none ó them flamín kids are mine anyroad!" However, this came to an abrupt end one particular evening. By now, Maureen was about fourteen, she was just getting ready to go out, when he made a comment about what she was wearing, telling her to change. She became defiant, refusing point blank, so he started to assert his authority.

At this point, she came out with something that left him completely deflated, "Why should I? You can't tell me what to do," then, she added the killer blow, "you're not my dad anyroad!"

You could have knocked him down with a feather, for the first time in his life he was absolutely speechless, just standing there with his mouth agape. He had mixed feelings ranging from anger and astonishment, hurt, to complete frustration.

After the initial shock, he managed to splutter, "You what … what did you just say?"

"You heard what I said!" she muttered rather sheepishly through clenched teeth and quivering lips, "You're forever telling mí mum that you're not mí dad, and that goes for all mi brothers and sisters as well."

He was absolutely shocked, and it wasn't only because of what she'd just said; it was the way in which she had expressed herself. She'd never spoken to him in this manner before … it took him completely by surprise.

In that instance, he realised the error of his ways, what a terrible mistake he'd made saying those awful things and so tried to make amends, "Oh, our Maureen, please don't say that … of course I'm your dad, and that goes for all mi other kids as well." There was a little pause, then he said, "So think on love … you won't ever say that to mi again will you? Please!"

"That's all very well Dad," she relented as she could now see the hurt in his eyes, "but why do you keep saying those terrible things to Mum?"

"Come here love and give your dad a hug, and I'll try and explain," he answered somewhat nonplussed. He then embraced her saying, "It's because I'm stupid, and when I've had a drink, I say things I don't really mean."

"But why Dad? I don't understand why you want to hurt Mum so much … don't you love her anymore?"

"Yes I do love … in fact, very much so, but like I said, I say stupid things when I'm drunk. You know the old saying don't you … you always hurt the one you love?"

"Oh, I don't know what to think Dad … it's all right you saying that but it's still not very nice for Mum is it? Anyway, there's something else whilst we're at it, our Jimmy and the others keep asking what you mean when you say those things to mí mum."

With these words, he put his head in his hands, "Oh my God! What have I done, how stupid can I get?"

At that point, Maureen started to reassure him, "Look Dad, don't fret about it cós we all know you're our real dad, and we all love you, but you've got to promise mi that you'll never ever say that to Mum again."

He looked at her pretty face, replying in the most sincere way, "Yes our Maureen, I promise with all mi heart … never again … never … never … never! And that's one promise that your dad's gonna keep."

"Thanks Dad, but whilst we're still on the subject, may I ask you just one more favour?"

"You certainly can love, what is it?"

"Well, it's just that you're not the only one who keeps saying it … your sisters do as well."

He screwed his face up a little at that remark, "U-um … I see your point. Don't worry your pretty little head about it any more, I'll sort it … I'll definitely sort it."

True to his word, those hurtful remarks never ever passed his lips again. It's just a pity that she didn't get him to promise to give up boozing at the same time.

13: junior school days

By 1948 Maureen was attending the senior school, Jimmy was in the top class at St Thomas's and the twins were in Miss Drennan's class.

Every morning, the first period was Catholicism, which was preceded and followed by prayers. This period lasted about an hour, which meant that in a week a total of five hours were taken up with religious instruction before getting down to the nitty gritty of real studying – the three Rs.

A fifteen-minute break followed, during which all the kids were given milk or orange juice prior to playtime in the yard. The yard was concrete, which soon became apparent, much to the children's plight if they got into a fight. Needless to say, Jimmy was one of these; he was constantly coming home from school with a split lip, busted nose and torn trousers. No matter, he gave as good as he got; he wasn't the only one though, as the twins found themselves the target of abuse, too, from many of the schoolchildren. There was no doubt about it, the schoolyard was certainly a good grounding for out of school education. Just like Maureen before them, all the Cowells soon learnt how to stick up for themselves.

They had no choice in the matter, as they were constantly on the receiving end of insults and barbed comments like, "Hiya, Cow-heel, how's it goín ... hasta bin on rag-cart lately?" "Hav ya bín to see thí dad in prison this weekend?"

To Jimmy, this was just like waving a red flag to a bull. John wasn't as fiery as Jimmy, and most of the time he would let it roll over his head; however, there were many times when he too was pushed too far and he also ended up fighting. The girls were just as bad with their sneering catty remarks but Mary had no trouble sorting them out. She was only slim, but like Jimmy she was fiery with a short fuse and she'd lay into them at the least provocation. She didn't mess about either, as she had a natural ability to fight like a lad, lashing out at them with clenched fists. At home, they would all talk about their scrapes at school, but Winifred never intervened so long as it was amongst children of their own age, and that's how they liked it. One thing though, she wouldn't tolerate bullying. It wasn't one-sided either; she'd taught all her kids never to bully any little ones, and God help them if they did.

Miss Gordon, the headmistress, was very strict and one of her rulings was no fighting; consequently she was forever sending for Winifred because of the constant brawls. Despite this, she had a soft spot for Winifred because she could see how hard she struggled to bring up her children, and what a good caring mother she was. There were many times when Winifred couldn't get to the school to talk over the situation, but on these occasions, she would always send a note with one of the children.

One day after one of the discussions, Miss Gordon turned to Winifred asking, "Mrs Cowell, could I just ask where you learned to write?"

"Certainly," she replied, "I did all my learning at St Mary's School in Bacup when I was a young girl. Why do you ask?"

"Well it's just that you always write an excellent letter, expressing yourself in the most explicit way," adding, "Have you had a further education?"

"No I'm afraid not, Miss Gordon, you see, due to my family and other circumstances, I've never had the opportunity. It's just that I've always loved reading, and I seem to have a natural flair for writing."

"You certainly have," replied Miss Gordon, who then came out with something that took Winifred by surprise. "Mrs Cowell, have you ever thought of writing your autobiography? I think it would make wonderful reading."

After some thought, Winifred replied, "Yes, Miss Gordon, perhaps it would, but I couldn't do that, as there are too many hurtful things that I wouldn't like to come to light, and not just for my sake, but for my children's as well."

"Yes, I can quite understand your feelings about that, Mrs Cowell, it just seems such a shame."

Well, that was it … the end of the story before it even began.

Miss Gordon did send for Winifred on other occasions and one of these caused Winifred quite a lot of concern. Miss Gordon pointed out that although Maureen was quite bright, she was struggling with her reading and writing skills.

"Yes, Mrs Cowell, I'm quite perturbed, as I feel that she is capable of doing much better."

"Right, Miss Gordon, I've got to agree with you there because I feel the same way; I promise you that from now on I'll take her in hand. If you could arrange some homework for her, I'll help her any way I can and I'll make sure that she keeps at it."

This she did; every evening when the other children had gone to bed, she'd sit with Maureen, going over things endlessly. Maureen complained bitterly, but no matter, she had to read a couple of short chapters from her schoolbooks or write a short essay or letter. But as time progressed, Maureen was eternally grateful, as she eventually became quite fluent and proficient. Miss Gordon was very pleased with her progress and on one of Winifred's visits, she was complimented on her achievement.

"Mrs Cowell, I am really pleased with Maureen's progress, it is plain to see that she is now much more competent. Although she is still a little way behind schedule, I feel confident that she will soon catch up. I'd also like to congratulate you, you must have the patience of Job, because it's obvious that you must have spent countless hours with her."

Winifred felt a little embarrassed, just replying, "Well it's my duty isn't it? She's my child."

"Yes that's all right, Mrs Cowell, but you've got all the other little ones to think about as well; it simply amazes me how you do it."

"Ah well, what it is, Miss Gordon, my children are my life, and nothing on this earth is more important to me. They're good kids, and each one of them is so unique in his or her way, and they give me so much love and joy. I can't really say why I love them so much, I just do."

Miss Gordon smiled at her replying, "You just did, Mrs Cowell, you just did."

Eventually all the Cowell kids learned how to stick up for

themselves, and ultimately gained the respect of their peers. In spite of everything though, the twins enjoyed themselves at St Thomas's, spending many happy hours there; lifelong friendships were formed and built upon. Mary had many friends, but her best one was a girl called Loretta Glover; they did everything together and sat next to each other in class. Little did they know then that their friendship was to last a lifetime through all kinds of toil and strife.

John also made many friends including Desmond Lee, David Whittaker, Kenny Clayton and of course Bobby Cheetham, the young boy who was born in the next bed to him in Bank Hall. Like Mary, he too had a best mate; his was called Ronnie Hopkinson. Actually, in some ways this caused John a problem, as he had a slight speech impediment, not being able to pronounce his Rs at all.

This gave rise to further jeering, as he was forever shouting, "Wonnie," across the playground.

Ronnie happened to be the fastest runner in the school, which created a big laugh in the classroom one day, as John blurted out, "I think Wonnie is a weally good wunner!"

But it wasn't just at school; he also got ridiculed by his own brothers and sisters, when he came out with remarks like, "I'm just goín' wound to Wonnie's to play out."

This caused Winifred great concern, so she arranged for him to see a speech therapist. For the next three years, he attended Elizabeth Street Clinic every Tuesday afternoon for a one-hour session. It wasn't easy and he made little progress in the first year; but the therapist was a very kind lady, who, with infinite patience and perseverance, employed many different methods. One of these was to inflate a balloon, which she then placed in between both their faces.

"Now put your mouth against the balloon, John," she would ask him, "and I'll put mine against this side and talk to you, and I'll make some funny sounds so you can feel the vibrations."

One of these sounds was the strong trilling Scottish "r-r-r-r-r" sound, rolling the "rs" from the back of the throat, which she followed with the sentence, "I ran the ragged rascals around the rugged rocks."

John couldn't get his tongue around these guttural sounds at all; when asked to repeat the sentence, it always came out as "w-w-w-w-w" and "I wan the wagged wascals awound the wugged wocks."

This went on for almost three years, until finally one day he realised he could make the trilling sound; it wasn't too good at first, but thereafter it was uphill all the way. His confidence grew; he never again had trouble with his pronunciation much to his delight, and Winifred's too.

In 1949 Jimmy moved to the senior school, but because of his hyperactivity, he went to the Open Air School within the grounds of Thompson's Park. Barry moved up into the first class in junior school, Mary and John into Miss Gordon's class. During his first year, Barry made his first Holy Communion, as the others had done before him, whereas it was now the twins' turn to be Confirmed. This meant that the children could choose their own names, which had to be the names of patron saints. At the time John was reading about St George and the Dragon, so that's the name he chose; Mary chose St Teresa.

In the school, there were one or two children from better-off families, but on the whole, the majority were from poor backgrounds; therefore most were quite happy because they didn't know any better. One thing perhaps more memorable than any other was that it was still very much the age of the clogs. These were worn by almost every schoolchild and adult; Winifred's children were no exception to the rule. Clogs may have looked and sounded cumbersome, but were in fact very comfortable; they kept the children dry shod in rain and snow alike and were far superior to most other types of footwear. In spite of this, there was a definite stigma attached to them for they were associated with poverty. Perhaps this was because a clogger's fund had been set up for the distribution of clogs to poor families in need, especially so at Christmas time. People of the upper class used to look down with contempt at anyone wearing them.

Girls mainly wore rubber soles and heels, but the lads preferred irons, so they could make sparks fly by kicking the ground; they liked the sound of them better too. Being a bit of a tomboy, Mary was one of the exceptions, preferring irons so she too could make sparks along with the lads. The sparking was much more effective when the clogs had just been re-ironed.

It's a far cry nowadays in the schoolyards to what it was like in the

1940s, as then the clanging of clogs was so distinctive as children played on the concrete surface. This was especially so as they all lined up in single file before marching into class to the sound of the bell with their clogs going clip clop, clip clop!

When it was snowing, the snow used to build up solid in between the irons; much to the kids' delight, this would make them two to three inches taller. Sadly, though, it had to be taken off by briskly kicking their feet against the school wall before entering the classroom.

At playtime, competitions were held to see who could make the most sparks in one dash across the schoolyard. The idea was to kick the ground whilst on the run as many times as possible, but it didn't count if sparks were not made. Most of the kids used to kick with their natural foot about once every third stride. This is where Jimmy came into his own as he became quite expert, managing to strike effectively every time on his right foot. This obviously made him quite happy, but Winifred wasn't too pleased as it meant a lot more trips to the clogger's.

Every district had a clogger's shop; the one on Trafalgar was next to the fruit shop near to Derby Street. All the local kids had to make regular visits there, but on the whole, they quite enjoyed it, as it was an enlightening experience and it was often the topic of conversation at school. There were dozens of steel hangers in the ceiling, each one containing many different sizes of irons. Usually there were about half a dozen people sat down on a wooden bench waiting their turn, while the clogger worked busily away on the other side of the counter. He always wore a long leather apron, and it was intriguing to watch him skilfully working away with nails in his mouth, using special tools doing everything from de-nailing, soling and heeling, to making a complete new pair of clogs. He worked on a special type of anvil called a last; his main tools were a special claw hammer, pincers, files and a very sharp knife with a curved blade.

Clogs were shod many times before their use was finished, and when the time came for a new pair, every precaution was taken to ensure they were comfortable and a good fit. The clogger would first measure the foot and then pick the correct wooden sole to match up to a leather upper. The wooden sole, being very comfortable, must have been specially prepared to make it weatherproof, as it rarely cracked or split.

There was a well-known saying that wearing clogs was good for strengthening the ankles and legs, and this certainly proved true in Winifred's children, as they all had good strong straight legs. They were also said to be good for health reasons and renowned for warding off colds and other ailments, and they certainly helped contain Barry's asthma.

It was still the age of the knocker-up, but on Albion Street, you only needed one if you had to get up about five o'clock. The reason being that from six o'clock onwards, you could hear the continuing clattering of clogs walking down the street, and could even determine what time it was by the different sounds or the number of them. For example, at six o'clock, a couple of colliers would go clip-clopping by; then, just before seven o'clock, there would be a cacophony of clog sounds as the weavers scurried towards the sheds; a little later, Joe Smithson, who had a limp, made a most distinctive sound. On hearing him, it was time for most schoolchildren to get up.

Many other games apart from clog sparking were played in the schoolyard, but one pastime that the girls enjoyed was making intricate bangles, rings and necklaces by plaiting and inter-winding different coloured coils of electric wire together. It was a custom handed down from their older peers and required a lot of skill, but once finished, they were quite pretty and sophisticated.

The most popular game by far amongst the lads was playing fag-packets. Every lad in the school collected cigarette packets; the idea of the game was to win as many of your opponent's as you could. It was played between two lads; one would stand a card up against the wall, then both would kneel down about six feet away, taking turns at trying to knock it down by flicking other cards at it. It wasn't too easy, therefore quite a lot of cards would finish up on the ground against the wall; the boy who eventually knocked down the target happily scooped up the lot. Being collectable items, these cards were a sort of currency amongst the lads and they could be exchanged for other commodities. Lots of kids came to school with some pocket money and would buy things at the tuck shop on the corner of Whittham Street and King

Street. They would then readily exchange part of this for fag cards. Winifred could never afford to give her kids any money, but no matter, both John and Barry became very adept at the game, so never went short of tuck.

During the school holidays, and at weekends, the local children found many different ways of enjoying themselves. The front street was filled with laughter, as girls gathered into groups playing hopscotch, tig, mug in the middle, spinning tops and skipping. They competed with each other by skipping individually on the spot doing intricate whips, over twists and crosses. Then, working together in groups, two girls would each hold one end of a rope spinning it faster and faster, making all the same intricate moves, whilst others jumped in and out. To make it more difficult and skilful, they would sometimes use two ropes, rotating them in different directions. Winifred, like many other parents, loved to sit on the front doorstep and watch all the children enjoying themselves.

The boys were more into football and cricket or playing knock and run. Cricket was always played on the back street using a dustbin for wickets and the lads were forever getting told off for knocking the ball into neighbours' yards. It was nigh impossible to play football on the front street, as the ball kept running down the steep incline and across Trafalgar into the factory yard. Hence, they used to play in the Piccadilly Tennis Courts but as this was out of bounds, the park attendant was forever chasing them off. The only place available for them to play the game was on Clifton Reckory, which was quite a long way off.

One game that was thoroughly enjoyed and played by both boys and girls on the front street was rounders; but, it was frowned upon by the neighbours, as many a window was broken, so this game was banned.

If one of Winifred's children happened to break a window, or anything else for that matter, she would willingly pay her share towards the costs. This was a constant source of controversy, as sometimes children would run off after causing some damage. Many a neighbour would knock at Winifred's door complaining about one or other of her children, demanding recompense.

Her reply would always be, "Right then, if my child has done it I will gladly pay for the damage, but first of all we must wait until the children come home so that I can ask them about it."

The usual response would be, "Nay come off it, Winnie, they're bound to say it wasn't them, aren't they?"

Much to their displeasure she would answer, "My children don't tell me lies; if they say it wasn't them, I believe them."

"Oh yeah, they're going to own up to it, are they? Umph, some bloomín hopes!"

"Like I said, my children don't lie; if one of them has broken your window I will know the truth and you will get your money."

Occasionally the offending child would appear on the scene during the conversation and Winifred would ask outright. "Right," she'd say in a determined voice, "this gentleman here says that you have broken his window ... is this true?"

If the child was innocent, the reply would always be a definite, "No, Mum, it wasn't me, honest!"

This usually left the neighbour feeling rather disconcerted and unhappy about the whole proceedings. Nevertheless, if the child was guilty of the offence Winifred always knew, as his or her head would drop with a quiet murmur of "ye-es" dribbling through tightly pursed lips.

This was the normal course of events and all the neighbours quickly learnt that they would get a fair response if any of Winifred's children had done anything untoward. As the children got bigger, Winifred would make them pay part towards the cost if they had been doing something they shouldn't.

Taking everything into account, play areas where the children could play peacefully were almost non existent. This meant that many of the kids had to make their own amusement, which in turn led them to getting into mischief. The canal was known to the local kids as 'The Cut'; it became a popular place for swimming and other escapades. Many a lad went home to face a good hiding with his clothes drenched after falling in off a makeshift wooden raft.

Another favourite place was a derelict piece of land, which was enclosed by high stone walls and bounded by Trafalgar, Dent Row and the Manchester Road Railway Station Paddock. Inside were the remains of demolished houses and cobbled streets; stored therein were lots of long wooden telegraph poles. It was designated as GPO private land, but despite the forbidding 'KEEP OUT' signs, it was a favourite haunt for many kids. Yes indeed, it was a place for gang huts, hide and seek, and general tomfoolery. If a person of authority like a warden, policeman or whoever came along, one or other of the kids was sure to spot him, then alert the others. It was very rare for anyone ever to get caught, as there were so many different escape routes over the high walls by scampering over the stacked logs.

Winifred used to keep empty jam jars and certain milk bottles under the sink. When she had a dozen or more she would return them to the shop and collect a small refund. This little scheme didn't bring in much money but all the same, it was a kind of emergency fund, which she sometimes fell back on. At the time, Mary was very keen on swimming; she was very good, too, and had actually been chosen to swim for the school team. To keep in trim, she needed lots of swimming practice and went to the Central Baths daily. Winifred encouraged her every way by giving her the entrance money and other things. The costs for this were minimal but all the same, there were many times when it was nigh impossible to find the money. Subsequently, there was one time when Winifred just couldn't afford it, and pointed this out to Mary.

"But, Mum," she responded, "you know I've got to keep up with my training if I want to compete with the other swimmers."

"Yes, I know that, our Mary, but surely it won't do any harm to miss going one day, you've been there every day for the past month."

"Oh but it's important, Mum, I can't miss going, I can't," replied Mary becoming quite flustered.

"Well you're going to have to, aren't you? I realise how important it is to you but all the same, I just haven't got any money to spare until your dad gets home."

"Umph, it's not flippín fair, we never have any money in this house," protested Mary.

"Now that'll do, you've had your fair share since you started this training lark," answered Winifred sternly, "and like I said, it won't do any harm to miss just once. Anyway, I haven't time to discuss it with you anymore, I want to catch the chemist before it shuts."

With no more to be said, Winifred went about her errand, leaving Mary sulking in the living room. Mary was mumbling something to herself when she noticed one of the milk bottles jutting out of the sink's curtain. Without giving it a second thought, she put six bottles into a paper carrier bag and took them back to Nora's shop. Now with sufficient money in her pocket, she happily made her way to the baths. Little did she know that her little ruse was going to be found out much quicker than she thought. Winifred returned from her errand shortly afterwards to find Maureen in the house. Maureen set about preparing something to eat for the younger ones when she noticed there was no bread in the food cupboard. On pointing this out to her mum, Winifred told her to get the empty bottles and jam jars, from underneath the sink and return them to the shop.

"There's enough to buy a four-penny loaf," said Winifred, "that'll put us on till your dad gets home."

"But, Mum," Maureen replied after looking under the sink, "there are no bottles, just one empty jam jar, that's all."

"Of course there are, I only cleaned out under there this morning, there were at least six."

"Well I'm sorry, Mum, but there aren't any there now."

Winifred looked for herself and was fuming when she realised exactly what had happened.

"It's our Mary, the little swine!" she rapped unable to contain her rage. "She's gone and took them so that she could go to the flamín baths with her friends. Right that's it, she's gone too far this time! I'll show her what for," she mumbled through gritted teeth whilst putting her coat back on, "I'll kill the little…!"

"Mum!" Maureen quietly protested. "Where are you going in that state?"

"I'm going down to the Central Baths to sort Mary out, and I'll drag her home by the scruff of her neck if need be; I'll not have her stealing from this house."

Meanwhile, Mary was quite unconcerned, happily swimming along with her mates. She was unaware that her little scam had been discovered and that her enjoyment was about to end very abruptly. She routinely did ten lengths of the bath without any trouble and had just completed nine when things came to a halt as the professor blew his whistle.

As the baths went all quiet he shouted, "Is there a Mary Cowell in the baths? If so, please come here now." Mary looked up and to her horror she saw her mother standing at the side of the professor.

"Oh no," she thought, "she'll kill me." Her fears were intensified because many of her mates were in the pool and she didn't like the thought of being shown up in front of them. Whether she liked it or not, that's what happened. She dragged herself out of the water and slunk up to Winifred dragging her feet.

Mary had good cause to be wary, as Winifred gave her one almighty crack across the face. "You little thief, you're nowt else!" she growled. "Stealing money from the house after all you've had."

"But Mum, I didn't think it was stealing," Mary protested, "they were only empty jam jars and milk bottles."

"It's still stealing no matter which way you look at it," she snarled, "anyway, which is your cabin?"

"Over there, Mum, on the other side of the baths." Winifred immediately grabbed hold of Mary's hair and dragged her to the cubicle and ordered her to dress herself.

"But, Mum, I haven't dried myself yet, I'm wet through."

"I couldn't care less, you can just put your clothes on top of your costume or I'll drag you all the way home as you are right now!"

Mary knew not to argue with her mum whilst she was in this sort of mood, and immediately did as she was told. Without giving her any time to dry or comb her hair, Winifred then frog-marched Mary out of the baths humiliating her in front of her friends.

Winifred didn't put a stop to Mary's training sessions, but she did ground her in other ways. Hence, Mary never did anything like it again.

It's true to say that the children got into loads of mischief and sometimes went a bit over the top with their pranks, but they were mostly brought up to respect other people's property and always showed due respect to elderly people. Winifred made sure that her children were always respectful to adults and they would address them as Mrs Burnett, Mrs Smith, Mrs Wilkinson, etc. Most folk lived in stark poverty and deprivation, but in spite of this they respected law and order to a fault. It was second nature to comply with the law; most people didn't just respect it, they liked it that way.

The local bobby used to walk the beat and although he wasn't the most popular person around, he had everyone's respect. He was never a friend as such, yet lots of folk felt more secure just to have him around. He didn't have direct contact with the police station, but there were police telephone boxes scattered around the town; these were in places like the one at the bottom of Albion Street. He was known by the local folk and, although not on a first-name basis, he was quite aware of their habits. He would turn up to let folk know he was around, and would often turn a blind eye to things so long as they were not too serious. If there was a fight going on, it quickly ended on the appearance of a policeman; then, many a lad would shake hands and make up.

Like many neighbours, Winifred never had cause to lock her front door, as it was unthinkable to walk into anybody else's house without first being invited. It wasn't drummed into one either, it was an unwritten law that was implicitly understood and respected by all. Despite the poverty and unemployment, muggings, burglaries and the like were few and far between. There was also a common understanding throughout the neighbourhood, as far as being protective towards children. If a child happened to stray from one street to another, one of the neighbours was certain to take it in hand and return it to the proper place.

If the child was a little older, they'd say, "Hey, young David (or whoever), does tha mum know tha's playín around here? I think tha'd best get thasél off home afore she starts worryín' about thi."

If any of the local lads happened to get copped by the local bobby for doing something untoward, he generally got a sharp clip behind the ear and that was the end of it. There was one time when this happened to John; he overstepped the mark with a prank that backfired on him. He was about ten at the time and he'd just acquired a toy plastic knife that had a retractable blade. At the time it was very popular with the local kids; they'd pretend to stab each other, then stagger about as though they were injured. When the plastic blade was retracted, then let go quickly, it made a distinct clicking sound. He was walking home one evening with his mate Ronnie and there happened to be two policemen stood in the Co-op shop doorway. The two lads decided to play a trick on them.

John said to Ronnie, "Just as we're going past them two bobbies, Ronnie, you pretend to be mad at me, and I'll pretend that I'm pulling a proper flick-knife on you."

"Good idea," replied Ronnie, "let's do it!" It worked all right, too well in fact.

They were just approaching the doorway when Ronnie blurted out loud enough for the two policemen to hear, "I'm tellín' thi, if you don't wrap up I'll belt thi one!"

"That's what you think," replied John as he pulled out the toy knife. He let go of the already retracted plastic blade, which made one hell of a click!

"Hey!" shouted one of the policemen. "What the flamin éck have you got there?"

John put it behind his back, still pretending. "Oh, it's nówt, officer."

"What do you mean it's nówt? Let me have a look... now!" The pretence was kept up for a little longer before John produced the toy knife to the officer, then burst out laughing much to the bobby's displeasure.

"Oh, you cheeky young bugger, you're nówt else!" he raved, then gave John one hell of a crack about his head that made his ears ring for a week; Ronnie received the same from the other bobby.

Needless to say, the toy knife was confiscated and the prank was never ever repeated. They never told their parents about the episode either, for fear of getting another crack.

One event enjoyed by every kid alike was the Saturday afternoon matinee, and for most kids, it was the day when they got their spending money. Winifred always gave hers ninepence each, which wasn't much, but it was all she could afford. Every district had its own local picture place; the one in the Trafalgar area was the Alhambra Picture

Winifred and Jack on their wedding day.

Below: A cast-iron fireplace, similar to the one in Winifred's mother's house. Note the raised fire-grate with an oven at one side and a water boiler at the other.

Above left: A treasured family photograph: Jimmy is perched on Mary's knee, Winifred is sat on the chair, and Katie is in the background.

Above right: Winifred's husband, Jack, stood at the top of the fourteen stone steps.

Below left: Barbara outside 14 Albion Street.

Below right: Barry, aged 14.

(From left to right) John, Malcolm and Ivy Davis and little Ann.

Newchurch Road, Stacksteads. No. 2.

Above: The ruins of Clocktower Mill, after it was destroyed by fire.

Below: A view of Stacksteads.

Above: Albion Street, looking up towards the railway bridge.

Below: The demolition of Albion Street. The exposed house is number 14.

Turn of the century dwellings in Bacup. © *Lancashire County Library: Bacup Library*

Above: A recent family photo. Back row, (left to right): Barry, John, Barbara, Jimmy. Front row, (left to right): Mary, Winifred and Maureen.

Below left: Mary and Matthew, Winfred's mother and father. This picture was taken during the second World War, when Matthew was serving with the home guard.

Below right: The amazing woman without whom this book would not have been written: my dear mother, Winifred.

House near to the Mitre Junction. It cost threepence to get into the pictures, leaving just sixpence to spend at halftime at the sweet kiosk. A packet of crisps cost threepence, but a tub of icecream was a staggering sixpence, using up all the spending money. John and Barry would buy a packet of crisps and save threepence for little luxuries later on, but Mary always threw caution to the wind, and would treat herself to a tub of ice-cream.

The matinee always showed serials, which invariably ended with the hero in some perilous state or other, leaving all the kids in suspense and eager to return the following week. The favourites were Westerns starring Johnny Mac Brown, Hoppalong Cassidy and Roy Rogers with his horse Trigger. Others were the Lone Ranger and Tonto, Zorro, Flash Gordon and the Clay Men, Captain Marvel and Superman; to complete the programme, there were always a couple of cartoons in between.

It was a time for letting off steam as deafening shouts of "Hooray! Hooray!" went up at exciting parts during the film, especially when the cavalry came galloping to the rescue. At the interval it was very boisterous and the usherettes were kept constantly on their toes in order to prevent any fighting.

It was obvious when a matinee had just finished because all the lads would wear their coats over their shoulders like cloaks, fencing with each other with little sticks.

Others would set off at a gallop along Trafalgar, slapping their backsides blurting, "Giddy up! Giddy up!"

On the way home, they made for Sunderland's Sweet Shop at the bottom of Sandygate, where they could buy penny, and ha'penny drinks of Sarsaparilla, Dandelion and Burdock or Lemonade. This is where Mary came into her own. Having spent all her money, she'd then look on with pleading eyes; either Jimmy, John or Barry would buy her a drink.

It so happened there was a little old fellow, who always carried a walking stick; he was a very pleasant old gentleman, known to all the children simply as Old Louie. Every Saturday afternoon after the matinee finished, he was always sat on the form facing the sweetshop on the other side of the road. He was forever setting riddles for the children to solve, then he'd reward whoever came up with the answer, by giving them a few coppers. It wasn't the done thing to accept money from strangers but Old Louie was well known and liked by everyone.

One particular afternoon he asked the waiting children, "Right, everybody, the first ún to tell me twelve coins that mék a shilling gets this here thrépenny bit."

Immediately, there were shouts of, "That's easy ... twelve pennies."

"Hang on to tha hosses! I haven't finished yet," said the old chappy. "What I was gonna say is that tha cain't use any pennies at all."

They all puzzled over it for a while before saying, "No, it can't be done."

Jimmy wouldn't be beaten though, and after some deep thought blurted out, "Yes, I've got it! I've got it!"

"Go on then, lad, gimme tha answer."

Jimmy stuck his chest out replying proudly, "A tanner, a thrépenny bit, two ha'pennies and eight farthings."

"By gum, lad, tha reight too; hasta heard it afore?"

"No, Louie, honest! It were just that ..."

"Not to worry thésen, lad, I believes thí; here's tha thépenny bit ... tha deserves it."

That was it! Back to the sweet shop for another penny drink for himself, and some ha'penny drinks for each of his brothers and sisters.

In spite of their poor surroundings, Winifred brought up all her children with good morals, and it is true to say that none of them ever used bad language of any kind or took the Lord's name in vain. Another fad she had was to always correct them on their grammar; she didn't even like them using slang words, which they did all the time. One example that springs to mind was that she constantly corrected them on the difference between teaching and learning.

For example, she might ask one of them, "And what have you been doing at school today?"

To which the reply would be, "Oh the teacher's bin learning us sums, Mum."

"No, that's wrong," she would respond, "she's been teaching you

... you're the one who's being taught."

Mind you, it did have its funny side like the day when she came home to find that one of the kids had knocked some sugar on to the floor.

Barry was the nearest to hand, so she asked him, "Who's done this then?"

"Not me, Mum, I haven't done nówt."

"No, Barry, you haven't done anything," she corrected him.

Much to the delight of his brothers and sisters, Barry innocently replied, "Yes, Mum, I know, that's what I just said."

One colloquial expression that was commonly used and readily understood by all and sundry in the schoolyard involved the word Agate. Whether or not it was used in Bacup as in Burnley is not certain.

One thing for sure though is that it used to confuse and displease Winifred immensely, as one or other of the kids was constantly saying, "He was 'agate'," "They were 'agate'."

Jimmy came home from school one day and he'd been fighting. When asked what it was about, he replied quite naturally, "It wasn't my fault Mum cós a lad in schoolyard was agate, 'Your dad's a rag chap, Cowheel,' and then he was agate that I was stupid!"

"Jimmy, what do you mean by he was 'agate'?" asked Winifred.

"Well he kept calling me names, didn't he?"

At this point, she became a little irritated. "Well why don't you just say that instead of agate? A gate is what hangs on a backyard wall or a farmer's field, do you understand what I'm trying to say?"

"Yeah, all right, Mum."

It didn't make much difference though, as she discovered to her bewilderment on asking him, "And what did you say back to him that caused the fight?"

Quite excitably he replied, "Oh straight away, Mum, I was agate ...!"

On many occasions though, Winifred had to smile to herself when they innocently came out with funny expressions or excuses. Barbara was about four and half years old at the time, Winifred was rummaging through the drawers for something when she came across a banana that must have been there for quite a while, as it was black, squashed and horrible. She knew it was Barbara's, as the little girl was forever hiding sweets and the like.

"Barbara!" she shouted. "Come here, what's this?"

On reaching the sideboard Barbara asked, "What, Mummy, what do you want?"

"Just look at this," rapped Winifred, "it's disgusting! What have I told you about hiding things in the drawers?"

To Winifred's surprise and amusement, Barbara just shrugged her shoulders, nodded her head, then in all innocence replied, "No Mummy, that's not mine … mine's yellow!"

Jimmy came home from school one day, feeling rather disgruntled. "Bloomín' éck!" he moaned. "We've been having a boring history lesson today all about the American Civil War," adding, "Why can't they teach us something to do with our own country?"

"But it is to do with our country," put in Winifred, "and especially so cotton towns like Burnley." She then went on to say that in the two decades from 1840 to 1860 the cotton trade was booming, and many factories were built alongside the canal as were many streets of terraced houses for the workers. The market for cotton was expanding rapidly; at first they couldn't produce it fast enough. Gradually, though, they had huge stockpiles in their warehouses that they couldn't sell, so panic started to set in amongst the wealthy. The greedy mill owners were facing ruin, but were let off the hook when the Civil War broke out. In fact, to them it was a blessing in disguise, as now the cotton products that they had been unable to sell could now be sold at highly inflated prices, thus making them very rich men.

However, although it was good for them, it had devastating effects on the working class. Raw materials could not be had; this inflated prices even more. Many mills had to shut down; thousands of workers were laid off, leading to the Great Cotton Famine.

Many families had to live in sordid squalid conditions on starvation rations; many resorted to begging whilst others died of malnutrition. The only person to profit, other than the mill owner, was the pawnbroker.

"Do you want me to go on, our Jimmy? There's much more."

"Yes please, Mum," he replied, "you make it sound much more

interesting than the teachers do!"

It was about this time when Winifred got a house-cleaning job for a wealthy lady in a big house on the outskirts of town. She worked during the school hours from 10am till 2pm so as to fit in with the children coming home from school. The mistress of the house was in her late seventies and a very typical lady of the manor type, having lived in rich surroundings all her life. She was called Mrs Cooper, and from the start it was made clear to Winifred what was expected from her and just what her position was in the household.

The pay was two shillings per hour and her first task of the day was to do the washing. The wash-house was out in a big yard next to a large coal-shed. It had no heating, and during the winter months it was a very cold place. Despite being a wealthy household, there were no modern facilities, which meant that Winifred had to use the same type of mangle and dolly-tub as in her own home. After draping the washing on a wooden rack she had the formidable task of cleaning several rooms, including a large games room that housed a full-size snooker table. She couldn't get through all the rooms in one session but did them all in the course of a week. On Fridays though she was expected to clean all the windows, which took at least two hours. If she happened to get through all her work with a little time to spare she was unable to relax because then she was expected to clean the yard, including the grates. In spite of it being very hard work, Winifred didn't mind, as it helped to support the children. She worked there for about six years.

But one thing that she did mind was Mrs Cooper's attitude, and the way that she looked down upon her treating her with high-handedness and even contempt. The only time she spoke to Winifred was to give orders and it was far beneath her to even consider saying 'Good morning' or 'Good-bye.' Winifred put up with this till one particular morning when she was a little stressed out because one of the children wasn't very well. She'd just finished the washing and was feeling rather low and decided that she'd had enough and was going home. As she walked to the hallway and started to put her coat on, Mrs Cooper asked her where she was going.

Not being in the mood for a cross-examination she simply

answered, "I've had enough for today, and I'm going home if you don't mind; I'll be back at the usual time tomorrow."

"But I do mind," retorted Mrs Cooper haughtily as she placed herself in front of Winifred, "now you just take your coat off and get on with your work!"

Winifred's mind was made up though and she said through gritted teeth, "Excuse me please, like I said, I'm going now, I'll be back tomorrow." She then left the building leaving Mrs Cooper shocked and dumbfounded.

Next morning, Winifred made her way to the wash-house and went through the normal routine before returning to her internal duties. She'd just made her way to the study when Mrs Cooper approached her.

"Right," she said acrimoniously, "and may I ask as to what sort of a mood you are in this morning and whether you will be staying to do your work?"

"Now now, Mrs Cooper, you may ask me anything you want concerning my work but please don't talk down to me."

"Don't talk down to you? Good heavens, I'm beginning to wonder just who the mistress is in this house and who's the servant."

At that, Winifred saw red but, without raising her voice to the old lady, she said, "Now that will do, don't you dare ever call me a servant! I come here for one reason and one reason only; I need the money to support my children but I am definitely not your servant or anyone else's for that matter. If you have any complaints about my work then I'm willing to listen."

"That's all very well but yesterday you left two hours early so I'm afraid I will be knocking four shillings out of your pay this week."

"You do that, Mrs Cooper, and you won't ever see me back here again."

"Oh so you expect me to pay you for work you haven't done then … that's not very fair, is it?"

"Right, if you want to talk about being fair, what about all the times when I've worked twenty minutes over my allotted time without receiving a penny piece extra?"

With that remark, Mrs Cooper had no alternative but to go along with what Winifred had just said.

She was still haughty though and replied quite smugly, "Right we'll let the matter go this time, but I hope that it's not going to be a regular occurrence."

This remark ruffled Winifred's feathers even more but still she kept her calm. "Of all the cheek!" she responded. "I've worked here for nearly four years now and that's the first time that I've ever left early. No, Mrs Cooper, it won't be a regular occurrence because as from right now I'm packing the job in."

"What, you mean to say you're finishing without even giving any notice; that's quite inconsiderate, isn't it?"

"Inconsiderate you say? Then maybe I'm taking a leaf out of your book; you haven't even the manners to say 'good morning' or anything else for that matter unless it's to do with work. I don't expect special treatment but it's only common courtesy to give someone a greeting on seeing them."

"Oh dear!" she responded rather taken aback. "I didn't realise I had to address my working staff in such a manner; I've never had to do so before."

"Well, it's about time you did, for I for one am not willing to put up with it any more. So if you'd please have my cards and my wage ready for Friday, I'll be quite happy to pick them up."

"Now now, Mrs Cowell, surely we can be sensible about this. I'll tell you what, you go back to your work and I'll try to be more approachable from now on."

Winifred agreed to this, as she needed the money. Mrs Cooper's attitude altered a little; she exchanged the odd greeting but the aloofness remained. She was now eighty-one years old and much too set in her ways to change. Winifred worked there for another two years and it was during this time that she did something quite out of character. It was a very cold winter's day and she was filling the coalscuttle from the large stock of coal in the coal-shed.

"Bloomín éck!" she thought to herself. "Just look at all this coal here and we're scraping for it at our house. These wealthy folk can relax in their nice cosy homes with blazing fires in two rooms whilst my kids have to go to bed early so that I can save a bit of coal." She pondered for a while before deciding to do something untoward. She filled a carrier bag full of coal and left it in the coal-shed ready to pick up on her way home. It didn't cause too much of a problem because she always left the house via the backyard. From that day on, she did this frequently, ensuring that there was always a nice fire blazing away in no. 14 Albion Street.

She felt a little guilty about it at first but after a while she convinced herself otherwise. "It might be wrong what I'm doing," she'd mutter, "but at least it compensates a little for the meagre wages I get."

She would have worked in the household much longer than she did, had it not been for another incident that thoroughly upset her.

Mrs Cooper was having one of the large rooms re-carpeted and the old carpet was laid in the hallway. It may have been old but it was still a good quality carpet with lots of wear left in it. When Winifred saw it, she felt a pang of excitement as she imagined it laid in her own home.

"Oh that would be wonderful for my children instead of having to live with the bare stone floors," she thought to herself. Rather than delay, she confronted Mrs Cooper about it immediately.

After broaching the subject the old lady replied, "Oh I don't think so, I've just been in touch with a salesroom and they've offered me £8 for it."

"Oh I'll gladly give you the same, Mrs Cooper, I don't actually have the money but you could take so much a week out of my wages."

After a moment's consideration, Mrs Cooper turned to her saying, "I'll tell you what I'll do, I'll think about it and tell you in the morning."

Winifred scurried home that day all excited; she couldn't wait to tell her children about it. Likewise, they all got excited too, at the prospect of having a fitted luxury carpet. But alas, their dream was shattered, as Winifred was to find out to her dismay the following day. On reaching the house, the carpet was no longer in the hallway, but she wasn't unduly concerned, as she thought it had just been moved. She worked heartily away and it was almost time to go before she had the opportunity to approach Mrs Cooper about it.

To her utter dismay the old lady replied, "Oh I'm sorry, I gave it lots of thought and decided to let it go to the salesroom."

Winifred couldn't believe it; she was absolutely devastated and for a moment just stood there in silence. "You've done what, after what you promised yesterday?" she said almost in tears.

"Come now, I promised nothing; I said I would give it my consideration and that's what I did."

"You gave it your consideration! I didn't leave till after two o'clock; you must have sold it within an hour of my leaving; you'd no intention of letting me have it, had you?"

"Yes that's right I did let it go, I wanted it out of the way. Besides, I got paid the money in full, which was far better than having to mess about for it."

"Mess about for it! What you really mean is you couldn't bear the thought of me being indebted to you for £8. All I can say, Mrs Cooper, is that you're a greedy, mean old lady; £8 is nothing to you, whereas to me, it is a colossal amount. The awful truth is that you've just deprived my children of a little comfort, which they truly deserve. I've worked for you now for just over six years and yet I still haven't been able to break down the class barrier which lies between us. Still, that's not the issue any more because I couldn't possibly work for you another minute under the circumstances." With no more to be said, Winifred took her leave and made her way home to her rather disappointed family.

It was 1949, by now Rosette was very old and far less capable, gradually becoming infirm; she had no close relatives, so had to be taken into care. It was a shame but it just wasn't possible to look after her properly at number fourteen, as it was already overcrowded.

The children missed her a lot, and used to visit her; even there she used to make them laugh with her funny expressions. Her condition deteriorated rapidly, needing lots of nursing care and she gradually became very confused.

Some days she could recognise people, whilst other days she would be asking, "Who the bloomín éck are you then?"

One day when Jack was visiting her, he had to smile to himself after asking her, "Is everything all right, Rosette, are they looking after you properly?"

Her reply was, "Yeah, it's all reight, but they keep puttín mí in wet beds."

Regretfully, within a few weeks, she died.

14: pastimes & ways of making brass

In the early 1950s, every fortnight or so, uncle Mat, Winifred's brother, would come over from Bacup and stop for the weekend. All the kids loved him. The house was overcrowded at the best of times but all the same, he was always given a rapturous welcome and made a fuss of by all. Like most folk, Mat got on well with Jack. Every Saturday afternoon, they would go out together to the pub for a traditional game of Don, a popular card game, and a game of darts; afterwards, they usually took a short nap in the chair. After tea, as they got ready for another evening session, the kids loved to watch Mat and tease him as he spruced himself up. He was thirteen years younger than Winifred and quite a good-looking bloke with dark wavy hair, and was always good-humoured.

"Right," he'd say in a right Bacup twang just prior to having a shave, "I'll get ready now and make myself bonny."

"Bloomin éck, Uncle Mat," one or other would quip, "you're asking a lot there, aren't you?"

"Go on, ged out of it, you cheeky young so and so!"

After he'd shaved, he quite enjoyed the attention that the girls paid him as they combed and brushed his hair. They'd try all kinds of styles but the favourite was a parting down the middle, then combed straight to the sides with little turn-ups at the front just like the old fashioned barber used to do.

Afterwards, they'd hold a mirror up to him and start laughing. "There, how do you like that then?"

Winifred looked forward to seeing her brother; she didn't mind Jack going out for a drink either, as he never got too drunk when Mat was with him. There was always peace in the home when Mat visited and she regularly met up with them for the last hour in the Labour Club.

the *broken biscuit*

Mat only stayed Saturday night and usually returned to Bacup after Sunday tea. Without fail, before he left, he'd give Winifred a hug and a brotherly kiss, and he generally gave her a little money to get by on. His parting left a little sadness in the house, but more so for Winifred, as she loved to have her own brother or sisters around her to hear news about home. It was a time when she felt rather vulnerable and insecure, as she nostalgically recalled her childhood, no matter how humble it had been.

She never had much time on her hands but whenever she got a chance, she loved to catch the bus and take a couple of the children to visit their grandparents in Bacup. They had long since left the little back to earth house and were now living in a three-bedroom semi-detached council house at 14 Mowgrain View, near to the Cricket Club. Her sister Katie had recently met and married a very nice Irish gentleman called John Walsh. Winifred was really happy for her. It seemed unusual though, as Katie's name remained the same, and was now her married one. Her little boy Tony was now sixteen years old, and Winifred made a fuss of him, as the young lad held a special place in her heart and there was a very strong affinity between them. Sometimes though, when she couldn't make the trip herself, she would see the children to the bus station and Maureen would take them. Aunt Mary would be waiting at the other end of the journey in Bacup.

On reaching the house, Grandma would always give them a hearty greeting, "Eh, it's our Winnie's kids from o'er Burnley, now sit thesél down, and I'll mék thi a cuppa tay and somét to eat." The kids loved it, as there was always a smell of baking about the house that made their mouths water. She made the most delicious biscuits they'd ever tasted before, or since. She now had long silvery white hair, which was tied up in a bun at the back. She had a very pale complexion with the most beautiful deep-set kind-looking eyes; she was only small and slim and very quietly spoken, with lots of charisma that just oozed from her.

Grandad was different altogether; although he was never cruel, he was invariably a little grumpy and rather strict. He was all right so long as the children behaved themselves and toed the line; in other words, he tolerated them. To be fair though, he was never a well man, suffering from chronic bronchitis, emphysema and severe rheumatism.

He was usually sat in the same creaky armchair crouched over the fire constantly wheezing, coughing and spluttering.

There were odd occasions though when he tried frollicking about with the children, but his shoulder caused him constant aggravation and he'd yell, "O-oh by gum, that's it, I've had enough, this flamín shoulder ain't half givín me some gip today."

Despite his nature and illness though, he was kind in his way, and used to tell them many stories. It was clear to all that he doted on Grandma, as he sat them on his knee talking about her.

"I'll tell thi what it is, our Winnie's kids," he'd say, "you're all bonny, but there's not one ó thi can hold a candle to what tha grandma was like; she was the bonniest thing that e'er walked on two legs. Aye, her long flowing hair was so dark, it were like ebony, and it shone like silk; I can just picture her now walking along Bridleway; by éck, but she was so pretty!"

At this point, Maureen or Mary would plead with her, "Oh come on, Grandma, let your hair down and we'll comb it for you!"

She'd oblige with a smile. It was still quite long and it didn't take a lot of imagination to see her as Grandad had described her.

The children loved visiting their grandparents but, sadly, the visits were few and far between because of the long trek over the moors.

Time passed and, by now, Jimmy was in his teens and the twins were eleven years old. Winifred could never give them much money but that didn't cause too many problems. In fact, if anything, it taught them the value of money and they all became quite canny and astute at making it. Unlike Jack though, if they had anything, they always looked after their mum. They'd all seen the way that their dad could make money, but also noticed how freely and unwisely he spent and wasted it.

One of Jack's favourite sayings was, "You've got to speculate to accumulate."

Even at a very young age, John got to thinking, "That's all very well, Dad, but what's the use of accumulating anything if you're going to throw it all away?"

The reasoning behind this derived from the fact that John loved nothing better than going out with Jack on the horse and cart, and was mindful of everything that his dad did.

As far back as the kids could remember, Jack had always had a horse; in fact, in the early fifties, he had two. They were called Tim and Peggy. He kept them in stables at the end of Rumley Road in the Healey Wood District. Tim was a small black horse and very old, twenty-five years, and he regularly put her out to pasture in a farmer's field at the bottom of Barden Lane; she actually ended her days there. He'd bought Peggy to take over from Tim; she was a brown mare just seven years old. Although not as large as a dray horse, she was quite big, but despite her size, she was very gentle and placid; one notable feature about her was that she was blind in her left eye. Jack had always dealt with horses from being a little lad and could really handle them; to his credit, he always treated them very well. He strongly believed that even horses needed a break; hence, he would put Peggy out to pasture along with Tim for two weeks during the Burnley Wakes' Weeks.

John had the same liking for them and, from an early age, he had the task of looking after Peggy in his dad's absence. At first, Winifred used to intervene, as she didn't like John going on the rag-cart with Jack because of the stigma attached to it.

John protested though, pleading with her, "Mum, please let me go, it's all right cós I love doing the job and I get lots of fun out of it, honest!"

He soon became quite adept as a stable hand and quite an expert rider too. He'd get up early in the morning even in the winter, then make his way along Trafalgar, down Manchester Road, along Healey Wood Road which ran alongside the canal, eventually leading to Rumley Road. The first thing he did was to feed Peggy from bails of hay that were kept in the loft, then fill her water trough. Next, he'd put on her bridle and bit, then lead her outside where she could graze in a small compound whilst he mucked out the stable. He'd put all the manure on to a compost heap at the side of the stable before scattering fresh straw on to the cobbled floor. He actually found the job quite interesting, all the more so, as there were many garden allotments round about; consequently, lots of people would come for manure to use as fertiliser. For this small service, he would charge between thrépence and sixpence per bag, which was on top of what his dad gave him; everything went towards his spending money and helping his mum.

If Jack happened to be working that day, John would dress Peggy in all her working regalia: bridle and bit, blinkers, collar with harness, breeching, girth and crupper before finally attaching her to the cart; he'd then jump on board, take the reins and proudly drive her home. Jack used to be quite pleased about this, as all he had to do then was to set off, which saved him a lot of time.

Another thing that John loved was taking Peggy to the blacksmiths, which was situated across from St Peter's Church on Gunsmith Lane. He was never prouder than when riding Peggy bareback down Manchester Road and through the Town Centre, for all and sundry to see, as he pretended to be Hopalong Cassidy or Roy Rogers. On odd occasions, there would be a couple of police horses inside the blacksmiths being shod. Even though Peggy was quite a big horse, she was certainly overshadowed when standing by their side.

Jack had lots of good connections; he would visit various factories where he had a standing agreement with the management to collect their scrap iron. He had a rota and would visit two factories a week, which meant that he usually visited each factory in turn about once every two months; this always assured him of a good cartload. He'd then weigh it in at Reeder's Scrapyard, which was near to the railway viaduct; ironically, it was also close to the Salford Pub. As they drew near to the pub, Peggy would automatically slow down in anticipation of a long rest.

The horse was happy but John always protested, "Oh, Dad, you're not going in there again, are you?"

"Hey cock, don't knock it, this is where your dad makes a lot of his living."

"How do you mean, Dad? I don't get it."

"Well, you know what I keep telling thi about speculating to accumulate? Well this is where I spend a bit so as to make good connections."

"How do you mean, Dad, good connections?"

"U-um let's see … do you know all them there factories that

we've just collected the scrap iron from? Well they won't let anybody take the scrap from there except me, as I have an agreement with the management."

"Oh I see, Dad, but what's that got to do with this pub?"

Jack gave a cheeky grin, "Good question, cock ... well you see there's a lot of them managers that like to drink in here, and I've got to keep ém buttered up, haven't I?" He then added, "It's not what tha knows in business, our John, it's who tha knows ... it's what's known as wheels within wheels."

"Yeah all right, Dad, I see what you're getting at, but please don't be a long while like you were the last time."

"Aye all right, lad, I promise thí."

John's request usually fell on deaf ears though, for once Jack was inside the pub, there was no moving him, leaving the young lad to spend many hours outside the Salford Pub with only Peggy for company. But it was his own fault, as he loved going with his dad despite his mum's disapproval. The long wait outside the pub was the only thing he didn't like. He'd wile away the time talking to Peggy, but on occasions, he'd take a peek inside and would see his dad at the bar flashing his wallet and spending lots of money.

There'd be quite a crowd around the bar and he could hear his dad saying, "Come on, lads, drinks all round, I've had a good day today!"

"Eh, I'll tell thí what it is, Barney, you're a great bloke too," one or other of the hardened drinkers would comment.

John thought how sad it was that he was so free with his money in there, yet so mean with his mum.

"U-um," he thought to himself, "I can see lots of speculating on your part, Dad, but I can't see much accumulating; there may well be an odd businessman in there, but they mostly look like plain boozers to me. No, I'm sorry, Dad, that might be your way but it certainly won't be mine." Even at his young age he used to think how clever his dad was at making money but how foolishly he spent it. With that in mind, he was determined to always be careful with money and spend it wisely in his future years.

John's brothers and sisters were all of a similar frame of mind. They mostly inherited Jack's canniness for making money, but never had the same desire for throwing it away. They all had their different schemes and here are but a few:

Just before Bonfire Night they'd go around town with a Guy Fawkes or singing door to door. They also went singing at Christmas time but then, unbeknown to Winifred, they'd go round all the pubs. One Christmas Eve, John, Mary, Barry and Barbara went into nearly every pub around the Town Centre. By the end of the night, they'd made a colossal £12, mostly in pennies. They weren't allowed in the pubs and were always thrown out as soon as the landlord spotted them; no matter, to overcome this, they each went in a different door so that whilst one was being thrown out, the others were busy singing and collecting the brass. On average, they took about ten shillings from each pub, which meant they'd visited about twenty or so pubs during the course of the night. On arriving home they put all the money on to the table, then gleefully stacked it into piles as they counted it. They were obviously delighted at making so much money but without any encouragement from their mum, they came to a unanimous decision to just keep £1 each and then spend the remainder on something for the house.

"I know what we can buy with it," said Mary enthusiastically, "and it's something that we've needed for a long time."

"What's that then?" enquired Barry.

"Well, I don't know about you but I'm fed up with drinking tea out of jam jars, so why don't we buy some pots and cups for Mum?"

Everyone agreed with her, so the very next day, they went down town and bought some new crockery from the Market Hall. After purchasing it, there was still four pounds left over, which they gave to their mum to help towards the cost of going to the pictures and other places during the holiday period.

Other methods of making brass included collecting wooden boxes from the market, chopping them up and selling bundles of firewood as Winifred had done in her childhood. Jimmy and John made a truck from pram wheels and used it to bring bags of cinders for the neighbours from the Gas Depot Yard on Parker Lane; the going rate was sixpence a trip.

Other schemes included going from door to door collecting empty jam jars, which used to fetch a halfpenny per jar at Nora's Grocery Store, or returning empty beer bottles to the Labour Club. Most of the local kids found it rather amusing as the enterprising Cowells would scale the high backyard wall of the Labour Club or the Trafalgar Pub, pick up a few empty bottles and then return them via the front door.

On rainy days, Mary, Barry and Barbara would put on inventive concerts and plays in the cellar, charging the local kids two pennies each; quite good they were too and many happy hours were spent there. The neighbourhood kids would congregate underneath the house, sitting on long wooden benches that Jack had procured for them. The front part of the cellar was used for changing and props. Sometimes, Mary would use some of the neighbouring children in her acts and pay them a few coppers, which they gratefully pocketed. In between performances, they would stand up and tell silly stories, or do comedy acts, or card-tricks, which Jack had taught them.

One of the more memorable acts involved just two people, Mary and Barry, and the only props used were a little wooden desk and a chair. To picture the scene, Barry was in another part of the cellar whilst Mary was sat at the little desk.

First of all, Mary addressed her audience saying, "Right, everybody … you've all got to pretend that this is a hospital, I am a nurse and Barry is a very old confused patient."

She then pretended to be studying something or other on the desk when Barry came doddering up to her from the back cellar with a paper carton in his hand.

On reaching the desk, he asked Mary in a tottery voice, "Ple-ease Miss, canna have a cuppa water?"

"Of course you can, Mr Wilkinson," she replied raising herself from the chair. She then went over to the chimney alcove and pretended to fill the carton with water and returned to the desk saying, "There you are, Mr Wilkinson."

"Tan-koo," he muttered, then tottered back to the other cellar.

Within half a minute he tottered back again. "Ple-ease ,Miss, cud I have a cuppa water?"

Once again, she got up and did the same thing as before saying, "There you are, Mr Wilkinson."

Off totters Barry into the darkness of the other room; once again, within half a minute, he came tottering back asking in a croaky voice, "Ple-ea-se, Miss, canna have a cuppa water?"

By this time, the nurse (Mary) was losing her patience. "My my, Mr Wilkinson! You are thirsty tonight aren't you?"

Then to the delight of everyone, Barry mutters, "O-oh no, Miss, I'm not thirsty ... it's just that my bed's on fire!"

Nearly all of the Burnley Cotton Mills ground to a halt during the Wakes' Weeks, which always fell on the first two weeks in July. Lots of people lugged their heavy suitcases and headed for Blackpool for a well-earned rest. This was yet another ideal opportunity to make some brass. Jimmy, John and Barry would make their way to either the Bus Station, or the Central Railway Station, and await the returning holiday-makers with their make-do trolleys, offering to carry the large suitcases for a nominal fee.

This weekend coincided with the time that the fairground came to town. Local kids would make their way to the allotted ground, behind the Odeon Picture House, eager to try out all the different amusements. One particular Saturday night, Barry was stood outside the boxing booth with a friend, Walter Baxendale, when a gang of rowdy youths started throwing out insults. One of them was called Bernard Spedding, who happened to do a bit of boxing for the Central Youth Club, and he was forever picking on Barry at school. Barry was never a fighting lad and wouldn't be drawn into an argument, but then Bernard did something that Barry wouldn't wear at all; he started to throw out insults about the rag-cart and prison. Barry threw all caution to the wind, and within seconds both lads were fighting.

The fight didn't last long though, as some fellows broke it up; one of these was a fairground worker, in charge of the boxing booth. "Naythen, you young uns, if tha wants to feight tha can do it in the boxing ring, and tha can mek half a crown for thasén while tha's at it."

"Oh yeah, and what do we have to do forrit then?" asked Bernard enthusiastically.

"Just three, three-minute rounds that's all, how about it?"

A little snigger came on Bernard's face as he turned to Barry asking, "I'm game, how about you, Cowheel?"

Barry wasn't keen on the idea but didn't like losing face, so reluctantly agreed.

The proprietor wasn't slow to seize his opportunity, immediately inviting the two lads on to the platform and announcing the forthcoming event to the passing crowd. "Roll up, ladies and gentlemen, we've got somethin' special on here tonite, two shows for the price ó one. These here two lads are gonna spar agen each other afore t'other boxers perform."

It worked like a treat and before long he'd attracted lots of paying customers.

Barry felt very nervous as he stripped to the waist, and especially when he glanced across the ring to Bernard's corner. The lads were as different as could be. Bernard was actually an inch shorter than Barry, but very well built with rippling muscles, whereas Barry was skinny and frail-looking. The crowd actually started laughing at the stark contrast between the two lads.

The fight got under way, and it didn't take very long for Bernard's expertise to show. During the first round Barry sustained a busted nose and hardly landed a blow in return. The second round started in a similar way, but Barry refused to yield in spite of a cut lip and a black eye. Although he wasn't a fighter, he wouldn't give up because he felt that he was in the right. Despite being in control of the fight, Bernard's enthusiasm started to wane because of Barry's unrelenting fightback.

The third round began and Barry's determination paid off, he managed to land a telling blow, busting Bernard's nose. By now the crowd was going mad, roaring loudly for the underdog; this became more apparent when Barry landed another blow on Bernard's nose, causing blood to trickle down his face. At the end of the bout there was no mistaking that Bernard was the overall winner, but this didn't bother Barry; the fact that he had stood his ground and given something in return was more important to him than anything else. The crowd showed their appreciation by applauding loudly, and the gaffer gave them both an extra shilling for putting on a good show. Another good thing that came out of it was that the two lads became friends thereafter.

On one occasion when Jack wasn't working, John was just about to set off for the stable when Mary asked if she could go with him.

"You can if you want, our Mary, but it's not all fun and games you know, and it can be quite hard and mucky."

"That's all right," she replied, "I'm not frightened of hard work and a bit of muck … I'd still like to come if I can."

"Yeah right, fair enough, let's go then." When they got there, Mary wanted to feed Peggy.

John agreed and gave her a few basic instructions, "Before you actually go up to the trough, our kid, just talk to her a little to let her know you're there, and especially if you approach her on her left blind side."

Mary was quite fearless and soon got the hang of it, tending to Peggy's needs whilst John did most of the mucking out.

Peggy was idly grazing in the paddock when a gang of boys and girls came into the grounds and began making abusive remarks. "Oh it's the rag tatters," shouted one of them and they all started jeering.

To Mary it was tantamount to a declaration of war and she was furious; her eyes narrowed and her fists clenched.

But John remained calm, reassuring her, "Take no notice of ém, our kid, they come round here regularly … ignore ém and they'll go away."

It may well have been good advice but Mary was having none of it, and she instinctively retaliated. "You bloomín cowards, you're nowt else!" she shrieked. "It's easy to be like that when there's a lot of you, you wouldn't be so brave if it was one on to one, would you?"

"Oh bloomín éck," thought John, "that's done it," as he knew only too well that one of the girls was notorious for fighting.

The girl, who was quite well built and slightly taller than Mary stepped forward asking, "Oh you fancy your chances, do you; how about having a go at me then?"

"What, just you and me, or will all your mates join in as well?" Mary responded.

The girl weighed Mary up and down, then started laughing. She looked back at her friends, who in turn started yelling, "Go on, Nellie, get stuck into her, you'll murder her!"

John was on his guard but wasn't overly concerned because although the girl was bigger than Mary in body, he knew she wouldn't match up to her in spirit. He also knew that in spite of being outnumbered, it wasn't the done thing for friends to join in when it was a straight one to one fight. Sure enough the fight started but from the outset, it was clear that Mary had the upper hand, there was no contest; they didn't even roll on the floor. Mary fought like a boy, lashing out with her fists, and after being knocked to the ground a couple of times and receiving a busted nose, the girl gave up.

It wasn't the end of the saga though, because then one of the lads shouted at John, "All right, pal, so your sister's a good fighter; it looks to me that she's gotta fight your battles for you as well!"

John quietly backed off, refusing to be drawn in. "I don't want any truck with you; I think it's best that you all go now."

Some hopes, for having just seen one fight, the crowd now wanted another, so they all started jeering, encouraging their mate on.

By now, Mary was getting riled up again so she encouraged John, "Go on, our kid, you're a good fighter, you can take him on easy."

John refused to be drawn in. "That's not the point, our Mary, I just don't want to fight."

Be that as it may, he had little choice in the matter, as the lad pounced on him knocking him to the ground; however, even though John didn't want to fight, he was quite prepared and on his guard. He was used to these situations, as he'd had to deal with plenty of them at St Thomas's, and he'd had plenty of skirmishes with his older brother Jimmy. They rolled about on the floor for a little while but, being quite nimble and very strong with lots of stamina, John soon overpowered him. Despite what had gone on though, he didn't want to hurt the lad, so merely held him in a vice-like headlock. Nevertheless, the lad, not wanting to lose face in front of his friends, kept struggling and striking out. John, sensing that this could go on indefinitely, managed to drag the boy over to the horse trough, then dipped his head in it. This didn't work either, as it infuriated the lad even more.

Still, John was in control, and he quietly whispered into the lad's ear, "Right, pal, this has gone far enough, I'm telling you now, if you don't give up, then the next time it won't be the water trough that I'll dunk you in … it'll be the horse muck!"

The lad still refused to back down but as John dragged him closer to the compost heap, it became obvious that he was on to a loser, so he reluctantly gave up.

"All right, all right," he blurted, "fair enough, I give in … you win!" After that, they both shook hands and that was the end of it.

Whilst the crowd were commiserating with their friends one of them asked John, "Hey, pal, is that your horse then?"

"Yeah it is … why?"

"Well, I was just wondering, is there any chance ó givín us a ride?"

John was unsure but Mary didn't miss a trick, "Come on, our John, why not … at thrépence a time?"

"Hey you're right there, our Mary … why not?"

Before they knew it, there were plenty of kids shouting, "Yeah, I want a ride as well!" Because of all the noise and goings on, many other kids had gathered around and they too eagerly took up the same cry, "I want a ride as well!"

Mary, being a right little organiser, took command. "Look everybody, you can all have a go but you'll have to form a queue."

She took charge of collecting the money whilst John took the reins and guided the paying passengers around the paddock. Threepence a time for just two rides around the yard with all the kids yelling for more; what a day, what a killing; even Peggy enjoyed it. It would have been better still but for being stopped by a rather big, rough-looking bloke, who was in charge of the stables.

John was just leading Peggy off when he heard the bloke bellowing, "What the flamín éck's goín on here, and what the bloody hell a ta doing wí that hós?"

"It's nowt to do with you," retorted Mary, "it's mí dad's horse."

"Oh it's nowt to do wí mi, is it not? I'll gív thí it's tha dad's hós; get the bugger back in stable now afore I kicks tha arses for thi!"

John told Mary that he knew the bloke and that he really was in charge of the stables, so they reluctantly had to do as they were told.

"Still, never mind, look on the bright side, our Mary … we haven't done too badly, have we?"

She chuckled agreeing, "Aye, you're right there, our John … it's bín a real day, an'it?"

The large man watched over them until they'd put Peggy back in the stable, and after locking the stable door he bellowed, "Now ged outa here and don't come back I'm warning thí! Aye, and don't think I won't tell tha dad cós I bloody well will!"

But they weren't too bothered about that as they happily walked home with their pockets bulging with money.

Jack did get to know about it but he wasn't too concerned; in fact, quite the opposite, he rather enjoyed the tale they had to tell and the way they'd used their initiative.

"I'm not bothered about you giving the kids a ride," he said, "cós at least it gave Peggy a bit of exercise, and I'm sure that she would have enjoyed it too … I'm only mad that I didn't think ó doing it myself."

Jack had many strings to his bow, and one of these was selling ice cream. In the 1940s/50s, there were lots of local firms in Burnley, who made their own delicious ice-cream. One of these was Allen's, whose main factory was situated on Standish Street. Jack had a natural talent for selling ice-cream and he had a good round within the Prairie Playing Fields in the Colne Road area and usually worked at weekends. He always took out the traditional horse and cart and would regularly take one of the kids with him; unlike the rag cart, Winifred didn't mind, as it had an air of respectability about it. The kids loved it, as he usually gave them sixpence and they were always assured of as much ice-cream as they could scoff. One summer's day when the sun was really cracking the flags, Mary asked if she could go with him.

"All right," he said, "but no moaning to come home afore I've finished, and tha'd best behave thaself."

After tethering the horse to the cart, they went to the little factory. Once inside, he said to Mr Allen, "Right, it looks like it's gonna be a scorcher today, and seeing that there's a festival being held on the Prairie, I'll take nine gallons."

"By éck, Barney, that's a lot of ice-cream, do you think you'll manage to sell that much?" asked Mr Allen.

Jack just looked at him. "Listen here! You just concern yourself with making it, leave the selling of it to me."

Jack then collected the nine gallons but then, whilst Mr Allen was in another part of the factory answering the phone, he added a couple more large scoops for good measure. On returning, Mr Allen handed over a cotton bag containing three pounds float, which Jack carefully checked before setting off. They'd only gone about half a mile when Jack pulled into a lay-by and emptied the float into a wooden cash box, which was on the inside of the cart. He took three two-shilling pieces from the float and put them into his pocket, then he replaced them with three foreign coins. Mary was watching all this, taking in everything but saying nothing.

He then set off for the Prairie Playing Fields and, on arriving, set up his stall. The day was glorious; he'd no sooner started to ring the bell than hordes of people began to queue up. Cornets and sandwiches with a touch of raspberry were the order of the day. There were three settings: large, medium and small, but whatever size they asked for, he always gave them a short measure.

Every now and again, he'd give Mary an ice-cream and she'd ask, "Oh, Dad, can I have a proper measure this time?" to which he replied, "Go on, you cheeky young bugger, watch your lip!"

The day went well, and he sold all nine gallons plus the extra unofficial bit; he worked on a commission basis, so taking everything into account, he'd had quite a good day.

On making his way back to the depot he turned to Mary saying, "Right, our Mary, when we get back to the shop, I don't want you to utter one word, just keep your trap shut! All right?"

"Oh yes, Dad, I know what you mean," she replied innocently. "I promise I won't say a thing."

Back in the shop, Mr Allen congratulated Jack on doing so well. "Well done, Barney, I didn't think tha'd do it but tha has ... I've got to put mí hand up to thí."

He was happy enough until he came to check the money, discovering the three foreign coins. "Hey, hang on a minute, Barney! What's these then?"

Jack gazed at the three foreign coins looking all surprised before retorting angrily, "Hey, never mind, 'hang on, Barney,' I hope tha not accusing me of anything! What the bloody hell do you take me for anyway?"

"Whoa, steady on, Barney! I'm not accusing anybody of anything, I just want to know where they've come from."

"I don't know and I don't bloody care," he rapped, "all I know is I've bín out working mi guts out all day and I've sold out everything over and above what you expected. Aye, and another thing whilst we're at it, I haven't had time to spit today let alone stop for a bite to eat; so I'm tellín thi now … don't even think about stopping anything out ó my wages!"

Mr Allen was taken aback, responding, "Oh come on, Barney, you must see my side of it as well; after all, the takings are down by six shillings," adding, "So what do you think about splitting the difference?"

"Splitting the difference my foot, you must be joking!" snapped Jack. "If you think for one minute I'm gonna drop mi wages for you or anybody else you're one off; you can bloody well think again! Aye, and if you so much as stop one penny, I'm tellín thí now, it's the last time that I'll ever work for thí."

Mr Allen was dumbfounded. "Eh, Barney, I'll tell thi what it is, you're an hard man. Go on then, I'll let it go this time seeing as how busy you've been, but just try and watch in future, will you?"

"Hey, don't give me that either, anything can happen on a busy day like today; and if I do have another one like it, then I don't want thi on mi back lookin o'er mí shoulder."

Young Mary listened taking everything in, but as promised she never opened her mouth whilst in the shop. However, being the precocious girl she was and never frightened of speaking her mind, or one for mincing words, she always got directly to the point.

Being crafty she waited until they were some distance from the shop, then turned to Jack saying quite bluntly, "Dad, do you know something?"

"What's that, our Mary?"

His jaw dropped when she replied quite openly, "You're a thief, Dad! I saw you place them three foreign coins into the float and put the six shillings into your pocket. You're always teaching us not to do bad things, but that's wrong what you did," she then added slyly, "Mí mum'll go mad if she finds out!"

A cheeky grin spread across his face as he replied, "Eh by éck, our Mary, tha misses nówt, I'll tell thi what it is, there's two shillings here ... now let's mék sure that she doesn't find out, eh?"

Two shillings was quite a lot but Mary was too crafty for that; she'd weighed everything up and knew only too well that her dad had made a killing; she wasn't for letting him off the hook that easy.

As far as she was concerned, he was ripe for the picking. "Oh come on, Dad, it's not just the foreign coins, is it? For a start, you put in more ice-cream than you should have, then you only served up small portions and besides ... you also got a wage on top of all that. And then, Dad, don't forget that you usually give us a shilling anyroad when you have a good day."

He really didn't have a good answer to that. "You cheeky young beggar, you're nowt else, who the flamín éck do you take after?" A cheeky grin spread across his face once again as he bethought himself ... he knew only too well the answer to that one.

He gave her another shilling, making it a good day for Mary; as she thought to herself, "Three shillings plus all the ice-cream that I've eaten; u-um, not a bad day, not a bad day at all."

Of all the kids in the family, Jimmy was the canniest of them all when it came to making money and saving it. Even in his early teens, he always had some stashed away in the post office; he even kept a little hidden in a secret place under the floorboards in the back bedroom. Unbeknown to him though, everybody in the house knew about it, but no one would touch it, as it wasn't theirs. He engaged in all the same scams as his brothers and sisters, but he also had a paper round. With the money he saved, he started up quite an enterprising scheme amongst some of the neighbours. There were about six people on the street who used to borrow a little money off him on a Saturday, then pay him back with interest on the following Wednesday or Thursday depending just when they got paid or cashed in their allowance. Each one on average borrowed five shillings and would repay six shillings;

this meant that after five weeks, they were actually borrowing their own money. Still, they didn't seem to mind and were only too glad to have Jimmy at their disposal.

Winifred encouraged the kids to use their initiative but, in this case, she wasn't very happy, as it put her in mind of Blakey, the moneylender. She showed her displeasure by having a word with both Jimmy and the borrowers, telling them of her disapproval. Still, the would-be victims, as Winifred put it, made it quite clear that they didn't mind and were only too glad of the service. Jimmy always seemed to have plenty of money but to be fair, he was never mean, and he would indulge his brothers and sisters with little treats now and again.

It was another scorcher of a day with brilliant sunshine; Jimmy was now sixteen. He'd just seen an advert in the paper for a weekend ice-cream man and he asked John if he fancied having a go with him. John went along with the idea, so Jimmy applied for and got the job. It wasn't the same firm that Jack had worked for but the transport system was still a horse and cart; on arriving at the depot there were a few carts just leaving. Jimmy thought that they might think it suspicious if two young lads went in together, so he asked John to wait a little way off and arranged to pick him up later. John waited patiently about two hundred yards down the road, then, sure enough, after about twenty minutes, Jimmy came along driving the cart.

"Would you believe it," he said as John got into the cart, "they've told me that I can only sell ice-cream in the Trafalgar area? Aye, and they stressed that I must keep to my own patch, as other carts are covering other areas."

John was actually pleased about this, as he wanted to show off to his many friends. As they were making for Trafalgar, a few people flagged them down but the horse was quite boisterous and hard to handle. Every time Jimmy stopped the cart to try serving anyone, it kept trotting off ... he just couldn't control it.

It was funny really because on a couple of occasions just as someone wanted serving, the horse set off of its own accord leaving Jimmy quite frustrated; turning to the would-be customer, saying, "Oh

I'm very sorry but we've sold out."

As he was used to handling Peggy, John suggested taking over, but at first Jimmy was too pig-headed, as he didn't want to lose face. Nevertheless, after a while he saw the sense of it and handed over the reins; it worked out a lot better, so they made their way to their destination.

Unlike Jack who could sell ice-cream to Eskimos, Jimmy and John were struggling. The customers in the Trafalgar area were thin on the ground and after about two hours, they'd only just about taken the top off the six gallons.

Jimmy was fast losing his patience. "Umph … this is no bloomín' good, is it? Come on, our John, I've had enough, I'm taking the flamín' thing back."

They'd just started back when John had an idea. "Hang on a minute, our Jimmy! Why not go to the Prairie Fields where my dad used to go, we're bound to sell a lot of ice-cream there?"

"Because like I've told you, our John, I'm not allowed because they gave me strict instructions not to encroach on to anybody else's patch."

"Yeah, so what, when has that ever stopped you doing things before?"

"Hey, it's all right for you!" he snapped. "It's me who has to face the consequences."

"Yeah all right, I agree with you there, our Jim but let's put it another way … are you thinking of doing this job again after today?"

"You must be joking! Why?"

"Well then, if that's the case, you've nówt to lose, have you?"

"Good thinking, our John, why didn't I think ó that? Right then, get the horse turned round and let's get up there now and make some brass!"

They arrived at the Prairie at about one o'clock but didn't actually go on to the field. Jimmy asked John to stop the cart on Colne Road near to the entrance gates where lots of people were coming and going.

"Right, John, we're pitching here, it looks as good a spot as any … I don't think we'll have any trouble selling ice-cream here."

He was dead right; within an hour, they'd sold about half of their stock. Things were going great until other angry ice-cream men, who had been alerted to their presence, confronted them.

They were furious, one rather burly-looking chap approached the cart shouting, "What the bloody hell do you think you're playín at, this is our flamín patch?" Jimmy didn't take any notice; he let it go in one ear and out the other and carried on serving.

"Are you deaf ó what, ó just plain bloody thick?" retorted the bloke.

"Thick am I? At least I'm selling ice-cream!"

"That's it!" rapped the bloke as he grabbed the horse's reins and started to lead it off.

Jimmy went mad, and even though he was a lot smaller than the bloke, he fronted up to him. To the surprise of all the customers, he jumped off the cart with the ice-cream spoon still in his hand and threatened to ram it down the man's throat.

The bloke, being much stronger, grabbed Jimmy, pinned him against the cart and threatened to banjo him.

Luckily for Jimmy, two fellows, who were waiting to be served, intervened, "Hey, mate, what the bloody hell do you think you're playín at? He's only a lad ... pick on somebody your own size!"

The bloke released Jimmy under protest but warned him, "All right, you clever little bugger, you think you're getting away with it, don't you? You know bloody well that you're not supposed to be round here!" then added, "Where is your flamín patch anyroad?"

"All right, we shouldn't be here," replied Jimmy defiantly, "but why should you have the best spot anyroad? Besides, there's plenty of people around here for everybody. I'll move but not for another hour, that should still leave you plenty of time to sell yours."

The bloke was fuming. "Right!" he warned, "I'm going to report you to your gaffer to make sure it doesn't happen again."

"Please yourself, mate, I couldn't care less!" replied Jimmy, knowing only too well that it was his last time anyway.

Consequently, they carried on serving, but within half an hour or so, a police squad car pulled up and two uniformed policemen got out and approached the cart. Both Jimmy and John were surprised to see them, as they didn't think they'd overstepped the mark that much;

however, it was nothing to do with the fracas or being on somebody else's patch. The policemen were a little surprised to see two young lads in charge of the cart, but after explanations, they advised Jimmy that Colne Road was a no-parking area and that he would have to move on.

It was a pity really, as there were still lots of people around; given another hour, they'd have easily sold up. As it happened, they still had about two gallons left.

"Ah well, never mind, our kid, we haven't done too badly, have we?" said Jimmy. "Let's call it a day and make our way back to the depot, shall we?"

On their way back, they decided to take a short cut through Stoneyholme, which, like Trafalgar, was a poor area of the town. They were going down Burns Street when a small boy flagged them down.

On stopping, the young lad asked, "Please, Mister, cudda have a penny ice-cream?"

The cheapest one was thrépence, so Jimmy answered, "I'm sorry, cock, but we don't have any penny ones."

The look on the little lad's face said it all; his bottom lip dropped as he muttered, "Oh, it's not fair! I never get an ice-cream."

Jimmy looked at John, who couldn't help but smile, then back at the little boy saying, "Oh all right, cock, give me your penny; it'll only be a little one, mind!" He scooped a small ice-cream into a cornet, then paused for a moment before saying, "Oh what the éck!" Digging deep into the canister, he gave the little lad the biggest ice-cream he'd ever seen.

By now, lots of other kids had gathered around the cart, their excitement was aroused when the little lad, who couldn't believe his luck, let out one hell of a shout, "Hey look, everybody, at my ice-cream what I got for a penny!"

That was it, all the kids clustered around the cart eagerly shouting, "Here, Mister! I've got a penny as well ... can I have a big ice cream like him?"

Once again, Jimmy looked at John, commenting, "Oh bloomín éck, our kid, I've started something here, haven't I?"

He didn't get much help there though, as John found it really

the *broken biscuit*

funny and couldn't help laughing. "You've done it this time, our kid, how you gonna get out ó this one?"

"I'm not sure but I can't help thinking that it doesn't seem fair to give one without the other. What do you think, our kid, don't they remind you of when we were kids and could never afford an ice-cream?"

"I know exactly how you feel, our Jimmy, and I know what I'd like to do but I can't really say because at end of the day, you've the responsibility of the cart, and you'll have to face the consequences."

"Oh sod it!" he exclaimed. "In for a penny, in for a pound!" He then turned to the crowd of children and to their delight he announced, "Righto, kids, get your pennies ready ... this is your lucky day!"

He started dishing out ice-creams to boys and girls alike, and thoroughly enjoyed himself; he even gave one to those kids who had no money at all. Needless to say, it didn't take very long to sell up. Before going back to the depot, Jimmy cashed up, but first, he took his wages out of the money.

"How come you're doing that, our Jim?" asked John.

"I'm taking what's due to me because Dad forewarned me that if there's any money short, it'd be stopped out of my wages."

On arriving back, the boss had heard all about the Prairie episode and was extremely annoyed; his mood changed though when Jimmy told him he'd sold out. Nonetheless, he soon became outraged again after the takings had been handed over.

"What the bloody hell do you call this, the takings are way down?"

"Oh well they will be because I've already taken my wages outa them," replied Jimmy quite unconcerned.

"What flamín wages?" he rapped. "I would have docked most ó them anyway for what's missing."

"Yeah, I thought you might," Jimmy replied casually, "that's why I took them first."

"You cheeky young bugger!" he barked, adding, "Anyway, all I can say is you must have been selling bloomín big portions."

"Oh yeah, maybe I was, but don't forget that this is the first time that I've ever gone out selling ice-cream."

"Yes," replied the bloke angrily, "and the bloomín last as far as I'm concerned!"

Jimmy and John went home in good spirits, it wasn't simply the money either; just remembering the looks of happiness on those little kids' faces made them both feel really good.

Barry was always keen on keeping pets ranging from fish, tadpoles and frogs, to rabbits. He was very caring but there was one time when this aspect of his nature caused quite a lot of consternation amongst the neighbours. It happened so innocently but got out of hand, growing out of all proportion.

He found a fledgling pigeon with a broken wing. He took it into his care tending to its every need, housing it in a disused rabbit hutch in the cellar. As the young bird progressed he took the hutch and placed it outside on the air-raid shelter. When it had recovered Barry released it into the wild. But, to his surprise and delight, within two hours, it returned to the air-raid shelter. The following day, his pleasure increased further when it returned again, but this time it was accompanied by a mate. He was quite fascinated by the amorous antics of the cock as it strutted and cooed about the hen pouting its neck feathers. One day he was cleaning out the hutch when he discovered that the hen had laid an egg. He couldn't contain his excitement as he vaulted straight over the steel railings on to the stone steps.

"Jimmy, John!" he shouted. "Come out here quick and have a look at this!"

Neither Jimmy nor John had been interested before but this stimulated their imagination. Together with Barry they set to and built an aviary adding two more huts. They made a really good job of it; it even had a specially designed landing platform, which took the weight of a pigeon but not a cat.

Subsequently, lots of other pigeons were attracted to the spot and, before long, there were six birds nesting there. Like the first two, they paired up laying eggs in the different huts. In the early stages it was very interesting to watch the birds caring meticulously for their chicks. It amazed everybody that, within days, the baby birds were as big as their parents.

the **broken biscuit**

Winifred put up with things for a while but then it became intolerable. She couldn't hang out the washing, as there were feathers and droppings everywhere. Neighbours started to complain because they couldn't open their upstairs windows during the summer months for fear of a pigeon flying into the bedroom.

The aviary created a lot of interest amongst the local youngsters throughout the Trafalgar area. This solved the problem of overcrowding for a while, as Barry sold off some of the young birds. However, this was only a temporary relief, as the birds continued to breed. Barry became quite concerned and it wasn't just because of the congestion; he had heard that some of the birds that he had sold were being mistreated, and he blamed himself.

"Right, that's it," he thought, "I'm not going to encourage cruelty." He immediately released all the birds and demolished the aviary leaving the air-raid shelter bare once again.

Winifred was much happier now but as yet, the washday problems were not quite solved. The reason for this was because for many months afterwards, the birds still returned to the area, nestling on the rooftops directly facing the Cowell household and they were clearly visible from the living-room.

Barry was never money orientated in the least. Of all the family he was the one, who most of all put Winifred in mind of her brother Jimmy ... like him, Barry also doted on his mum. He still earned a little money here and there but was never interested in accumulating it.

There was the time when he went to a pantomime that was showing above the Co-op Showrooms in Hammerton Street. He was about ten at the time and was a member of the Police Youth Club. The top official Youth Club Leader was a gentleman called Mr Powel, who thought a lot about Barry, as he was always a polite well behaved lad. Special invitations had been sent out to different clubs, and the Police Youth Club was the first to attend. It was a Monday evening, and the pantomime being performed was Cinderella, Barry went along with lots of other youths. The show started at half past seven, he was enjoying it along with the rest of them, then at half past nine, it came to the part when the Two Ugly sisters invited six volunteers out of the audience to come up onto the stage.

Barry was rather shy but one of his mates egged him on, "Come on, Barry, if you go up, I'll go up as well."

He was a little reluctant but with a little coaxing he agreed, "Yeah, all right then, it should be a bit of fun shouldn't it?" he felt a bit awkward at first, as the Two Ugly Sisters made fun and teased them but then at the end of the act he got a pleasant surprise.

One of the Ugly Sisters turned to the audience saying, "Well ladies and gentlemen, what do you think of these young lads ... didn't they do well?"

The audience responded by heartily clapping.

Then to the boys delight the Ugly Sister added, "I totally agree with you there and I think they all deserve a good reward." Turning to the boys, she gave each of them a silver shilling prior to leaving the stage.

Barry was sat about six rows from the front and to get back to his seat, he had to pass by Mr Powel, who was sat on the third row against the aisle. The club leader seemed quite pleased with the event, giving a little smile as Barry passed by him.

Barry was highly delighted about the shilling; he couldn't wait to get home and tell Winifred about it. He got a lot of pleasure from being able to help his mum. He knew that the pantomime was showing every night that week, which got him to thinking that should he attend every show, he could possibly make another four shillings. It was a bit off-putting though, as he knew Mr Powel would be attending every time, and that he would be sat in the same seat; still, he wasn't to be put off. He made his way to the Co-op building on Tuesday evening, but as there was an attendant on the door he had to ask to be taken in by an adult. Once inside, he made his way to an empty seat, then waited patiently for the part when the Two Ugly Sisters made their request. He knew just what to expect and was up onto the stage whilst the others were still thinking about it. They went through the same rigmarole as the first night, so once again Barry ended up with a shilling.

To get back to his seat, he had the daunting task of passing by Mr Powel, whom this time showed his obvious disapproval. On Wednesday and Thursday evening, he did exactly the same, but on the Friday night it didn't quite go to plan. By ten past nine, nobody had offered to take him as he waited patiently by the entrance door. He kept slipping upstairs to peep through the door and could see the stage quite clearly but he couldn't dodge in, as the attendant was still there. At half past nine, he was just about to give up and go home when a rather official looking gentleman entered the building.

As he began to climb the stairs, he said to Barry, "Hello young fellow ... if you're thinking of seeing the show it's a bit late now, it'll be finished in about ten minutes." To Barry's delight though, just as he'd reached the top of the stairs he asked, "Still, if you want to go in all the same, then just follow me." Barry scurried up after him as fast as he possibly could, but as he entered the theatre he thought it was too late, as there were already some kids on the stage.

"Oh flippín éck," he muttered to himself, "all that waiting for nówt."

Then to his surprise, one of the Ugly Sisters asked, "Naythen come on children, surely we've got one more boy or girl, who's brave enough to come up here haven't we?"

Without hesitation Barry ran down the aisle and clambered up the steps on to the stage. Both of the Ugly Sisters glared at him through their makeup but they couldn't refuse him, as by now the audience was clapping loudly. After the performance, he was really pleased with himself; he'd actually made five shillings. But now he had the daunting task of passing by Mr Powel, if looks could kill then Barry would have collapsed there and then on the spot. The weekend came and Barry wanted to go to the Police Youth Club on the Sunday night but he didn't look forward to the prospect of facing Mr Powel.

It troubled him creating a little anxiety, "Oh éck!" he thought to himself, "I want to go up there but I don't fancy being reprimanded." He set off but the closer he got to the club, the more nervous he became. The nerves almost got the better of him; he was about half way there pondering over it when he turned around to make his way home.

He'd only walked a few yards though when he bethought himself, "Oh sod it! If I don't go now, I'll only have to face up to him another time so I may as well go and get it over with."

So, he made his way to the club full of foreboding.

He was playing table tennis when Mr Powel interrupted, summoning him to the office; Barry warily made his way there, feeling very nervous.

Once inside Mr Powel soon made his displeasure known, "Right Barry, I'm not going to mess about ... you know only too well why I've called you."

Barry had his head bowed a little as he felt rather awkward; he could well understand why Mr Powel felt the way he did, but his awkwardness also stemmed from the fact that he liked and respected him.

"Ye-es I do know Mr Powel," he answered rather clumsily, "it's to do with the pantomime isn't it?"

"Too right it's to do with the pantomime!" he rapped, "What I want to know is what have you got to say for yourself?"

Barry just shrugged his shoulders and said nothing.

"Right Barry ... I don't like what you did ... not one little bit, and I can tell you now that I felt like dragging you off the stage myself. Have you still got nothing to say for yourself?"

Still ... Barry said nothing.

"Right then, in that case, I'll say it for you. I want you to promise me that you won't attempt anything like this again or I may seriously consider suspending you from the club."

Barry pondered just a little while longer, then came out with something that took the official by surprise, "Well, Mr Powel, all I can say is that I'm sorry if you don't like me anymore, but I cannot make that promise to you. You may not like what I did but all the same ... I didn't do anything dishonest."

"Now just hang on a minute Barry! It may not have been dishonest what you did, but all the same ... It wasn't very nice was it?"

"Maybe not Mr Powel but what matters most is that I made five shillings and that went towards helping my mum, and that is more important to me than anything. The reason why I can't make you the promise is because I know that under the same circumstances, I would do exactly the same thing again. I like coming up this club but if it means that it stops me helping my mum, then you'll just have to ban me ... I don't want you to but there it is."

the *broken biscuit*

Mr Powel was taken aback with Barry's candid answer, so being a fair-minded person he pondered a little before saying, "All right Barry, I still can't say that I go along with what you did, but at least your intentions were good. Under the circumstances, and because your reason for doing it was such, I'm willing to let it go this time." He paused a little before adding, "However Barry if you do anything like it again ... please don't do it so openly in front of me."

Barry left the office feeling much happier now that it had been sorted.

Barbara was different again from all the others. Whether it was because of the promise that Winifred made when Barbara was born or because she was the youngest is not clear, but one thing for certain is that Barbara was rather spoilt. She tended to get away with things. It went on like this until she was ten years old, but then it came to an abrupt end when she did the unforgivable; she actually stole something from the house.

It happened in 1953 just before Queen Elizabeth's Coronation; by then, Barbara was in the top class at St Thomas's. Every year the school held a charity-raising event when the teachers gave each child a donation card that contained twelve small squares. The collection was for the St Joseph's Penny Collection Fund. The idea was to ask someone to prick a square on the card and then kindly donate a penny. On completion of the card, it was handed over to the teacher along with one shilling. It was only pennies, but filling in the card was no easy task, as there was always a lot of competition from all the other children.

The children's enthusiasm would reach fever pitch, as running in conjunction with the fund raising was a visitation by the Bishop of Salford to all the Catholic schools. After the visit, the convent always held the Bishop's Party, and anyone who had sold three cards or more was automatically invited. It was an unfair rule really, as it meant that the more privileged children from better-off families never had any trouble achieving their goal, whereas it was nigh impossible for many of those from lower-class families. Subsequently, every year it was always the same children who attended the party.

Barbara wasn't having any of it; come what may she was determined to go to the festivities. What made it worse in her eyes was that she had a friend called Rita, who had three older working brothers, and they all used to spoil her. As Rita always had plenty of money, it didn't present a problem for her to fill in the charity cards, which meant that she was always amongst the privileged ones invited to attend the party. On the other hand, Barbara was struggling as she went from door to door with little success; as the deadline got closer, it became apparent that she was not going to reach her target.

Meanwhile, back at home, Winifred had left half a crown on the end of the sideboard for the clubman. It was a weekly routine, as she bought clothes for the children from a club, then had to repay it at so much a week.

Barbara happened to come home at dinnertime this particular day, and there was nobody else in the house. As she looked at the shiny new half a crown just sitting there, the thoughts of the party flashed through her mind. She didn't succumb to temptation straight away but the longer she was in the house, the more her bad thoughts got the better of her. Before she left the house, she picked up the money, put it in her pocket, then made her way to school. She'd already collected one shilling and sixpence, which meant that she was still left with a shilling after handing over the three full cards. Call it fate or whatever, that shilling was to be her undoing; but for it, her misdeed may never have come to light.

It was almost the end of May and Princess Elizabeth was about to be crowned Queen the following week, and people throughout the town were preparing for the occasion. Many of the young girls were wearing red, white and blue multi-coloured hair ribbons. The fact that her friend Rita had always been able to spend so freely had created a little resentment within Barbara, and she had become envious. The shilling seemed to burn a hole in her pocket, as she too wanted to be as popular as Rita. The ribbons cost tuppence each, but no matter, she invited five of her school friends to join her and bought each one a ribbon and one for herself. This was to be her downfall, but still, her little peccadillo did not come to light immediately.

Back in the house, the missing money was not noticed till the week after when the clubman came around collecting again, and he pointed out to Winifred that two weeks money was due.

This alone caused a bit of a stir, as Winifred insisted he'd been paid. "I beg to differ, Mr Thorpe," she affirmed, "but the money was left as per usual on the end of the sideboard inside the book."

"Oh the book was there, Mrs Cowell, but I can assure you that there was no money inside it."

"Hey, now just wait a minute, Mr Thorpe! I can definitely remember putting it inside the book before I left the house because it was my last half a crown."

"I can't argue with you about that, Mrs Cowell, all I know is that the book was there, but there was definitely no money inside it."

"I can't believe this," she muttered, then asked, "Was there anybody in the house at all when you came?"

"No I'm afraid not; not a soul," he insisted and went on to say, "Look, Winifred, I know this looks bad and it puts me in a bit of a predicament, but surely you know me from old. I've been coming here to your house for many years now and I understand your plight only too well, and I would much rather help you than hinder you."

Winifred knew he was sincere, so apologised for placing him in an awkward position. "Yes I know you would, Mr Thorpe, and I'm sorry if I've caused any embarrassment, it's just that I don't know what to think; I've absolutely no idea what's happened to the half a crown."

She had to leave it at that but all the same, she was determined to get to the bottom of things. Jack was the obvious suspect, as she couldn't visualise or bear the thought of any other member of the family taking it. In spite of her thoughts though, she had a deep inner feeling that he wasn't the one responsible.

All the same, she questioned him about it but he threw a tantrum and started to yell, "What the bloody hell do you take me for, woman? You know flamín well that I haven't done ówt like that ever since our Maureen was born, so I'm tellín thí now ... don't come it! Anyway, have you asked all the kids about it?"

She had to admit that she hadn't, so he suggested asking each one of them as they came in. This she did but each one in turn emphatically denied it; almost everyone came up with the same answer. "Umph no,

Mum, not me, I wouldn't ever steal anything, you know that."

Even Barbara's answer was convincing. "Oh no, Mummy, not me … you've always taught us never to steal anything."

Winifred racked her brains but she couldn't come up with an answer. She felt so frustrated because never before had she been faced with this sort of situation where suspicion was thrown on to the entire family. She knew that she couldn't pinpoint the culprit, and as she had no idea where the money had gone, she had no alternative but to let the matter drop.

So Barbara got away with it; she even went to the Bishop's Party. Even then, Winifred hadn't suspected her, as she knew that Barbara had collected quite a lot before the disappearance of the half a crown. Also, Barbara had been crafty, covering her tracks by scrounging pennies here and there from her brothers and sisters, making folk believe that this is where some of the donated money came from. Three weeks passed, and Barbara was by now feeling quite smug to think she had outwitted her mother and all the others. Little did she know, though, that fate was now taking a hand in things; her theft was about to be discovered.

Winifred had to go shopping down town; she caught the bus at the bottom of Albion Street and in the seat facing sat Rita's mother Emily.

They exchanged greetings, then Emily said something which made Winifred's heart turn cold. "All right, Winnie, I believe you've found out what happened to that half a crown then?" It wasn't so much what had been said, as the fact that she knew she was about to learn the truth, also that an outsider knew of it.

Accordingly, she reacted rather coolly to the question. "And what do you know the half a crown then, Emily, may I ask?"

"Ah well, our Rita mentioned something about it, and she said that your Barbara had been buying ribbons for some school girls just before the Coronation."

Winifred could feel her blood boiling but didn't answer straightaway. She then accused her of spoiling her own daughter Rita and turning Barbara into a thief.

After the exchange of words, Winifred was rather distraught, so decided to make her way back home. On arriving there, Jack and

Maureen were sat by the fireside having a pot of tea; they were both surprised to see her back so soon. During the conversation that followed, Maureen made herself scarce, slipping out of the house so as to forewarn Barbara, who she met on the footbridge as she was coming home from school. But in spite of the warning, Barbara wasn't for owning up; she swore blind to Maureen that it wasn't her.

"Listen to me, our Barbara," Maureen tried to tell her, "mí mother knows because Rita's mother has told her everything; even that you spent some of the money buying ribbons for your school friends."

Still, Barbara wasn't for coming clean, fervently protesting her innocence. "It wasn't me, our Maureen … honest!"

"Look, our Barbara, I'm saying no more except that on your own head be it, if you tell Mum lies on top of everything else you're really asking for it; she's fuming as it is and she'll bloomín well kill you if you make it worse than it already is."

Barbara dragged her feet going up Albion Street; she was really wary at the daunting prospect of facing her mum. Nevertheless, despite Maureen's advice she chose to lie, defiantly pleading her innocence.

But Winifred wasn't having any of it and really tore a strip off her. "Right then! So that's your answer, is it? Well, Barbara, all I can say is you're not only a thief, you're a liar as well; I'm going to ask you just one more time … did you take that half a crown?"

Barbara was quivering but still refused to own up and resolutely stood her ground.

Despite lying through her teeth, Winifred knew she was guilty, so reverted to other tactics. "Right, Barbara, get your coat on right now cós I'm taking you to the police station, and I'll let them sort you out!" she rapped. "And tomorrow morning I'm going to the school and I'm going to show you up in front of all your class mates."

"Oh no, Mum, please don't do that, I promise I won't ever do it again … honest!"

"What's that you just said?" asked Winifred. "You won't do what again?"

That was it … Barbara knew it was pointless to carry on lying, so started to cry, "Oh, Mum, I'm sorry! I promise I won't do anything like it ever again."

"You sneaky little swine, you're nówt else!" Winifred screeched, "You've watched us turn this flamín house upside down looking for that half a crown and you've even pretended to look for it yourself. The worst thing though is that you cast suspicion on all your brothers and sisters even as they were trying to help you get to that blasted party!" Then for the first time in her life, Barbara got a good hiding and sent straight to bed; she was also grounded for a fortnight. That wasn't the end of it because for at least two years after that, she got loads of ribbing from her brothers and sisters. Poor Barbara really did get punished because if anything got lost or even misplaced after that, she got the blame!

"Oh our Barbara's been about, she'll have taken it," one or the other would say. It had the desired effect. Barbara learned her lesson, never ever stealing anything again.

Winifred was now working at Bank Hall Colliery Canteen where she'd been employed since leaving her cleaning job for Mrs Cooper. It was a very arduous job and the working hours were from 6am until 2-30pm. Things were more burdensome because there were no buses running from Trafalgar so early in the morning, so she had to trudge to the Town Centre to catch one at 5-50am in order to get to the canteen on time. This meant having to get up at 4-45am, before leaving the house at 5-30am. She always tried her very best to keep the children well-dressed but tended to neglect herself a little. There was many a time when she made her way through the snow wearing very thin shoes that let in water; she'd think nothing of stuffing a piece of cardboard into them for added protection. Some winter mornings, she would rise to find it had been snowing heavily during the night. On these occasions, she was afraid of slipping on account of Albion Street being so steep, so she would actually remove her shoes and walk barefooted until she reached Trafalgar.

The job itself was very difficult, catering to the needs and whims of all the colliers. She'd to make up lots of sandwiches, which the miners used to take with them down the pit in their bait tins. The sandwiches were made up of cheese, ham and other fillings. This meant she had first to hump around large fifty-six-pound cheeses and heavy joints of ham before carving them up. Everything had to be prepared for both the miners starting the early shift at 7am and those just finishing the night shift. After the first initial rush hour she had to start preparing meals for the pit-top workers and in between there were piles of washing-up to do. From dinnertime onwards it was non-stop because then the afternoon shift had to be catered for. Taking everything into account it was a very demanding job with no time for relaxation.

Hard work or not, she stayed there for seven years. Whilst there, Jimmy left school and began work at Hapton Valley Colliery. Like the Bank Hall miners, he too started at seven o'clock but he was lucky because Hapton Valley laid on transport for its workers, which meant that he could catch the bus at the bottom of Albion Street at 6-20am.

Despite Winifred leaving the home at 5-30am she'd have a blazing fire going before giving Jimmy a shout to get up and there was a breakfast awaiting him of egg, beans, bread and butter, and a cup of tea. Her energy was boundless and she was totally dedicated to her family. She liked the job in the canteen but the hours were unsuitable, so she asked for permission to start at nine o'clock and work through until five. This was refused, so eventually she decided to leave and went to work at Massey's Brewery, which was much nearer to home situated as it was at the bottom of Sandygate. She settled in quickly and made a few friends and worked there for several years.

15: *the* fifties

In 1951, John passed his eleven plus examination; he didn't get high enough grades for Grammar School but qualified to go to Towneley Technical High School. Nobody was more suited than Maureen; she reacted like a little mother with lots of enthusiasm and was very proud of him. She eagerly went with him to help choose his new uniform, which included a maroon blazer with a badge depicting Towneley Park Castle Gates. John will always remember the first morning when she saw him off to his new school, waving after him as he strutted down the front street carrying a new leather satchel over his shoulder. Sadly, though, her expectations were never realised because John didn't do quite as well as she had hoped, the main reason being that he was required to do a lot of homework, and was never encouraged in this department. Jack didn't like this aspect of John's schooling, and rather than help him, he would actually reprimand John, totally disheartening him.

The young lad would be trying his best to tackle his homework on the end of the sideboard, but Jack would say, "What the flamín éck do you think you're playing at cluttering up the house with them books? That kind of work should be done at school, I don't want you bringing it home here!"

John protested, but to no avail and his education suffered. His marks were always poor and, ultimately, he lost interest in his studies.

It was about this time that Jimmy and John bought three second-hand bicycles out of their paper round money, one each for themselves and one for Barry. They were forever breaking down but, as luck would have it, some new neighbours, Mr and Mrs Davis, had moved into number twelve next door. The gentleman's name was Malcolm; it turned out that he was a biking enthusiast and also a dab hand at repairing bikes. He got on very well with the lads, teaching them how to repair punctures and other little breakdowns.

A friendship evolved and together they toured miles of the surrounding countryside. A favourite run was doing a round trip, first cycling to Rawtenstall over the moors, then on to Bacup via Stacksteads and finally returning home to Burnley via Weir. It was great once they'd reached the Deerplay Pub, as it was downhill all the way from thereon in. They'd think nothing of doing this trip in the morning and another one to somewhere else in the afternoon. Sometimes, they'd set off early in the morning and do a round trip to Blackpool and back in a day. As the years progressed, the lads took up motorcycling and, once again, Malcolm took an interest, helping them to sort out any mechanical problems.

In 1953, Maureen, now aged eighteen, was actually engaged to be married to a young local lad called Bill Howley, whom she'd been courting for over two years. Bill was a reserved lad and very shy, but in spite of this, he got on well with everyone in Maureen's home and the family really brought him out of his shell. He had no brothers or sisters of his own, therefore number fourteen Albion Street was entirely different to what he'd always been used to. He had an endearing sense of humour and was readily accepted as part of the family. He got on well with Winifred too, despite the fact that she laid down strict ground rules – one being that all the courting was done from the house. She made it quite clear that Maureen always had to be picked up from her home and escorted back there at a reasonable hour. On Saturday nights the young couple would go dancing at the Weaver's Institute on Charlotte Street or at the Empress Ballroom and perhaps go to the pictures once a week. But most evenings were usually spent in Maureen's home getting to know the family.

There were no airs and graces put on and Bill had to take things as he found them. Nearly every night was wash night, so there was always plenty of activity in the house, as Winifred set on the gas boiler and got out the dolly-tub and posser. Nonetheless, he didn't seem to mind; on the contrary, he seemed to enjoy the stark contrast to his own home. His personality began to blossom and he loved to crack jokes as he turned the handle of the wringing machine prior to Maureen hanging the clothes on the rack.

Bill may have been a very naïve young man as far as the outside world was concerned but his horizons were certainly broadened in Maureen's home. Everything was open and above board, the fact that Jack had been in prison and the job he did was not hidden from Bill. To his credit, though, he didn't mind; he loved Maureen and that's all that mattered to him. It was just as well because, one evening, his love was really put to the test. He was in the house with Maureen and some of the family when Jack walked in with a cardboard box containing a dozen bottles of whisky. The first thing he did was to put them behind a rocking chair that was placed near to the cellar top.

"Oh no!" Winifred complained bitterly. "You're not up to your old tricks again, are you?"

"Oh come on, Winnie, I couldn't let these go, I got them for a song."

"I don't flamín well care if you got them given, I don't want them in my house."

"Oh just for once, why don't you relax and let your hair down?" He gave a cheeky grin, jesting, "I'll pour you a nice tot if you want one, love."

"You'll do no such thing, you can take them back to wherever you got them from."

There wasn't much chance of that, so an exchange of words took place for about twenty minutes only to be interrupted by a loud knocking on the front door. Maureen answered it and on returning to the living room, her face was ashen.

"There's two men at the door, Mum," she stuttered, "they say they're police officers and they want to have a word with Dad."

"Oh my God!" Winifred exclaimed. "Now we're for it."

On going to the door one of the men said, "Good evening, Mrs Cowell, is your husband in please?"

"He is, why do you ask?"

"Well we have reason to believe that he is in possession of some stolen goods and we have a warrant here to search your property."

"Stolen goods! And what would they be then?" she enquired shaking in her shoes.

"Well, a warehouse was broken into a few nights ago and a shipment of whisky was stolen."

"Oh I see, and just what has that got to do with my husband?"

The detective in charge gave a little smirk saying, "We have our sources, Mrs Cowell; now if you don't mind, can we come in please?"

She wasn't happy about it but knew she had no option. On reaching the living room, everything appeared normal; Jack was still sat in the rocking chair behind which the whisky was hidden, Bill and Maureen were sat on the sofa and the others were sat around the table.

"Hello, Barney," one of the detectives sneered sarcastically, "you know why we're here, don't you?"

Winifred was afraid that Jack might trip himself up so forewarned him by blurting out before he could answer, "Someone's broke into a warehouse, Jack, and stole some whisky and they think you've got something to do with it."

"Oh yes, I know all about that … it happened last week, didn't it?"

"And how would you know that, Barney?" asked the detective in charge.

"Oh come off it, everybody knows; it's common knowledge around the pubs down town."

"Aye maybe you're right there," mumbled the officer rather disgruntled at the answer, "but all the same, we have reason to believe that you have purchased some of it and we intend to search this house."

"Please yourself, I've nothing to hide; search where you like," he replied quite coolly. He may have looked cool but he was trembling inside, as he knew that if they charged him he could go to jail for five years this time. The two policemen thoroughly searched the upstairs and the parlour using their flashlights, but only glanced around the living-room with everything appearing so normal. Throughout all this procedure, Bill couldn't believe what was happening.

"Right, Barney," said the detective in charge, "we can't find anything this time but we still have our suspicions and we'll be keeping an eye on you."

"Yeah righto, please yourself," he replied still keeping his calm.

Winifred saw them both to the door saying, "Right, officers, goodnight, I hope you find the ones responsible."

"Right, thank you, Mrs Cowell, sorry for any inconvenience caused."

"That's all right, you're only doing your job." With that, she quietly shut the door, gritted her teeth, took a deep breath and then stormed back into the living room. "Jack," she screeched, "if you ever put us in that kind of predicament again, so help me, I'll swing for you!"

"Shush," he whispered with a grin on his face, "keep your voice down ... make sure they're well away from the house before you start." He had a way with him and despite being furious about what he'd just put them through she was unable to suppress a smile.

"By éck, Jack, you could get away with bloomín murder and that's the Gospel Truth."

"Eh that's better, love, I like it when you smile, it really lights up your face. Now how about having that drink cós I'm telling you straight, I'm having one, my nerves are shattered." Turning to Bill he asked, "How about thee, lad, would you like a little one?"

"I think I'll just try one at that; I don't usually drink but after that episode my nerves are a little on edge as well." At that, everybody had a good laugh.

Then came the happy day when Maureen and Bill got married, on July 18th, 1953. It may have been a happy day for the young couple, but there was a tinge of sadness in the home that morning as she put on her wedding gown. Emotions were running high and very mixed; to think that Maureen was leaving the family home never to return seemed unbelievable. Each one in turn gave her a big hug, even Jimmy had tears in his eyes at the thought of his big sister leaving.

"Don't worry about it," she reassured everyone. "I'll always be close at hand so that you can come and visit me whenever you want, and I'll come and see you all regularly."

She was married in Christ the King Church and the reception took place at the Mitre Hotel. True to her word, she always kept in touch, and there was always a hearty welcome for her brothers and sisters at her new home on Napier Street. It never seemed the same again in Winifred's home now that Maureen was gone.

Still, another era was dawning and before they knew it, the twins were fifteen and ready for leaving school. Mary began work in Barden Mill and John at Thorney Bank Colliery whilst Winifred was still working at Massey's Brewery. It was during this time that she put her writing skills to good use; however, she mainly used them to help others, not herself. She regularly used to write letters to official bodies on behalf of elderly neighbours who were infirm, or if they couldn't manage to put a good letter together for themselves. These letters were mainly in reply to awkward questions from government officials or to claim benefits or entitlements for the claimant.

One Sunday morning, whilst reading the *News of the World*, Winifred noticed a competition entitled, "Competition for amateur writer of the year". The award was an up-to-date prestigious television set fully licensed and maintained for five years. The article went on to say, however, that the prize would not go to the writer; the conditions of the competition were as follows:

You may choose your own title.

It has to be your own story.

It has to be the story of a real person.

It has to be true in every aspect.

The prize will go to the person who the story is about.

Winifred thought long and hard about this for there was someone she had in mind; it happened to be a little old lady, who lived directly opposite on the other side of the street. The little lady's name was May; she lived all alone except for the companionship of a very old dog called Rex. It was a very unusual dog having the body of a sausage dog but the head of a spaniel. Still, to May, Rex was everything: her child, her constant companion and her loyal obedient friend. May was always very poorly dressed with a frayed shawl around her shoulders and half-heeled shoes on her feet. Every day, weather permitting, she would sit on the doorstep with Rex by her side just mumbling away to the old dog. The poor lady had a terrible skin complaint and both her arms and legs were full of boil-type blisters, which she was forever scratching and picking at. She didn't appear to have any friends at all; in fact many people ridiculed her because of her condition; it wasn't just children either, as many grown-ups did the same. Winifred's children knew better; they had always been brought up to treat other people with respect, and especially so if they were elderly or had a disability. They treated her with the respect she deserved, running errands or doing other little chores for her.

After reading the article, Winifred thought to herself, "Yes, that's a good idea, Winifred, it would be lovely to be able to win the prize for May, and I'm sure it would bring her lots of happiness. Mind, there's not much chance of winning it, but who knows, anything can happen; there's one thing for sure, she won't win anything if I don't enter." These thoughts stimulated her, so she immediately got down to writing.

The first line of the story was, "She sat on a cold doorstep talking to a very old dog," then went on to tell of the loneliness and ridicule of poor old May.

Winifred got rather carried away by her enthusiasm and before she knew it she'd finished the story and given it the title of "The loneliest person". On reading it through she was quite happy with the outcome until she realised that in her eagerness to write it, she hadn't asked May's permission. As it happened, May didn't mind at all; in fact she thought it was a nice idea. So the story was posted and Winifred didn't give it another thought.

That is until she was stopped on Trafalgar one day by a lady who asked, "Winnie, don't mind me asking but have you written a story about old May in the *News of the World*?"

"I have, Betty, why do you ask?"

"Well, I got the paper this morning and I happened to spot this article about an old woman, who sits on the doorstep every day talking to a funny old dog, and it said that they'd dwindled this here contest down to the last four contestants."

"Was it a competition for Amateur Writer of the Year?" asked Winifred now becoming rather curious.

"That's right, Winnie, and it says somét about the old lady living on Albion Street in Burnley. It didn't say much else except that a Mrs Winifred Cowell wrote it. Anyway, Winnie, it didn't take much figuring out, did it? I just put two and two together, old May is the only person I know who lives on Albion and fits that description, and she lives just facing you, doesn't she?"

"Yes, that's right she does, and yes, it was me who wrote the story. Mind, I'm as surprised as you are that it's got down to the last four; are you sure you've read it properly?"

"I'm certain, Winnie, because I couldn't believe it myself at first, so I read it three times to mék sure and I right enjoyed what bit they'd written about it."

"Right, Betty, thanks a lot anyway for telling me." Winifred's curiosity was by now getting the better of her, so the first thing she did was to buy a newspaper; sure enough, there was a brief extract of her story in the centre pages along with three others. She was quietly pleased to have reached this stage of the event, feeling a shiver of excitement rushing through her body.

"Goodness gracious," she thought to herself, "I never expected to get this far; it seems strange to see my name written there amongst the four finalists." It suddenly dawned on her that she might even possibly win it, and the excitement within her built up even more. "No that couldn't happen surely to goodness, not from all those entries from all over England. Then again, who knows? God's good and if that be His will, then so be it."

One thing that struck her though was that she hadn't heard anything from the newspaper itself. Be that as it may, the very next evening there was a knock on the door, and standing there were two reporters.

"Excuse me, madam, would you be Mrs Cowell?" asked one of them.

"That's right, what can I do for you?"

They explained who they were and asked if she was the person who had written the story?

After replying that she was, they went on to say, "Right, Mrs Cowell, the reason we're here is to confirm that you have applied yourself strictly to the rules laid down."

"Oh yes, I certainly have, every single word written down is the gospel truth, I took special care to see to that. Anyway, if you want living proof for yourself, just glance across the street."

Sure enough, there sat on her doorstep, stroking and talking to her dog Rex was poor little May. After satisfying themselves that all the rules had been adhered to, the two gentlemen informed Winifred that the newspaper liked her story very much and that the winner would be notified within the next fortnight prior to printing.

"Oh well, one never knows," pondered Winifred, "I may win even yet ... I hope so for May's sake."

She did hear, just a week later to be exact; the same two reporters came but this time there was another official-looking bloke with them. They'd come to give her the verdict and to her astonishment ... she'd actually won!

They explained that the prize would be given to May the very next day, and they would be taking photographs of her and Winifred for the following Sunday newspaper when the full story would be published.

"Excuse me," said Winifred, "but I'm afraid that I don't want my photo taken, it's not my day; the day belongs to May."

"But, Mrs Cowell," replied the official, "you're the author of the story, surely you deserve some recognition for that."

"Maybe so but all the same, if you don't mind I'd rather not; like I said, it will be May's day and I don't want to take anything from her." They tried to convince her otherwise but she remained adamant.

The officials made arrangements to deliver the television at eleven o'clock, pointing out that there would be reporters and a cameraman coming at the same time. Before their arrival, Winifred went across to May's house to make sure she was dressed and ready for the occasion; she then very discreetly slipped back to her own house. Notwithstanding, she may not have wanted any publicity, but all the same, she was still curious and eager to see the outcome of her efforts; therefore at the appointed time, she went up into the front bedroom and peered through the netted curtains. The television arrived along with the reporters and cameraman; but so too did lots of the neighbours eager to get their photographs in the newspaper alongside May. They were gathered outside May's door making a right fuss of her; many of these were the self-same ones who had ridiculed her and given her grief. No matter, the day still belonged to May; it was one that she was to remember for the rest of her life; besides, she now had this wonderful television set to help her pass the lonely days. Winifred felt really good about all this, she'd achieved her goal, which gave her a great inner feeling of satisfaction.

"Well that's it," she said to herself as she descended the stairs, "I just hope now that all the neighbours give poor old May the same respect once all the glamour's finished and done with."

The episode wasn't finished yet by any means ... at least not for Winifred, After the story was highlighted in the Sunday paper, it became the topic of conversation throughout the Trafalgar area.

People would say, "Hasta seen that there article that Winnie Cowell's written; by éck she's gone and won a brand new television for old May, the old lady that talks to that ole dog?"

"Has she now, by éck, who'd a thought she cudda done that?"

It actually created quite a lot of work for Winifred; it was as though she'd made a rod for her own back.

For a long time afterwards, she was forever being stopped in the street by elderly people, asking, "Oh, Winnie, dusta think tha cud write a story about me, I cud do with a new telly?"

"But, Nellie," she would try to explain, "this was just a one-off situation, I don't think it'll actually happen again."

"Aye, all reight, Winnie, but dusta think tha cud write a letter to claim some extra benefits for me, I believe tha does that as well?"

"Yes all right, Nellie, just give me a few details and I'll try my best for you."

Well, that was it, she now had more clients than ever.

A few months later came another sad time for Winifred. She received word from her sister Katie that her mother was ill; she immediately dropped everything and caught the next bus to Bacup. Her mother Mary had been suffering with phlebitis in her legs for a while and was on various medications. She had got very run down contracting pneumonia and didn't seem to have the strength to fight it off; sadly, she died within two weeks of becoming ill; she was sixty-nine years old.

Mat was at a complete loss; Mary was his world, his universe, his only reason for being; there was no consoling him, he just wanted to die alongside her. He didn't actually die in body but definitely in spirit, as his heart was broken into a thousand pieces. From that day on, the only thing he looked forward to was the day he would join her.

Winifred was heartbroken at the loss of her mother; she also had a terrible feeling of guilt, as she felt that she hadn't visited her parents half as much as she should have. She made a resolve there and then that she would keep more in touch with her father from then on; true to her promise, she visited him whenever she got the chance.

Like she had done for some of her neighbours on Trafalgar, she got in touch with the social services and other departments to help her dad both financially and physically. However, Mat was still the same stubborn proud man that he'd always been; he wasn't too keen on the idea and took a lot of persuading.

Throughout all his grieving though, he was still very kind to Annie; she was now thirty-five years old, but still only had the mind of a child. She was actually working at Ross Mill as her sisters had done before her; in fact, she'd worked there for twenty years since leaving school. One day, whilst carrying a box, she slipped on a patch of oil, injuring her arm so badly that she was unable to work again. Winifred took over, filling in all the necessary forms and making a claim on Annie's behalf. She also represented Annie at various medicals where she argued for, and won, an industrial pension for her sister. Even Mat accepted this, as he too thought it only fitting that Annie should receive some kind of compensation. Every six months or so, Annie's pension was reviewed by either an official body or a medical board, and on each occasion, Winifred represented her. Winifred didn't mind at all; in fact, it gave her a lot of satisfaction. Ironically, her efforts, on behalf of Annie, resulted in her being ostracised from her father.

One particular day, she had taken Annie to the doctor's surgery for a routine examination, and everything was fine as far as that was concerned. Just before leaving the surgery, the doctor asked Winifred how her father was coping.

She was rather concerned about Mat's condition, so pointed this out to him. "Well, to tell you the truth, doctor, he's not feeling very well; in fact, I personally feel that he's failing and badly in need of a holiday or some kind of convalescence."

"Right, Winifred, I'll see what I can do for you, just leave it with me."

"Oh that's good, doctor, but do you think you could send all communications to me, you know how stubborn my dad can be if he thinks he's getting something for nothing, and in the meantime, I'll try my best to talk him round."

Winifred didn't give it another thought till one day when she went over Bacup to see her dad. On reaching the house, he was sat in the same old chair close to the fire.

"All right, Dad," she said, "would you like a brew and something to eat?" He didn't answer; there was a stony silence.

"That's strange," she thought, "he mustn't have heard me," so asked, "Are you all right, Dad, are you not feeling so well?"

"I'm all reight," he grunted, "just leave me alone, that's all!"

"U-um, I wonder what's to do," she said to herself, "something must have upset him." She finished making the brew, then handed it to him saying, "Here you are, Dad, drink that up, it'll make you feel better."

"Ték the flamín thing away, I don't want ówt off thi, and nówt to do with thi either!"

"Whoa, just hang on a minute, Dad!" she retaliated. "What are you mad at me for, what have I done wrong?"

"It doesn't matter, if tha doesn't know, I'm not gonna tell thi."

"Now come on, Dad, if you're going to be mad at me, the least you can do is tell me what it's all about."

"Look, just go away wilta, there's no more to be said!"

"Right, if that's the way you want it, I will then," she snapped, then stormed out of the house and made her way back to Burnley.

Nonetheless, she was very unsettled and fidgety about the whole affair, so decided to go and see her dad again the following day to settle the issue; still, when she got there, his mood was unchanged.

She couldn't fathom out why he was so angry with her. "Surely," she thought, "he can't be mad at me for hardly visiting whilst Mum was alive; he must have known it was nigh impossible for me to get over here much?" She bethought herself, "No that can't be it, because he was quite nice to me for a while after Mum died; what can it be then, what can I have done to upset him so?"

She was determined to get to the bottom of things, so approached him again; but despite asking many times, her efforts were in vain; he completely ignored her saying absolutely nothing! She was quite downhearted about the whole thing, so decided to go and have a word with her sister Katie about it.

Winifred opened up her heart to Katie who replied, "Well, our Winnie, you've really surprised me ... you mean to say that you really don't know what it's all about?"

Winifred's ears pricked up. "No, our Katie I haven't got a clue, please tell me and put me out of my misery."

"Well, knowing you, our Winnie, you're not going to like what I have to tell you but here goes; it's all about the last time you took our Annie to see the doctor; according to her you tried to get Dad put into a home."

Winifred was flabbergasted answering, "Oh no, that's not true, our Katie; surely you know I wouldn't do anything like that and especially so behind his back." Winifred's mind flashed back to the day she was in the doctor's surgery. "Oh that's it," she thought to herself, "our Annie was listening to the conversation and she's gone and got hold of the wrong end of the stick."

She went on to tell the true tale, to which Katie replied, "U-um that sounds more like you, our Winnie; I've got to admit, though, that at first, I was quite shocked myself and I thought you were well out of order."

"Oh thanks, our kid, I feel better now, at least I can go and sort things out with Dad." She immediately went to see him but to her despair, he was still unrelenting and wouldn't listen to a word she had to say.

"But, Dad," she stressed, "you've got to listen to me, there's been a misunderstanding; I only wanted to help you because you weren't so well." Her pleas fell on deaf ears, and he wouldn't be swayed at all; she didn't want to involve Annie but felt that she didn't have much choice.

On mentioning her name, though, Mat went wild. "You leave our Annie out of it!" he growled. "This is your doing not hers."

Winifred's mind flashed back to her teenage years when he wouldn't listen to her side of the story then. "Yes," she thought, "you're still exactly the same, Dad, you haven't changed one little bit." She'd forgiven him for that over the years, knowing only too well what he'd been through; but at this moment, she felt very angry. "Right, Dad, if that's the way you want it, then so be it; you're just as stubborn now as you ever were." She turned to open the door but just before leaving she stressed, with tears rolling down her cheeks, "Right, Dad, I'm going home now to Burnley, but I'm telling you, if you make me leave under these circumstances, I will never return!"

He was still unmoved, just muttering under his breath, so off she went.

The next two weeks were very troublesome for Winifred; she was really tormented by the thoughts of not being on friendly terms with her dad, so made up her mind to visit him at the first opportunity. Sadly, though, the opportunity never came; unfortunately, she got a message from Bacup that her father had peacefully passed away whilst sat in the chair. She was absolutely devastated; the thought that her father had died whilst she wasn't speaking to him was just too much. She kept telling herself, though, that she'd had every intention of making it up to him and felt that he would have come round eventually. She didn't know how she was going to cope with her thoughts over the coming months but then, she got a little help. John Walsh, Katie's husband, told her something that eased her conscience, making her feel much better inside.

"Hello, Winnie," he said the moment she arrived in Bacup after hearing the news of her father's death, "could I have a word, there's something I think you ought to know?"

"Certainly, John, what is it?"

"Well, I was in your dad's house this morning just a few hours before he died, and he wasn't feeling too good; he must have known he hadn't long left, because he appeared to be bothered about something, and he kept asking for you."

"For me, John, oh please tell me, what did he say?"

"He kept muttering, 'Oh will somebody send for that lass ó mine o'er Burnley, she's ne'er done me a wrong turn in her life,' aye, and he kept on saying that it wasn't your fault, it was his."

"You're certain that it was me who he was talking about, did he mention anything else?"

"Oh it was you all right, Winnie, because he kept mentioning your name, saying how you'd tried to help him and how he'd turned on you. Anyway, Katie was going to get in touch with you about it just before we found him in the chair."

No other words could have made Winifred happier, at least she knew her father had forgiven her knowing the truth. "Oh thank God for that!" she replied tearfully. "He'd forgiven me and wanted us to be friends again. Oh thank you, John, for telling me, thank you very much indeed, you don't realise just what that means to me."

It was still a very sad time for her though, but at least she now felt that she could live with herself. Matthew was just turned seventy-three, and it was three and a half years since Mary had died; he was buried with her alongside his four children.

As Winifred made her way home after the funeral, she couldn't help thinking, "Well, Dad, you've finally got what you wanted, you're at peace now with Mum." She reminisced about her own little brothers and sisters, who'd passed away all those years ago; little Martin, the babies, Teresa and Nellie, and finally, Jimmy. She had to smile to herself as she imagined them all waiting to greet him.

Jack's lifestyle didn't change very much and one particular evening he did something very foolish; lots of people found it rather amusing but all the same it was still foolish. He was out on one of his many boozing sessions, and as per usual, the effects of the beer completely took over. On this occasion though, which happened one summer's evening, he overstepped the mark playing a silly prank that cost him the loss of his beloved horse Peggy. Two months previously, he'd actually gambled Peggy away in a silly game of cards; all the same, the man who'd won the horse had agreed to rent Peggy back to him at a nominal fee.

This particular night, Winifred, Jimmy and John were sat around the fire drinking tea. It was coming up to eleven o'clock when there was a commotion on the front street. The front door opened, then there was a loud clomping noise in the lobby; the three of them wondered what on earth it could be, making such a noise. First of all, Jack popped his head around the living-room door and staggered into the room drunk out of his mind; then, to their amazement, Peggy, the horse, followed him. How on earth the floor didn't collapse, heaven knows;

it's just as well that they were well supported by very large joists. Jack was in a rather mischievous mood and Winifred was too flabbergasted to argue with him.

Jimmy and John took care of Peggy, backing her out on to the front street and settling her down. Nevertheless, the damage had already been done, as Jack had been seen riding Peggy at a gallop along Trafalgar, and someone had reported the incident to the police. Jack hadn't been in the house very long before a police car arrived; he was arrested and kept in custody overnight. As he was taken away there were lots of people on the front street whose curiosity had been aroused by the rumpus. John had the responsibility of taking Peggy back to her stable and bedding her down for the night; little did he know that he would never see her again. It's not quite sure whether Jack was charged with being drunk and disorderly, being in charge of a horse whilst under the influence of drink, or riding Peggy without lights, maybe all three; one thing is sure though, he got a hefty fine. It turned out that Jack had done it as a prank; however, the new owner was not the least bit amused, and he wouldn't let Jack use her again and sold her shortly after.

Jack was at a bit of a loss at first, but not for too long though, as Jimmy came up with something. Nine months previously, he'd joined the airforce and, being thrifty, had saved quite a bit of money in the Post Office.

"Why don't you buy a wagon, Dad, I think it would be more practical than a horse and cart anyway?"

"Good idea, our Jimmy, except for one snag, where do I get the money?"

"You could buy a second-hand one, Dad, I know where there's one goín in the Mitre Area for two hundred pounds," adding, "And you'd probably get it for less than that if you bartered with ém."

"Aye perhaps I would but like I said, where do I get the money?"

To Jack's surprise, Jimmy replied, "I'll lend it to you, Dad, I've saved up quite a bit since I went into the forces and I reckon I could just about raise that much."

"By éck, lad, you're a canny ún too, tha never ceases to amaze me. Anyway, would you really lend me that much?"

"Course I would, there's no use me havín it if I don't put it to good use is there? Mind, tha'd have to pay me back so much a week, Dad, with a bit of interest."

Jack shook his head a little. "That's my lad," he said, "right you're on, our Jimmy, let's go and have a look at this here wagon." Jack did buy the wagon, and that was the end of the horse and cart era as far as he was concerned.

Mary was now seventeen and a very pretty teenager she was too. It was a pleasant summer's evening; her best friend Loretta was on a date with her new boyfriend Burt Myers and Winifred was out somewhere. Subsequently, Mary was in the house feeling restless, not knowing what to do with herself.

Out of the blue, Jack said to her, "Oh dear, what a gloomy face, it's enough to stop the Town Hall Clock."

She muttered a little something or other under her breath before saying, "Well, there's nothing much to do around here, is there?"

"Right, I'll tell thi what, cock, get thaself ready and tha can come out with your dad."

"Umph," she mumbled adding, "Oh yeah, Dad, sure, and where will you take me ... around the pubs in Burnley I suppose?"

"That's right, have you any better ideas?"

"Don't forget, Dad," she quipped, "I'm only seventeen, so I'm not allowed in pubs anyway."

"Oh righto, please yourself, I was only trying to help; but for crying out loud, our Mary, straighten your face afore wind changes, or it'll stop like that."

Mary pondered about what he'd said, then asked, "Do you mean it, Dad, are you really serious ... would you really take me round the pubs with you?"

"Yeah, of course I'm serious," he replied, "mind you, tha won't be able to have a beer or the like, tha'll have to drink orange juice or something."

In a flash, Mary made her decision. "Right, Dad, that's it, I'll go upstairs and get changed."

It took her half an hour to get ready but when she came down she was beautiful. She was wearing a royal blue dress fitted to the waist with a V-neck and short sleeves. Her light brown shoulder-length hair was swept mainly to one side of her face with a quiff complementing her blue eyes, and she was wearing a pillbox hat with a white veil effect; for accessories, she had white matching high-heel shoes and a handbag. She was always a very pretty girl with perfect features, but at this moment she looked absolutely stunning (and she knew it).

Even her brothers paid her compliments. "By èck, our kid, you look really nice," commented John, and Jimmy and Barry made similar remarks telling her how pretty she looked.

Jack was taken aback by her beauty and let her know. "Well, my love, I'm really impressed, you look like a picture and you make me feel real proud." He offered her his hand saying, "Come on then, sweetheart, let's go."

She walked off down Albion Street holding his arm with her head held high; many of the neighbours, who were sat on their doorsteps, looked on in admiration. They were both dressed smartly enough for the grandest occasion but still, he took her to the most dingy pubs in town to show her off; she obviously felt a little wary, so constantly clung to his arm for a feeling of security.

She felt uneasier as the night progressed, so let him know, "Oh, Dad, is there any chance of going anywhere else? I don't feel right in here."

"Aye all right, our Mary, I'll tell thi what, I'll tèk thi to the Prince of Wales on Sandygate; it should be all right in there, and it's a lot closer to home." It certainly was a lot nearer, and it wasn't quite so notorious either.

On reaching there, Jack asked, "Naythen, our Mary, what would you like to drink?"

"Is there any chance of me having a Babycham, Dad?"

"You can have anything you want, my little princess," he replied as he made his way to the bar.

He brought the drinks back and had just handed Mary the Babycham, when a rather smart gentleman tapped him on the shoulder asking, "Is there any chance of having a word in private, Barney, it's about business?"

"This is my daughter," replied Jack, "you can discuss it here if you like."

"I'm sorry, Barney, but it's quite confidential, I'd rather discuss it alone with you in the tap room if you don't mind," stressing, "It is important and very good."

Jack turned to Mary saying, "I'm sorry, love, but do you mind coming with me for a moment?" He took her into the lounge, which was quite full with only a couple of available seats, then said, "If you just sit in here and wait for me, I promise thi I won't be long; I have to go an' talk a bit ó business with that bloke."

"Oh, Dad, don't leave me for so long please!" she protested. "I don't like being in a pub on my own."

"Aye all reight, just hang on a minute," he said and introduced her to some of his friends in the room asking if they would keep an eye on her for a short time, whilst he was in the other room. The vacant seats were directly facing, opposite a big fat man called Pey and his wife, who was a very small lady. Mary sat down and wasn't feeling too relaxed, but then something happened.

No sooner had Jack left the room than Pey starting mouthing off in a loud voice for everyone to hear, "Don't they make you laugh though ... bragging and boasting," then added sarcastically, "Aye, and bringín in their beautiful daughter to show her off; they make me bloody sick!"

Mary was listening to all this wondering, "Is he talking about my dad?"

A silence fell over the room, then the fat man started again. "Yeah, next news, he'll be goín home, and his wife Winnie'll be hittín him oe'r t' head wí fryín pan, they're allus at it."

This time, Mary was certain who he was talking about; she felt the hackles rising on the back of her neck. She was fuming as the thought went through her head, "Who does he think he is, talking about my mum and dad like this, and in front of so many people too?" In spite of her anger, she kept her cool; she stood up picking up her untouched drink, then calmly walked directly across the room to where Pey was sitting. The room went deadly quiet as she momentarily stood in front of him defiantly gazing into his eyes.

"Aye, and what can I do for thi, lass?" sneered the big fat man.

A wry smile came to her face; it turned to a little snigger just before suddenly throwing the Babycham right into his face. "So much for you, fat man!" she rapped, then emptied his pint of beer over his head and coolly left the room.

The last words she heard were, "I'll f'fing well kill the little bitch if I get my hands on her!"

There was no chance of that; Mary removed her high-heel shoes and legged it down Sandygate and along Trafalgar as fast as she possibly could.

On reaching home she blurted out to Winifred what had happened adding, "Oh, mí dad'll go mad, Mum, I've really shown him up ... what am I going to do?"

"Never you mind yourself about that," put in Winifred, "he'd better not start, he shouldn't have taken you there in the first place. Anyway, I think you'd best get yourself to bed before he comes home, he'll probably have forgotten all about in the morning."

"Oh please, Mum! Please let me stay up till he gets home, I'd rather face him now and get it all over and done with."

"Yes all right then, please yourself; I don't want any bother, mind, I'm telling you now!"

Mary didn't have to wait very long, it was just about half an hour later when she heard Jack's voice at the front door, then he came walking through the lobby. Once again, Mary was feeling defiant, standing there with her hands on her hips determined to stand her ground. She was ready for a good rollicking from her dad but instead, something quite unexpected happened.

Instead of bellowing at her, he just stuck his head around the living-room door; a big toothless grin spread across his face as he enthused, "Aye, our Mary, sticking up for tha dad; I'm reight proud ó thí ... come here, lass, and give tha dad a big hug."

He went on to say how everybody in the pub had turned on the fat man saying, "It serves thí bloody well right, you were well out of order goín on the way tha did; tha shouldn't a bín callín her mum and dad in front ó lass."

"Aye, and they all said they were delighted to see such a young girl sticking up for herself. Mind you, I don't hold with swearing as you know, and I'd a clocked fat Pey on the snout for swearing in front ó thí if I'd a bín there." He then repeated proudly, "Eh ... stickín up for tha dad, tha's a reight little good un." He never did forget it.

The following day was Sunday, and Jack approached John asking, "What shift are you on this week, our John?"

"I'm on nights, Dad, how's that?"

"Well I was wondering, how would you like to have the week off and come working for me instead?"

John wasn't too keen on working nights, so was easily swayed, "Yeah, righto, Dad but what about my wage? If I don't go to work, then I don't get paid."

"That's all right, lad, I'll mék up tha wage and happen a bit on top, depending on how well I do."

"Right, Dad, fair enough, you're on. Anyroad, how come you need me, Dad, have you got a good deal going?"

"I have that lad and it's all credit to our Mary."

"Our Mary, how's that then?"

"Well, but for her I'd a never a gone into Prince of Wales last night; but as it turned out, that's when I made this deal."

"Oh last night, that was great, wasn't it Dad, really funny too, our Mary was telling us all about it this morning; we had a really good laugh about it."

"Yeah, me too, our John, it was really funny; mind, fat Pey didn't think so."

They had another good laugh about it before Jack changed the subject back to business. "Oh just one snag, lad, can you lend me fifty quid till end ó week? I'll pay you back along with your wage."

"You must be joking, Dad, I don't have that sort ó money! You'd best be asking our Jimmy rather than me."

As it happened, Jimmy had just returned to camp; he was stationed at Kirkham, so that was out of the question.

"Oh not to worry," replied Jack, "I can always borrow it off Reeder."

Sure enough, on Monday morning John set off in the wagon with his dad; the first place they headed for was Reeder's Scrap-yard. They went into the office together and Jack negotiated a deal with the businessman, who then handed over £50.

"Right then, our John, let's go, we've a lot of work to do."

"Fair enough, Dad, but where are we going?"

"We're going to a factory reight o'er moors above Todmorden near to a place called Hepstonstall; it's a good drive from here so we'd best get our skates on."

The drive there was through moorland country, a pleasant journey taking about one hour. On arriving at their destination, John once again accompanied his dad into the office and further negotiations took place. The deal was obviously about scrap-iron and Jack agreed to pay them £45 for the lot.

Once outside, John commented to Jack, "Hey, Dad, it seems a lot of money what you've just paid; how do you know how much stuff there is?"

"Don't worry about it, lad, I'm not that daft, I nipped out and had a reight good look whilst you was having a bite to eat in the canteen."

"Oh right, I thought it wasn't like you to hand o'er money just like that."

Jack gave a little chuckle murmuring, "You'll see, our John ... you'll see."

He saw all right, he couldn't believe his eyes; they'd been replacing some old looms, and great big heaps of scrap iron were stacked all over the factory yard.

"Bloomín éck, Dad, I didn't think there'd be this much, it'll ték us a month never mind a week to shift this lot."

Jack just chuckled again. "Aye you might be reight there; anyway, let's get cracking, we've got a busy time ahead of us."

They both got stuck in, and worked very hard. Jack was only small and despite his illness he did his fair share. Mind you, the fact that he'd just struck a good deal stimulated him, spurring him on. They got back to Reeder's Scrap-yard just after one o'clock and weighed in the first load.

Jack turned to John saying, "Come into the office with me again, our John, I want you to see how things work." For that single lorry load he got £32.

"You can knock that off what I owe you," said Jack, "and I'll be back with another load this afternoon."

Sure enough, father and son did another trip that afternoon and the load was similar to the first. Not only that, they did another two trips on Tuesday and two more on Wednesday as well. John was absolutely flabbergasted, six trips in three days, which meant his dad had taken about £190. After repaying Reeder and giving John £25, he'd still made £120 profit. John was more than satisfied, as he'd only worked three days and his weekly wage at the pit was only about £8. £120 was an enormous sum of money; even colliers working on the coal-face only earned about £20 a week.

John was really proud of his dad for being so clever and astute but, sadly, Jack didn't put the money to good use. He did give Winifred about £40 but then he went out on the rant treating all his bosom companions. Once again John thought just how clever his dad was, yet how foolish; he would have loved to have left the pit and gone into partnership with him but never had the confidence, always feeling that Jack would let him down.

It was after Jack had been out on one of his boozy escapades that something very amusing happened. One particular night, Winifred decided that she'd had enough of his antics; it was turned midnight and there was no sign of him so she decided to lock the door and go to bed.

At around two o'clock, Jimmy was awakened by his dad's voice shouting, "Winnie ... Winnie, please help me!"

Jimmy nudged John asking, "Can you hear mí dad, our kid, he seems to be in bother?" John was half-asleep and couldn't hear anything at first, but then there came a kind of wailing sound.

"Oh yeah, I can hear something now, our Jim," he replied, "but where is it coming from?"

Then, they heard a loud howling followed by an ear-splitting yell as their dad cried out, "Oh come on somebody, help me please!"

By now, Barry was awake. "Hey that sounds like mí dad," he said, "he must be in trouble; let's go down and help him."

"Yeah right," replied Jimmy, "but where is the noise coming from? I can't tell if it's from inside or outside the house."

"No, neither can I," responded Barry, "but there's only one way to find out."

the *broken biscuit*

All three of them crept downstairs trying not to disturb Mother and the girls, who slept in the back bedroom. Nonetheless, they soon found out that they were left with little choice. Jack wasn't in the house and on opening the front door he wasn't outside either. Nevertheless, there was a distinctive animal-like wail, which rent the night air, and it seemed to be coming from the ground level and, on looking down, they saw the most hilarious sight they'd ever seen. They didn't know whether to laugh or cry, as their dad was stuck in the cellar chute. He'd obviously tried to get into the house via the cellar after finding the front door securely bolted.

"Come on, you lot," he pleaded, "stop your laughing and get me outa here, it's not flamín funny!"

"Righto, Dad, don't worry about it," quipped Jimmy, "we'll have you out in a jiffy."

Jimmy then started issuing the orders. "Right, our Barry, you stay here and help me. John, you take a chair down the cellar to stand on and try shoving him out whilst me and our Barry pull from here."

They tried but after twenty minutes of huffing and puffing they still hadn't budged him. The trouble was that one of Jack's arms was stuck fast by his side, and it seemed to wedge even more every time they tugged and shoved. They were frightened of pulling him downwards for fear of wedging him deeper; the logical thing seemed to be to pull him out the same way that he'd gone in.

By this time, Winifred was downstairs awakened by the commotion. "Oh my God!" she exclaimed. "Now I've seen it all; I thought the escapade with the horse was the final straw, but now this!"

"What are we going to do, Mum?" asked Jimmy. "Are we going to have to send for the Fire Brigade?"

"No we're not, I've been shown up enough around here as it is. As far as I'm concerned he can stay there all night, it'll teach him a lesson."

"Oh no, Winnie, you can't do that," wailed Jack, "please get me outa here!"

"It's all right, Dad," put in Barry, "Mum's only joking, she wouldn't leave you like this."

"Oh yes I would if it means sending for the Fire Brigade; he's not bringing disgrace on to this house again."

"Oh come on, Winnie, do something please, it'll kill me if you leave me here all night!"

"You should have thought about that before you went out on your boozing spree, shouldn't you?"

Despite what she was saying though, she encouraged the lads to try again. Nevertheless, after another ten minutes it seemed hopeless; he was completely jammed in. By now, Mary, Barbara and many of the neighbours had been aroused by the rumpus.

"Oh, Mum, we're going to have to call the emergency services," said Mary, "or Dad might die."

"Yes all right, I suppose you're right," answered Winifred who was now quite concerned herself.

"Just hang on a minute, Mum, before you do that," said Jimmy. "I think I have an idea that might work."

"What's that then?"

"Well, if we fill a bowl with warm soapy water and douse Dad with it, it should lubricate him, and maybe we'll be able to pull him through then."

"Hey! If you're gonna wet me through make sure the water's not cold!" protested Jack.

Jimmy ran into the house and came back with a full bowl. Standing above his dad he said, "Right, Dad, just shut your eyes and put your head to one side and I'll let you have it."

"Thank you very much, our Jimmy; maybe I'll be able to do the same for you someday. Anyway, get the flamín thing over and done with!"

"Right, Dad, here goes," replied Jimmy as he threw the water straight at the chute.

John couldn't help laughing which in turn triggered off Barry and the girls, with Jimmy trying his best to keep a straight face. When they'd regained their composure, they got down to the serious business of trying to free their dad. There were obvious signs of movement but he kept crying out that his arm was still jammed.

"Sorry, Dad," muttered Jimmy, "but I'm going to have to douse you one more time, I think that'll do the trick."

the *broken biscuit*

"Aye all right but be quick about it and make it a bit warmer this time!"

Jimmy went through the same routine making sure this time that he reached parts not previously soaked. After this, Jack felt himself sliding gradually downwards but once again came to a full stop. Winifred knew then that there was no alternative but to call the Fire Brigade, so reluctantly made her way to the police telephone box. When they arrived it took them about forty minutes to free him, but luckily he was no worse for wear. He was as black as soot and looked like a drowned rat, but everybody had a real good hearty laugh now, including Winifred. It was a late night for everyone but nobody minded; it had been a night to remember for many a year.

Two more years passed, then it was Mary's turn to get married. It took place on St Valentines Day 1959. Eighteen months previously she'd met a handsome young man called Jack Clancy, whom she'd courted ever since.

It was shortly after this that Jack, Winifred's husband, did the unforgivable as far as Winifred was concerned: he actually had an affair with one of the neighbours; it wasn't too serious and didn't last long but for Winifred it was the final straw. She told him straight that he'd now killed off the last spark of love that she'd held for him over the years, and that he had to go. It happened shortly after the twins' twentieth birthday. He moved into a little house on Healey Wood Road just lower down from his sister Beatie.

John used to visit him regularly helping him to decorate the house. It was during this time that Jack asked him whether he was interested in taking over some of the factory contracts. John didn't take a lot of persuading; in fact, he was so keen on the idea that he gave in his notice at the pit. Ironically, though, within two months he received his call-up papers and had to go into the army to serve two years National Service. He was enlisted into the Royal Army Medical Corps, which incidentally had a bearing on his younger brother's life. Barry had always been inclined to train to be a male nurse but he'd never had the confidence. The fact that John was now in the Medical Corps finally persuaded him and, shortly after John's enlistment, he started his training at Burnley General Hospital.

In the meantime, Jack was still trying his best to get back on good terms with Winifred but she adamantly turned down his flirtatious advances. There was only Barry and Barbara at home now with Jimmy still in the air force; they both tried persuading Winifred to take their dad back but to no avail. Eventually though, in September she relented a little; it happened to be Barbara's birthday. Jack came round to the house with a present and a bunch of flowers.

He'd just put them on the table wishing Barbara a happy birthday, when Winifred made a comment, "That's nice of you, Jack, but I think the present would have sufficed. I don't really think she was expecting flowers as well."

"Oh the flowers are not for her, they're for you, my dear!" At that remark, both Barry and Barbara started laughing; it even brought a little smile to Winifred's face.

"Now that'll do, Jack, it's finished, you know it is."

"Eh, Winnie, how can it be finished after all we've been through? Anyway, this is the time of life when we should be enjoying ourselves, what with all the kids nearly fully grown and off our hands. Just think, love, we could start all over again, wouldn't that be nice?"

She was just about to retaliate, when both Barry and Barbara intervened, "Oh go on, Mum, give Dad another chance … please!"

"Anyroad, Mum, you have been rather unhappy just lately, haven't you?" added Barry.

Being outnumbered she relented, but there were conditions which she pointed out there and then. "Right, Jack, so you'd like us to start all over again, would you?"

"Oh that I would, love, more than anything, you know that."

"Right then, we'll try yet again but this time I'm going to take you at your word."

"How do you mean, love?"

"Well, we'll start right from the very beginning; in other words, you'll have to court me again, and that means picking me up and bringing me back here and then … going back to your own place."

"Oh but, Winnie, I …"

"Never mind, 'oh but, Winnie,' they're my conditions … take ém or leave ém!"

"Yeah right, Winnie, I'll ték ém, I'll ték ém!" He actually thought though that, like always, he'd be able to worm his way back into her affections not realising that this time, it wasn't going to be quite so easy.

She literally kept him to his word. They did start courting again just like young sweethearts and were like Derby and Joan reminiscent of their courting days in Morecambe, and he treated her like a lady in every respect. However, Winifred was older and much wiser now; she knew him too well and wasn't willing to stand for any of his old wily ways. It was funny in a way, because he'd take her out for the night and escort her home; she'd invite him into the house for a nightcap but afterwards, she'd politely ask him to go.

"But, Winnie," he protested, "this seems silly, haven't we just had a really good night and enjoyed each other's company?"

"I agree with you, Jack, we have but that's the way I want it to stay for now."

"Nay, Winnie, you're not really going to make me go all the way back to that lonely house on my own, are you?"

"I'm afraid I am, Jack, those were the conditions."

"Oh éck, love, you and your bloomín conditions, don't you love me any more?"

"Yes I do, Jack, I wouldn't go out with you, and you wouldn't be here right now if I didn't; but you've got to understand that I'm not willing to take anymore of your wanton ways. Quoting your own words, all the kids are nearly full grown now, and this is the time of our lives when we should be enjoying ourselves together; I just want to make sure that things are right, that's all."

She wouldn't be swayed, leaving him no alternative but to make his way back to Healey Wood Road. One Saturday night, John happened to be home on weekend leave and it seemed really strange to him. He arrived home about half past eleven just five minutes prior to his mum and dad arriving; the kettle had just boiled, so he made them both a brew and something to eat.

"All right, our John, it's grand to see you, lad; by éck but the army life must be doing you good, you haven't half filled out."

"Thanks, Dad, it's good to see you too; have you and mí mum had a good time tonight?"

"We have that, lad," he said turning to Winifred, "haven't we, love?" After finishing his brew, he turned to John again winking and dropping a hint, "Eh, I'll tell thi what, our John, that was a good brew too, I could just do with you bringín me and your mum one upstairs in the morning."

John was a little surprised as Winifred interrupted, "Never mind in the morning … you won't be here then."

"But, Mum," put in John, "surely mí dad's still not living on Healey Wood Road is he?"

"Oh yes he is and that's where he stays until we've got things sorted. And as for you, Jack, don't get yourself all nice and cosy because it's nearly time for you to leave."

Sure enough, five minutes later, he had to leave feeling all dejected.

John understood his mum's feelings, yet felt really sorry for his dad saying, "Come on, Dad, I'll walk along with you."

On the way, John mentioned how he felt about the situation. "Never mind, Dad, I think Mum's coming round a bit, it shouldn't be too long now."

"I don't know so much, lad, you know how stubborn your mum can be once she digs her heels in; I'm not calling her, mind, it's all my own doing." As they got almost to Healey Wood Road he added, "Right, our John, tha's walked far enough, thank you very much, that was very nice ó thi."

"Oh I enjoyed it, Dad, I don't get the chance much nowadays, do I?"

"You're reight there, lad, we don't see each other a reight lot, do we; how about having a drink with me tomorrow dinner in the Healey Wood?"

"I'd love to, Dad but I can't, I've got to be back in Plymouth by tomorrow night and I have to hitchhike all the way."

"All right, lad, fair enough. I'll tell thi what though, it's bín nice seeing thi."

John gave his dad a big hug replying, "Yeah, me too, Dad; anyway, next time I'm on leave we'll have a real good night out, right, Dad?"

"You're on, son. You're on."

At that, John set off for home after saying, "I'll see you later, Dad."

Sadly, although John did see his dad again, their planned outing together was not to be.

A week later in mid-December, Winifred moved out of Albion Street into 76 Moorland Road on the Rose Hill Estate. She spent her first Christmas in her new home; Jack kept up his calling and the courting continued. They spent many happy hours together and Winifred thoroughly enjoyed it. So did the rest of the family; they were all glad to see them so happy. Winifred was beginning to mellow and there was talk of Jack moving into Moorland Road with her; but it was not to be, as he was taken ill just before his fifty-second birthday. He collapsed suffering with abdominal pains and was rushed to hospital where he had an emergency operation for a burst appendix. His condition was so critical that he was transferred to Intensive Care where he remained for over a week.

John and Jimmy were both called home from the forces, and together with the rest of the family, they kept a constant vigil over him throughout the critical hours. To everybody's relief, he seemed to recover and was transferred to the main ward. However, complications set in; he had a blockage of the bowels, so had to have another operation and, once again, had to return to the Intensive Care Unit. After this second operation the whole family was in total shock, as he looked absolutely dreadful. The constant vigil was maintained by all members of the family, and there was never a time during this critical period when he was alone. Consequently, he did improve slowly, even to the point where he was once more transferred to the main ward. He was still very poorly but was quite aware of everything that was going on around him. It was during this time that he became rather sentimental, having all his family continuously by his bedside. His sisters visited him but he realised one thing: not one of his phony friends from the pub came to see him ... not one!

The really sad part was still to come. His condition improved and he appeared to be on the mend, leaving John no alternative but to return to his barracks. He'd only been back in Plymouth two days when on Saturday morning at nine o'clock, on the twenty-seventh of February 1960, he was told to report to the commandant's office where there was a telephone call awaiting him. On answering it, his sister Maureen was on the other end with the terrible news that their dad had just died! John was absolutely devastated and completely stunned; he went numb, it was just so unbelievable; as he put the phone down, it was obvious to everyone that something was wrong. His commanding officer was very understanding, immediately granting him compassionate leave.

The following is an account of Jack's last days as seen through the eyes of his son Barry, who at the time had just started his nursing training:

I had only been working at Burnley General Hospital for four months when my dad took ill with abdominal pains. I was actually on duty at the time when I heard that he'd been rushed to theatre for an emergency operation, then afterwards to Intensive Care. My family and I (including my two older brothers, who were both serving in the armed forces) stayed constantly by his bedside during this critical period. Within ten days, his condition improved, so he was transferred to the main ward. It saddens me to say this, but up till this time in my life, my father had never really taken to me, for what reason I do not know. However, a bond was formed between us whilst he was in hospital that will remain with me for the rest of my days. He was in the first bed on the left as one entered the ward, and although much better, he was still quite poorly. I carried out my everyday duties, but went to his bedside at every opportunity during my off-duty periods to encourage or even help to feed him. As the days went by, it became obvious that his condition was not improving, as he began to show apparent signs of abdominal obstruction. His stomach became quite distended, his wound was festering, appearing very inflamed, and he was in a lot of pain and discomfort, not being able to take anything by mouth. I was informed that he needed another operation immediately, so I went along to the ward just prior to him going to theatre. He appeared so small and frail in the little white operating gown, and he had a definite pinched look about him. He seemed pleased to see me giving me a nice tender greeting, then said something that took me by surprise.

He gently murmured, "Eh, our Barry, you look really good in that nurse's uniform, I'm reight proud ó thi."

"Oh thank you, Dad, that means a lot to me."

He then went on to say, "Do you know, our Barry, they want me to have another operation? I don't really want go to theatre again but I'm in so much pain that I've gone and signed a consent form; anyway, according to the nurses, I'm going to have it done this morning, and to tell you the truth, son, I'm really frightened."

Seeing the dismayed expression on his face, I felt choked, but I held back my feelings, trying to reassure him. "You'll be all right, Dad, it's for the best really."

"I don't know so much, our Barry, I don't think that I'll come through this operation,"

"Of course you will, Dad, of course you will. Listen, I'll ..."

He interrupted me, "No, I don't think so, it took every bit of my strength to come through the first one and I definitely feel much weaker this time ... I simply won't have the strength to fight it."

"But you will, Dad, I can assure you, and all the family's going to be there behind you, willing you on."

"Thanks, cock, thanks a lot, I've got to admit that helps. Anyway, will you please do something for me?"

"Course I will, Dad, anything; what is it?"

"Well I'm a bit nattered cós with it being such short notice, there's bín no time to get in touch with your mother. Will you give her this from me and tell her I love her," he said handing me a rather large Valentine card on which, he'd scrawled on the front in the most spidery handwriting, "I love you Win."

I could feel the tears welling up in my eyes but I managed to suppress them saying, "I will if you want, Dad, but you could give it to her yourself later you know."

By now, the pre-medication was taking effect; his eyes were starting to close, yet he still carried on murmuring, "I haven't bín a good dad to you, have I, cock?"

"Of course you have, Dad," I reacted. "Most of the time you were great, it was only when you'd had too much to drink that you got a bit stroppy."

"No no," he persisted, "I know you're just trying to be kind, but the truth is I haven't bín a good dad at all, but I promise thi, when I get better I'm goín to make amends. I'm gonna take you and the others out; aye, and I promise thi too, there won't be any more drinking either."

I felt really touched, as never in my life before had I known my dad like this; to me, he'd always been the macho type, never showing any outward signs of emotion. At that moment I thought that nothing could affect me more than this, but then he came out with something else that took me even more by surprise.

"Our Barry, what's that prayer that tha says when tha's really sorry for tha sins? I would like to say it now."

"Do you mean the Act of Contrition, Dad?" I answered quite dumbfounded.

"I don't know the name of the prayer, son, it's the prayer that tha says when tha's sorry for doing wrong."

I couldn't believe my own ears that Dad was actually talking and acting like this; I did know though that at this very moment, something very special was taking place.

"Right, Dad, if that's what you truly want."

"Yes, our Barry, that's what I truly want." He joined his hands in prayer, slightly bowed his head in reverence, then waited for me to commence.

He had a childlike appearance about him as I started to pray, "Oh my God, because Thou art so good." I paused a little whilst he repeated word for word very slowly and reverently; then continued in stages, "I am very sorry that I have sinned against Thee, and by the help of Thy grace, I will not sin again!"

After the Act of Contrition we both proceeded to say the "Our Father" then to my astonishment, he asked me to say the "Hail Mary". The reason that this took me back was because I didn't know that Dad had even heard of this prayer. I started, "Hail Mary," etc. and just like the first two prayers, he slowly and deliberately repeated it word for word after me.

Shortly after that, the nurses came and placed him on the trolley; I went along with them and held his hand up to him going into theatre.

"You'll be all right, Dad, you'll see," I reassured him once more.

By now, he was almost asleep, yet gently mumbled, "Yeah right, son, right."

It wasn't very long after that our Jimmy and John arrived, then Mum and my three sisters. Dad was in theatre quite a long while, but every one of us sat patiently and diligently awaiting the outcome. Once again, he was taken to intensive care; we had to wait a while longer until the nurses had settled him down before being allowed to see him. We all expected Dad to be in a poorly condition, but none of us were prepared for what we saw.

"Oh my God!" I thought, as his body was so full of tubes. There was one in his left arm giving a blood transfusion, one in his right arm for nourishment and a Ryles tube up his nose; oxygen was being administered via a face mask, he had another tube draining blood from his wound and also had a catheter in. He looked so frail and helpless as he fought for life with every breath he took; it didn't seem conceivable that he could possibly live.

Clearly remembering what he'd said to me just before going to theatre, I prayed silently, "Oh please God, please let him live, please don't let Dad die." As I looked around the room, it was obvious that all my family felt just as I did; we were all completely shocked.

Once again we all kept a constant vigil by his bedside; but then after a few days, to everyone's delight, he started to show signs of recovery again. Within a week, he was once again transferred to Ward One. I felt much happier now, and like before, I went to see him at every opportunity.

It was during one of these visits that he once again astounded me asking, "Our Barry, could you do me a special favour?"

"Of course I can, Dad, anything, just ask."

You could have knocked me over with a feather as he said so innocently and simply, "Could you send for a priest for me please, I would like to be baptised into the Catholic Faith."

"Are you sure, Dad, do you know what you're asking?"

He paused for a moment before replying, "Oh yes, our Barry, I know all right, I know only too well; you see, son, I want to be as one with my own family."

I felt choked trying my best to contain my emotions answering, "Righto, Dad, I'll arrange it for you."

The christening actually took place on the ward in the presence of a couple of nurses and me, who acted as witnesses; I felt completely honoured.

Throughout his illness, he hardly complained despite being in obvious pain and discomfort. One thing that was particularly touching to all the family at this critical time was that Mum, who had been temporarily separated from

Dad, tended to soften towards him during his suffering. They appeared closer now than they had been throughout my lifetime; they talked openly of their courting days together and I felt that there was a poignant rekindling of the embers of their young love.

Another very touching moment for me was one day whilst I was just readjusting his pillows for him, he took hold of my hand saying, "Do you know, cock, you've done more for me than all the other nurses put together?"

This wasn't strictly true, but I felt that what he really meant was the personal contact that had passed between us as father and son; not so much the moving of his pillows or other little things that I had done for him.

"Thanks, Dad, but I think you're trying to be kind now, all the nurses have worked extremely hard."

"Yeah they have, lad, but none more so than you."

It was then that he mentioned that none of his friends from the pubs had been to visit him adding, "You know, son, I've been the most stupid bloke in the world; I've had gold at my fingertips and just thrown it away. I've simply wasted lots of money on phony friends; they soon came out of their closets when I was spending freely, but where are they now? I've been blind, our Barry, I've had eyes, and yet I've been blind."

"Oh don't talk like that, Dad, you've been a good ..."

"No, our Barry, it's all right, cock, don't try to protect me. You see, the truth is I've been going out all these years buying friendship in the pubs when all the time my true friends were all around me in my own home." A little tear came to his eye as he added, "My own family."

After that, I went about my everyday duties and the rest of the family visited him every single day.

As he made progress he was taken off the critical list, therefore my brother John had to return to his barracks in Plymouth. I plainly remember him giving

Dad a hug and saying, "I'll see you later, Dad."

Two days later I was on the evening shift and I went to see my dad before going home. He was rather sleepy and appeared quite comfortable as he'd been settled down for the night. Not wanting to disturb him, I just whispered to myself, "Goodnight, Dad, see you tomorrow," not knowing that this was the last time I was going to see him alive. When I got home, Mum asked me how he was, and I told her everything seemed fine.

Nevertheless, next morning at three o'clock we were awakened by police officers, who conveyed the terrible news that he'd passed away.

I had the awful job of getting in touch with my sisters Mary and Maureen, who in turn got in touch with Jimmy and John.

I was completely devastated, losing my dad like this when, for the first time in my life, we'd just got to know each other and we'd been so close. The feeling was mutual throughout the family; we all drew comfort from one another.

Dad was buried from my mother's home on Moorland Road; for two days we all kept a constant vigil around the clock by his coffin. It was during this sad period that I confided in my brother John about my feelings towards my dad and what he had said to me on the ward.

"Eh, that was nice, our Barry."

"Yeah, it was, and especially so cós I always thought he didn't like me."

"Oh come on, our Barry, he more than liked you, he loved you, he just didn't show it, that's all."

"U-um, maybe, our John, but how come that he showed it with you, cós he did, didn't he?"

"Yeah, that's right he did but don't forget, our kid, that I used to help him a lot more than you did; don't you remember how I used to go on the cart with him and how

I used to look after Peggy? Mind you, our Barry, I'm not trying to say that I did more for him than you cós I didn't; you always seemed to care for Mum a lot more than I ever did, which in a way was helping Dad just as much. We're all made in different moulds, our kid, and I couldn't have done things the way you did. Anyway, I think that that's the way my dad saw it during his last few days; in other words, our Barry, he saw you for the real person you are."

The funeral took place on Wednesday, 3rd March; afterwards a reception was held in the Co-op tearooms; Mother put on a brave face ordering a nice meal and drinks.

She gave a little speech trying to make everyone feel better. "Right, I want everybody to have a little drink and enjoy this occasion, as that is what your dad would want. He wouldn't want to see any sad faces."

Like Mum, we all tried our best to put on a brave face but it was obviously easier said than done.

After that day, we all had to get on with our everyday lives; it was never ever going to be the same again; still, my dad left me with memories that I will always cherish for the rest of my life.

16: *the* retirement years

After the funeral, Winifred returned to her new home on Moorland Road. It seemed so strange that Jack would never again come calling on her. Despite herself, she couldn't help but reflect on her life since meeting him in Morecambe.

"Well, Winifred," she thought, "whatever happened to those dreams you had as a young girl, things didn't work out just as you planned, did they?" Her emotions were mixed; she was happy, sad and angry all at the same time. Dreaming on, she said to herself, "He was certainly right when he mentioned, 'everything we've been through', u-um, most of that wasn't very good either; anyway, I'm just forty-seven years old and look at me, a widow already. Still, God's good and works in mysterious ways; I wouldn't have had my children but for him and I wouldn't swap them for anything in this world."

Facing up to reality, she realised that things were not going to be easy for her. This became more apparent the following week when she received notification of her widow's pension from the social services department. Due to Jack never putting on any National Insurance stamps, the total allowance was a paltry four shillings a week, paid monthly in arrears. Nonetheless, Barry and Barbara were still at home, helping her as much as they could, and Jimmy and John sent her a small allowance from the forces. John had been posted abroad to the Cameroons in West Africa, where he stayed for the duration of his time in the army up to being demobbed.

It was about this time that Winifred went working at Bellings on an assembly line making electric fires and other appliances. It wasn't exactly the job of her choice but still, she was to work there up to her retirement. Whilst there, she still put her literary skills to many good uses; one of these happened to be another writing competition sponsored by the *Lancashire Evening Telegraph*. The rules of the contest were similar to the one she had won previously in the *News of the World* in that:

It had to be a true story in every aspect.
It had to be about a real person.
The prize went to the person being written about, not the author.
The two main differences were that it had to be brief and the title had to be 'HAPPY HOUSEWIFE'.

This got Winifred to thinking about her daughter. Mary had been married to Jack Clancy just a few months when he collapsed at work, having to spend quite a long time in Marsden Hospital. During his stay there, Mary went into Bank Hall Maternity Hospital where she had a little son, whom she called Michael. It was a very happy event but all the same, she felt a little despondent as all the other young fathers called upon and paid tribute to their wives and doted on their new babies. This put Winifred in mind of when Barry was born and Jack hadn't been able to visit her. Nevertheless, Mary put on a brave face throughout her stay there.

On reading the article, Winifred decided to write about Mary, who was expecting her second child. Before the evening was through, she had written and posted off the following:

I know a little housewife, just twenty-one years of age, mother of a thirteen-month old boy, and soon to be a mother again.

She had only a few months of happy married life when her husband collapsed at work; consequently, she carried on with her job as a weaver until the birth of her child.

In the maternity home, she must have felt most unhappy when she saw other young dads admiring their first babies whilst her husband was in hospital.

But the bright, flashing smile was always there ... and she was compensated by the gift of a baby boy.

Although they have a great worry paying their way
in life, they are a very nice and happy couple. Always,
the girl feels for and tries to help anyone in need of help.

Various events and fashion shows were presented as a prelude to
the final; Bryan Johnson, a singer, was host to more than fifteen-
thousand East Lancashire housewives. The grand finale was held at
King George's Hall in Blackburn where there was a banquet for the
finalists and their relatives. The Mayor and Mayoress of Blackburn
were in attendance, as were many more prominent figures who were
acting as judges. Mary's new baby was due to be born that same day,
so she was actually quite large; still, the bright smile was forever
present.

As it happened, Winifred didn't go to the occasion, as she was
babysitting for Mary. She'd declined the invitation, letting Mrs.
Clancy, Mary's mother-in-law, take her place. Still, Mary's husband
Jack was with her holding her hand and giving her lots of support.

The moment of truth arrived and to the delight of everyone
present, the judges proclaimed Mary the winner. Even the runners-up
were happy stating that she truly deserved to win; her bright happy
smile had captivated them all. Mary went up on to the stage where the
Mayoress presented her with a cheque for £25 and a great big hamper,
which was lined with blue silk and contained many varieties of food
plus some wine.

"Now I'll be able to buy the new baby a complete layette," she
exclaimed after getting over her surprise.

"But, Mary," teasingly commented one of the judges, "the money
is supposed to be spent on yourself."

"Oh all right then," she replied with a contented smile on her face,
"I suppose I'll buy myself a frilly negligee then."

The entire crowd readily laughed at that and especially those sat
near to her husband Jack.

Winifred was thrilled when Mary told her the good news and they
embraced each other affectionately. The prize-money and the food
hamper helped out the young couple a great deal towards the
impending happy event. But babies take no heed of calendars and

the **broken biscuit**

Mary actually went nineteen days past her due date before giving birth to another baby boy. She had chosen the name of her first son, so on this occasion her husband picked the name – Dale.

After finishing his stint in the army, John was hoping to take over the factory contracts that Jack used to have, but regrettably this was not to be, as many other contractors had already done just that. He visited the management of all the different firms, which Jack had dealt with, but to no avail, there was no chance of getting the contracts back again. He was rather disappointed but didn't dwell on it too much, and began working for Bruce Leaver, a building contractor.

Two years passed since Jack's death, Winifred had started to go out for the odd game of bingo at the Empire, the Mechanic's Institute and other places. Still quite slim and attractive, she had quite a few admirers but was never really interested in any of them. One gentleman in particular, who was ten years older than her, kept asking her out; he was a retired businessman, always very smart and his name was Alec. After a lot of wooing she finally relented and from then on they spent quite a lot of time together. He was a very nice person with a pleasant personality and he absolutely doted on Winifred. He took her over to Bacup many times where they had a few good nights out in places like the Conservative Club with Winifred's sister Mary and her husband Harold. Alex lavished everything upon Winifred; as far as he was concerned, she could have had the world. She only had to gaze into a shop window and make a passing remark about something and it was hers.

He was clearly quite well-off, having a large beautiful bungalow in Worsthorne, and a brand new Rover car. He was generous to a fault and not just with Winifred either; when they were in other people's company, he wouldn't let anyone else buy a drink. Nevertheless, this was one aspect of his nature that Winifred didn't like at all; in fact it used to infuriate her, as she thought it a complete waste of money. There was one particular event, which almost brought matters to a climax. It happened on his sixtieth birthday. He hired a room in the Bacup Conservative Club and put on a special buffet. She was quite enjoying the occasion, as all her relations were invited; but then, he did something that she didn't like. The club was packed to capacity, and he went and ordered drinks all round, including the committee men and the bar staff.

In spite of his good nature, Winifred did not take advantage of him; in fact, she put a stop to him buying her anything at all. Not only that, she asked him not to spend money so freely in her company, as she felt he was just trying to impress her.

"But, Winifred, that's not true; it's just that I really think the world of you and I want to spoil you."

"U-um, is that not the same thing?" she quipped.

"No, not really, at least not in my eyes."

"Look, Alec, I know your intentions are good and that you mean well, but you've got to understand that I've never been used to having much money, and it grieves me to see it spent so freely on frivolous things."

"All right, Winifred, I take your point, but can I just say, what's the point of me having plenty of money if I can't spend it on somebody who I think the world of?"

"Yes I can see that, but all the same, I can't help feeling the way I do; it's just something inside me."

"Righto, Winifred, I'll see what I can do, I promise; I don't want to get on the wrong side of you, do I?" he said with a boyish smile.

Poor Alec, he didn't stand a chance, Winifred was too set in her ways and far too strong a character for him. He tried his best not to spoil her but it just seemed to be second nature to him. It didn't take too long before he got on the wrong side of her again, finally putting an end to their relationship; it began so innocently too. He was sat in her house one day and overheard a conversation between John and Barry, who were stood in the kitchen. John had recently bought a car on hire purchase and the engine had seized up.

"Hey, Barry, do you know if our Jimmy's coming home today?" he asked. "I could do with borrowing £140 off him."

"No I don't think so, cós he said that he would be on guard duty this weekend," replied Barry.

"Oh blast, it would happen this week! Oh well never mind, I'll just have to nip down to the bank to see if I can borrow it."

At that remark, Alec intervened, "Excuse me, John, I wasn't listening in but I couldn't help but overhear what you were talking about. If you're stuck for some money, I'll lend it to you; you can repay me back at so much a week."

Before John had time to reply, he heard Winifred's voice, "You'll do no such thing, Alec, if he wants his car repairing, he'll either save up for it or take out a loan himself."

"Oh come on, Winnie, it's only a loan, he'll still have to repay it; it's just that it'll save him quite a lot of money on bank charges and interest."

"That's not the point, Alec, he's young and strong, and fit enough to go out and earn it; I don't want you making it easy for him."

She was actually cross with him but John spoke up on his behalf, "Oh come on, Mum, Alec didn't mean anything by it; he was only trying to help out in his way, and I would have paid him back, you know that."

"Yes you would, I'd have seen to that," she said rather sharply.

"Now don't be like that, Mum, there's no cause for it," he replied slightly annoyed.

"Whoa, just hold on a minute, I don't want you falling out on my account," interrupted Alec. "I get the message, it won't happen again."

This was the way of things; even though Alec was a decent man, Winifred didn't have any loving feelings towards him, and she couldn't pretend otherwise. It was a shame really, but she actually found him rather dull and boring; despite taking her to many nice places and shows, she found it a very uninteresting and monotonous relationship. She didn't take advantage of his wealth and generosity though, telling him in the best way she could that she wanted to finish their association. He was heartbroken begging her to carry on, implying that their love would grow over the years. John hadn't been too keen on his mother going out with another man when she'd first met Alec, but over the months he'd grown to like him. He pointed this out to Winifred but it made no difference; she'd made up her mind and that was it. Despite not wanting to hurt Alec, she unintentionally did something rather hurtful as she engaged in a little bit of idle chatter.

She was stopped one day in the street by a lady, who asked, "All right, Winifred, are you not going out with Alec any more?"

"No, Ada, I'm not, we finished about two weeks ago."

"You must be crazy, Winnie, he used to lavish gifts on you left right and centre; I only wish I could find a fellow like him."

"Well, you're welcome to him as far as I'm concerned, I'm just not interested."

"Are you serious? You could live in comfort for the rest of your life if you married him, you'd want for nothing."

"U-um, maybe so, but I couldn't do that, I just don't have any loving feelings towards him at all."

"Bloomín éck, Winnie, what difference does that make? I know what I'd do if I was in your shoes?"

"Ah well you're not, are you, Ada? Anyway, if you like him so much, why don't you ask him out yourself?"

"I'll tell you what it is, just tell me where he lives and I'll do just that."

Without thinking, Winifred gave the woman Alec's address.

She didn't hear any more about it till one day, when she was shopping in the town centre. Whilst she was looking in a shop window, someone tapped her on the shoulder; on turning, she saw Alec.

"Hello, Winifred, how are you keeping?" he asked very politely.

"Oh very well, Alec, and you?"

"Oh, I'm all right, Winifred, but I've got to say that I am rather disappointed in you; I thought our friendship meant more to you than it obviously did."

"But, Alec, I thought I'd made my feelings perfectly clear to you."

"Oh I'm not talking about you packing me up, Winifred, I could go along with that; but what I don't like is you trying to pass me on to one of your friends." His tone changed as he quietly told her off, "What did you think you were playing at, sending that woman around to my home, and who the flamín éck was she anyway; she made me feel like an old dishcloth being handed down?"

Winifred realised she was in the wrong, and felt a little ashamed. "I'm sorry, Alec, it was unintentional and I promise that it won't happen again."

Alec smiled a little saying, "Oh well, I'm glad that's out of the way; it's been weighing on my mind quite a bit, I thought it seemed out of character. Anyway, Winifred, is there any chance of you coming for a coffee with me for old time's sake?" She accepted his invitation and they went to one of the local cafés. They'd been sat down about ten minutes when he brought up the subject of their recent association.

"Well, Winifred, it's really nice to see you again, I've got to admit that I've been thoroughly miserable ever since we finished our relationship." He paused a little appearing quite nervous, then added, "You know something … you'd make me the happiest man in the world if we could put this behind us and start again; how about it, Winifred, what do you say?"

Under the circumstances she felt rather awkward but still wouldn't be swayed, replying, "No, I'm sorry, Alec, I think you are a very nice considerate person, but I just can't do as you ask; I like you as a friend but nothing more." The despondent look on his face said it all as he realised that this really was the end of their alliance; sadly, she hardly ever saw him again after that.

The years rolled on and one day Winifred was reading an article in the *Burnley Express* that changed her life yet again. It had been written by one of the nuns of St Mary's Convent and the heading was "The rights of the unborn child." The nun's name was Sister Mary Veronica and, according to the article, she was acting on behalf of the unborn child, who in her opinion had no voice. It went on to talk about the true horrors of abortion and the far-reaching consequences. Sister Mary Veronica was not condemnatory, in her way she merely tried to give guidance to the poor expectant mothers. Her words did not fall on to infertile ground, but became embedded at the very moment of reading into the mind and soul of Winifred. She didn't realise it immediately though; in fact it seemed to have the opposite effect, as it made her remember the time when she had been pregnant with Barbara. The more she read, the angrier she became; by the time she had finished reading the passage, she was furious.

"What does she know about suffering?" she mumbled to herself all choked up. "She's a nun, she's had a sheltered life within a convent; how can she possibly have the remotest idea what it's like to be a young pregnant mother with all the anxieties that go with it? She can't possibly know what it's like to be hungry, not knowing where the next crumb's coming from." Her mind went back to when she was pregnant with the twins and then the awful time when she took quinine when she was pregnant with Barbara. "Yes, I almost killed myself at the time but all the same, under similar circumstances, who knows, maybe I would do the same again! Anyway, where was the Church and the nuns when I needed them?"

Barry happened to be in the kitchen and he could hear his mother murmuring away to herself, so asked, "Is everything all right, Mum, has something upset you?"

He noticed the hurt, bitter look on her face as she replied, "Yes, something has upset me, it's this flamín article in the paper. There's a bloomín nun, who's gone and written a column on abortion and the rights of the unborn child; who the flamín éck does she think she is?"

Barry read the item before saying, "She's not condemning anyone, Mother, she just appears to be speaking up for the unborn child, who has no voice of its own."

"That's not the point, our Barry," she answered in a shaky voice still full of bitterness, "she has no right to say things like this because she's never been in the position and never likely to be either. Another thing, they come out with these things but they're never there when you really need them; they make me bleeding sick!"

Barry could see that she was becoming quite worked up over the issue, so tried to placate her. "Look, Mum, it's no good upsetting yourself over it; besides, there's not a right lot you can do about it."

"Oh is there not? Well, we'll see about that," she replied fiercely as she started to put her coat on.

"Oh no," Barry quietly protested, "you're not going where I think you're going, are you, Mum?"

"If you mean the convent, then yes I am, I'm going to give this here Sister Mary Veronica a piece of my mind!"

Barry tried to talk her out of it, but there was no stopping her as she stomped out of the house. By the time Winifred reached the convent she was angrier than ever because she'd been brooding all the way there on the bus. Not to help matters, one of the nuns was quite formal, asking her to wait in the reception, thus making her more resentful by the minute. Her imagination took over as she conjured up an image of a rather large boisterous dominant nun with a holier-than-thou attitude. The more she thought about it, the more furious she became; by now, she was absolutely fuming inside and determined to give the nun a piece of her mind.

Things didn't work out exactly to plan though. At that moment the door opened; Winifred was quite taken aback by the unassuming frail little Irish nun, who introduced herself as Sister Mary Veronica. For a moment, Winifred's anger seemed to subside and she was actually at a loss for words. Nevertheless, after the initial setback, the resentment within her returned and she set about her task.

"Excuse me, Sister, but could I have a word with you about the caption you've written in the paper concerning abortion?"

"Certainly you may," she replied very politely, "just come with me please and we'll discuss it in the lounge."

Winifred really gave the little nun a piece of her mind, telling her of her own past when she'd been pregnant with Barbara and how she'd tried to abort her. She just went on and on telling her of all the poverty and hardship and how her own little ones had missed out on so many things; also about Jack and the constant struggle to survive, when she didn't know where the next meal was coming from. Sister Mary Veronica sat there so passively just listening to everything that she had to say. The tranquillity of the little nun had a strange calming effect on Winifred but still, she wanted to get her point across.

"With all due respect, Sister," Winifred pointed out in a voice so choked up she could hardly speak, "what do you know about suffering, and what right have you to write about these things? You've never been married, or ever known the pain of childbirth; you can't possibly begin to understand what motherhood is like. Your article brought back the nightmare of my irrevocable past when I was a young pregnant mother under terrible duress. The frightening truth is that under similar circumstances, I would probably do the same thing again." She went on a little more until finally the painful memories caused her to break down. She had said her piece and got it off her chest, but in no way was she prepared for the little nun's reply.

"Mrs Cowell," she said with simplicity and sincerity, "but for the grace of God, it could so easily have been me."

It was such an honest non-judgmental reply that it touched Winifred's heart right to the very core. She felt in that instance that this little frail unassuming nun was indeed someone very special. She also felt very humble and was overwhelmed by a need to apologise for saying the things she had.

"I'm awfully sorry, Sister, for going on at you the way I did, it's just that your write-up really did upset me."

"That's all right, Mrs Cowell, you'd every right to be upset; I'd have probably done the same thing myself if I'd been in your shoes."

"Thank you for understanding and listening to me the way you did."

"Oh think nothing of it, Mrs Cowell, it's me who should be thanking you, the way you've enlightened me about so many things."

"That's nice to hear, but whilst I'm here do you think you could tell me a little about your cause?" She then added, "Oh by the way, you may call me Winifred if you like."

"I'll do just that, Winifred, now let's see, where do I start? First of all, the most fundamental part is that the unborn baby has not got a voice of its own, therefore it cannot speak up for itself. I feel very strongly that there is a need to act on its behalf; in other words, we have to be its voice and speak up for it. Quoting your own words, Winifred: you have just told me how when baby Barbara kicked in your stomach, you felt as if she was screaming out loud, that she was ready to come into this world."

These words touched Winifred; she was now completely won over and ready to join forces with this unique person. "In what way do you intend to help these unfortunate young women?" she enquired.

"I have lots of plans for them but first of all I would like to open a refuge for battered wives and other unfortunate ladies, where they can retreat to in dire emergencies."

Winifred's first response to this was not very enthusiastic as she pointed out, "Oh I don't know if I could help with that, Sister; in fact I actually feel a little resentful. That may sound awful but you see, I never ever got help from anyone when I needed it."

"But, Winifred, can't you see, that's my very point? Wouldn't it have been so much better for you and your young ones if only the help had been there for you?"

Winifred couldn't argue about that and decided there and then that she would help out in any way she could. From that day on, they teamed up working in partnership together running raffles, jumble sales and many charitable events for the cause of the unborn child and many other deserving causes.

Meanwhile back home in Moorland Road, Barry had been patiently awaiting his mum's return. She arrived about two hours later and, to his delight, she was in a much more placid mood. It wasn't just her change of mood either; there was something different about her. She appeared to be deep in thought and there was a perceptible change in her whole countenance.

"Did you see Sister Mary Veronica, Mum?" he asked.

Winifred didn't appear to have heard him so he repeated the question.

Almost imperceptively she replied quietly in just one word, "Yes," followed by silence.

After a moment, Barry asked curiously, "Well, Mum, what did she say?"

She paused in thought before saying quietly, "It was strange, Barry, really strange; I went down to the convent so full of fire and fury, and I was completely bowled over by this tiny slip of a person. She's not in good health herself apparently, suffering from kidney problems, and yet all her thoughts seem to be for others in need. Sincerity and goodness just shone from her, completely winning me over, and I've decided that I'm going to help her from now on."

"And how are you going to go about that, Mum?"

"Oh well, she's got a few schemes in mind, one being that she's planning to open a refuge for battered wives and expectant mums. At first, I wasn't too keen on the idea, as nobody helped me during my difficult times, but she pointed out just how much I would have appreciated it, had help been available."

"There wasn't a right lot you could say to that, was there, Mum?"

"No there wasn't; in fact, that's what decided me."

"That's all right but going back to the question, how are you going to help her?"

"Well, I've promised that I'll write a few letters to different bodies and we're going to organise a few jumble sales and things like that. She also wants me to try and arrange the picking up of furniture from certain addresses and its transportation to people in need. That's where Jimmy and John will come in handy; I'll be able to call upon them to help out."

This was the start of Winifred and Sister Mary Veronica's special friendship and wonderful partnership together. It was to last for many years and they would forever be organising raffles, jumble sales or any other type of charity event enabling them to raise money. The money not only went to the cause of the unborn child but also to many other worthy charities in many different parts of the world. Wherever there was a need, Sister Mary Veronica and Winifred were there to help as much as they possibly could.

It was during one of the charity events that John made his acquaintance with the little nun, and an unforgettable experience it was. Winifred and Sister Mary Veronica had organised an auction in a large club on Manchester Road near to St Mathew's Street. Winifred asked John to collect some furniture and deliver it to the auction room. After unloading his wagon, he decided to stay a while to watch the proceedings. During the bids he acquired a little picture frame for £4. It wasn't worth that much but he wasn't bothered, as it was for a worthy cause. He might not have been, but Sister Mary Veronica was sat next to him and she was.

"Oh please, may I have a look at what you have just bought?" she enquired curiously. John turned to see this little pale-faced nun by his side and was immediately struck by her frail, yet friendly face.

"Certainly, by all means, scrutinise it at your leisure!" he joked.

"Oh it's a pretty little thing," she said in a pronounced Irish accent, "but surely to goodness, you didn't pay £4 for this, did you? It's not worth that much."

"Yes, I know that, Sister, but it doesn't matter, it all goes to help the cause, doesn't it?"

"Oh that's all very well, but it matters to me, young man, I'm not having that," she responded. To his surprise, she rummaged through her purse, and then thrust £2 into his hand.

"There, that's more like it, we don't want to rob anybody, do we?" John protested but to no avail, for the little nun, though only frail, was very persistent. After the initial meeting, she asked, "Would you be Winifred's son by any chance?"

"That's right," he replied, "and you must be Sister Mary Veronica, I've heard quite a lot about you from my mum."

"Oh that's nice, all good I hope?"

He gave a little smile. "Yes, Sister, that's for sure."

At that moment, Winifred approached them. She was pleased, as the sale was almost finished and they had done quite well. "Hello, Sister, I see you've already met my son John?"

"Yes I have, Winifred, and a pleasure it's been too."

The compliment made John blush. "Take no notice, Mum, I can assure you, the pleasure's been mine."

"I'm sorry to break up your conversation, our John, but could you run me home? I have an appointment to keep."

"Yeah, of course Mum, but I'm in my wagon."

"I'm not bothered about that," she replied adding, "Could you possibly give Sister Mary Veronica a lift down to the convent as well?"

"Yeah, of course I can, Mum, I don't mind if she doesn't."

"Of course I don't mind," put in the little nun, "that would be wonderful, I've never been in a wagon in all my life."

It turned out to be rather awkward because the lock on the passenger side was stuck and the door wouldn't open. John explained that they would have to get in the driver's side and scramble over to the passenger seat. It was a sight to behold as the little nun climbed over the gear-stick clutching her habit as her rosary beads dangled in mid-air. He dropped his mother off first before making his way down Manchester Road to the convent.

To his surprise, Sister Mary was in her element and kept repeating, "Oh this is marvellous, I've never been in a wagon before, never, never, never!"

What amused him even more was that she asked if he would drive through the Town Centre explaining that it would be wonderful if some of her colleagues espied her. "I'll be the envy of the convent for weeks," she laughed. "I've never been as excited in the whole of my life before, I think this is absolutely wonderful ... oh if only the Reverend Mother could see me now!"

John couldn't help but smile and was very impressed by her playful sense of humour. "My, she's so down to earth, so human, no airs and graces at all," he thought as he made his way through the heart of the town.

This was their first meeting, but from that moment on they became very close friends. After that, she called upon him many times in connection with the charity work. He could now understand why his mother loved this little nun so much. His relationship with this unique person was also to be very special; in fact, he thought she was the kindest, gentlest, most sincere person that he'd ever met.

As the years passed, Sister Mary Veronica and Winifred's friendship blossomed all the more and a strong bond was formed between them. Winifred never did socialise much but Sister Mary Veronica introduced her to a different social circle altogether. On odd occasions, they would go to the Opera House in Manchester along with other nuns and guests. Winifred never felt as pampered, as Sister Mary Veronica would take a picnic basket containing sandwiches, fruit and a flask of coffee.

On odd occasions the little nun would say, "Here's your coffee, Winifred, and seeing that it's such a cold day, I've just added a touch of rum."

Another time Winifred went to the toilet at half time and was away for quite a while.

On enquiring where she'd got to, Sister Mary Veronica replied, "Oh knowing Winifred, she's probably down in the foyer doing a sale."

This was the kind of friendship they had, but sadly, the poor little nun's illness worsened, gradually turning to chronic renal failure. Consequently, Winifred had a lot more responsibility and ran everything from her own home. Still, Sister Mary Veronica battled on helping out whenever she could, but as time passed she was confined to her bed more and more. There was one very special honour in particular that was bestowed upon her but due to her failing health, it was too hard a task. Nevertheless, not to be beaten, she called upon Winifred.

"Winifred, I know you're extremely busy but could I possibly ask you to do a great favour for me and the cause?"

"Of course you can, Sister, what is it?"

"Well you know that I've been selected as a delegate for Nelson to present a petition for the unborn child to the Houses of Parliament?"

"Of course I know and in my opinion, they couldn't have chosen a better person."

"That's just the point, Winifred, you see I'm not well enough to travel all the way to London and I was wondering if you would take my place?"

"Oh I'm sorry, Sister, but I couldn't do that."

"Come come, Winifred, of course you can do it; you write well; you speak with authority and certainly know how to get your point across."

"Yes maybe so, but that's not the reason; you see I don't think it would be fitting because of my past; I'm sure you could find a much worthier person than me."

"Nonsense, Winifred!" she replied in her rich Irish accent. "I'm afraid I don't go along with you there; I don't know anyone more fitting and worthy than you. It is precisely because of your experiences, both good and bad, that you above all others should go. Nobody else in this world realises the sovereignty and dignity of the unborn child more than you yourself."

Once again, Winifred was won over by the serenity and humility of the little nun and agreed to do as she asked.

The day of the delegation arrived, which turned out to be eventful in more ways than one for Winifred. She wasn't in the best of health herself, as she had been suffering quite badly from arthritis and was shortly due to go into Wrightington Hospital for a hip replacement. Still, she made her way to the convent where there were other lady delegates, who were representing various towns. It soon became clear to Winifred that most of them were well versed in this kind of activity. It also became quite clear to her that they were rather aloof and not very welcoming.

"Never mind," she thought as she made her way to the coach, which was to take them to Piccadilly Railway Station in Manchester, "my mission today is much more important than making friends of the elite."

She was actually struggling to get on the coach until a kindly gentleman assisted her. He introduced himself as Mr. Mee saying he was in charge of the party of delegates for the surrounding areas. Her seat on the coach was amongst the other ladies but she wasn't really brought into the conversation. No matter, she didn't mind; in fact, she preferred it that way. Be that as it may, once they'd reached Manchester, she needed their assistance.

"Excuse me, ladies, do you mind if I join you?" she asked. "I'm not too sure what to do or where to go!"

"No not at all," one curtly replied, "just follow us, we're heading for platform four."

Winifred tried keeping up with them but struggled, as her hip was giving her a lot of pain. Consequently, the main party scurried up some steps leaving her on her own. She was a little concerned because she hadn't quite heard what platform number the lady had said.

"Oh dear," she muttered, "I'll have to rest, this flamín suitcase is bloomín heavy."

She just sat there looking at the steps ahead wondering how she was going to climb them. The platform was almost deserted now, but there was a solitary gentleman standing just a few yards away. Without giving it too much thought, she approached him and explained her dilemma to him.

"Oh you'll be all right, my dear," he kindly replied looking at his watch, "don't worry yourself, the London train doesn't leave for another thirty-five minutes yet. Allow me to carry your bag for you and I will escort you there."

On reaching the steps, he could see she was struggling, so took her arm and gently helped her. As they walked over the bridge Winifred noticed that quite a lot of people were staring at them.

"What the bloomín éck are they looking at?" she thought to herself. "He's a very smart gentleman, I know that, and quite good-looking. U-um, perhaps they're wondering what he's doing with an old woman like me."

When they reached the platform, it was packed with lots of delegates from other towns. The first group was from Liverpool, and very friendly people they were too.

The kind gentleman approached the group asking, "Excuse me, I presume that you are all delegates making your way to London?"

"That's right sir," replied one of the ladies, "how can we help you?"

"Well, could you please take this little lady under your wing; she's a delegate but seems to have lost her companions; she requires some assistance, as she has difficulty in walking."

"No problem at all, she can come along with us."

"Thank you very much, that's very kind of you," he said, then turned back to Winifred politely saying, "Cheerio, my dear, it's been very nice meeting you, I hope your delegation goes well; I've no doubt that it will."

As soon as he'd gone a small crowd gathered around Winifred asking, "Hey, where did you meet him, did you get his autograph then?"

"His autograph, why, who the bloomín éck was he anyway?" replied Winifred naively.

This created a lot of laughter as one woman said in a broad Liverpool twang, "You must be joking! Who was he? ... That was Charlton Heston!"

"Oh was it?" replied Winifred quite unimpressed. "All I know is that he was a perfect gentleman."

From that moment on, the group really took to her, and vice versa. She travelled along with them all the way to London, thoroughly enjoying their company. On reaching London, however, there was a rather bemused Mr Mee waiting for her on the platform.

"Oh thank goodness for that, Winifred, I wasn't sure whether we'd left you behind in Manchester or not, I was getting quite worried."

"Oh thank you very much for your concern, Mr Mee," she replied courteously, but couldn't resist adding, "I don't suppose anybody else was worried though."

They all gathered together and headed for the Houses of Parliament where they had a long wait in the House of Commons reception hall prior to lobbying their MPs. Eventually, it was Winifred's turn to state her case, during which she both asked and answered many questions precisely and confidently. By the end of the session, she was very tired and decided to find somewhere comfortable to rest, which happened to be close to where the Burnley group of ladies was sitting.

"Excuse me, Winifred, you look tired, did you find the ordeal rather trying?" asked one of them.

"Yes, I am tired and yes, I did find it rather trying," she replied quite indignantly, "in fact, I have found quite a few things rather trying today."

She started to walk away but then bethought herself, "It's no good being sarcastic with them, Winifred, that achieves nothing. No, if you're going to say something, then do it properly."

Turning back to them she very calmly and politely said, "Excuse me, ladies, you all appear to have been given a gift, as you all seem to have a great deal of confidence in these sort of matters." She paused for a moment before adding, "It's such a shame that you lack the quality to share it with others. Anyway, that's all I have to say, I must rest now because like you've noticed, I am very tired."

Winifred didn't give it another thought until they were ready for boarding the train back to Manchester. There she met up with the friendly Liverpool group again and decided to join them on the return journey. Just before boarding the train someone tapped her on the shoulder.

On turning, it was one of the Burnley ladies who said, "Winifred, will you please accept my apology? I didn't realise that you had a bad hip and were awaiting surgery. I've just been having a word with Mr Mee and he's put me in the picture."

"Now now," replied Winifred, "why should that make a difference; surely it was plain to see that I was at a loss this morning, yet none of you offered your hand in friendship?"

"All right, Mrs Cowell, I own up, I was in the wrong; I see that now. Could I please offer my hand in friendship now and ask you to come and sit with us?"

"Thank you very much, I accept your apology, but if you don't mind, I came here with these friendly people and I intend to return with them."

Notwithstanding, when Winifred rejoined the Burnley group on the coach back to Burnley, they were all much more receptive.

"Mr Mee has been telling us about all the work you do with Sister Mary Veronica," one of them enquired.

"That's right," replied Winifred still on her guard, "why do you ask?"

"Well, we were just wondering, are you in with the Ladies' Committee?"

"No, I'm afraid not, I do all my own organising, running everything from my own home."

"Good heavens! How do you go about all the jumble when you're having a jumble sale then?"

"Oh I get different members of my family to collect it for me from various places and I have a spare bedroom in my house where I store it till the day of the sale. I then call upon my family again to take it all to the sales rooms."

"How do you manage then; surely, you need a lot of assistants to help during the sale?"

"Oh that's no problem either, the family help out plus I have lots of willing neighbours, who help out making tea, working on the stalls or even taking money at the door."

"Oh, Mrs Cowell, do you think you could put our names down on your list of helpers? We'd love to join you in your cause."

"Of course I will, but you will have to muck in like everybody else, working on the stalls or whatever is required of you."

The ladies agreed to this and from that day on they were regularly in attendance.

A little more time passed and in 1982 Sister Mary Veronica's condition worsened to the point where she had to be admitted to Burnley General Hospital. Whilst a patient, she had many visitors, who took her floral tributes. Amongst these was a single white rose from Winifred denoting the innocence of the unborn child. The little nun, who was quite aware that she was dying, was very touched by the kind gesture.

"Oh, Winifred, thank you ever so much; this means more to me than anything else."

"Sister Mary Veronica, my little friend," replied Winifred as she gently clasped her hand, "all I can say is that when the good God decides to call upon you, the holy unborn innocents will escort you to His heavenly kingdom."

The little nun raised a smile, saying, "You know something, Winifred, I feel at ease now because I know that I am leaving my cause in good hands."

Sadly, this was the last time that they ever spoke to each other, as Sister Mary Veronica died the following morning; she was just sixty-five years old. Ironically, of all days, she actually died on St Patrick's day, the patron saint of her beloved country Ireland.

Winifred placed another single white rose on her coffin once again saying, "Sister Mary Veronica, this little white rose represents the innocence of the unborn child." It really was a fitting epitaph to such a wonderful unique person.

True to her promise, Winifred did keep up the good works; in fact from that day forward, her house was constantly cluttered with everything from clothing, toys, bicycles, music centres to pieces of bedding and furniture. She didn't just stick to jumble sales either; she had many private sales from her own home.

Despite all the work that her own family and neighbours did in helping her, there was no special priority given. If there happened to be a certain article of clothing or whatever that a member of her family or one of her neighbours wanted Winifred would put a price on it and they would have to donate that amount. It didn't matter if one of them had just brought a bag of stuff from miles away, they still had to put in a donation if something took their fancy. To be fair though, she also applied this rule to herself.

It was rather funny at times and could also be a little frustrating, especially if one happened to remove their jacket or any other article of clothing. The reason being that if they forgot it, it would then get mixed up with the rest of the jumble and sold on. Jimmy happened to leave a new designer jumper lying around the house one day, but by the time he got back next day, it had been snapped up. The saying that 'Charity begins at home' took on a literal meaning in Winifred's case.

The proceeds went to many different parts of the world including Ethiopia, Biafra and many more just as they had done before Sister Mary Veronica's death. Wherever there was a just cause, Winifred would do her bit to help out. She even organised for clothing and food to be sent out to war torn places like Bosnia; in fact on that occasion she'd so much stuff that it was impossible to store it all in her own home. Box loads of food came from many different sources along with lots of woollen clothing; many articles were still in their original packaging. All the stuff completely filled a large wagon, which joined a convoy of others. She obviously couldn't help every single cause but she strove to share things out the best way she saw fit. She'd send donations to dialysis units, cancer units, research centres, hospices and many more organisations. On top of all this, she still used her writing skills for the charities or in trying to right any wrongs. She had long since become a well-known character but still didn't like any publicity.

Besides all the charitable works, she also did something else that was quite an achievement; but this time it wasn't for other people, it was for herself. She was fifty-eight at the time and she booked herself into college. From being a little girl, she'd always wanted to take her O level in English and this she did. It wasn't a remarkable achievement by her standards but all the same, it gave her a great deal of pleasure and satisfaction.

Another sad time was the death of Winifred's namesake Winifred Clark, the young girl who had been born in the Workhouse just before Maureen's birth. She had been ill for a few months and had been receiving radiotherapy treatment in Christie's Hospital, Manchester. During her illness, John took his mother to visit Winifred in Marsden Hospital. Winifred Clark was only five years older than John, yet she'd always called him young Johnny Cowell; the fact that he was now fifty-two years old didn't seem to matter to her; this was still how she referred to him. She looked so frail as she lay in the hospital bed but she still had a sense of humour.

They'd been there just a little while when she turned to John asking, "And how are you, young Johnny Cowell, what are you doing with yourself lately?"

"I'm doing all right, Winnie, thank you very much. As a matter of fact, I'm trying my best to write a book."

"Oh yeah, and what is it going to be about then?"

"Well actually, it's about my mother's life"

"Oh bloomín éck, Johnny, that should make interesting reading; there's certainly plenty to write about."

"Well, I hope so, Winnie, I've been trying for years to get my mum to write it herself but she won't, as she says there's too many hurtful memories. The funny thing, though, is that she doesn't mind me writing it."

"You do it, Johnny, I think there's definitely a good story there to be told," she encouraged him, adding, "By the way, what is the title of your book?"

"I don't know yet, Winnie, I just can't think of one."

Without any hesitation she replied, "Oh that's easy, 'The Broken Biscuit'.

"'The Broken Biscuit'?" John queried looking rather puzzled.

"That's right, Johnny, they were the only ones that we ever got in your house, weren't they?"

He just stood there dumbfounded thinking, "By éck, she's right and I like it too, it has a nice ring to it."

John took his mother to see Winifred just one more time after that. A short time later she died peacefully on the ward. It seemed fitting that Winifred had been on the scene when her young namesake was born and now she was there at the end of her life.

It was shortly after young Winifred's death that Winifred was taken ill and had to go in hospital to have an operation for a strangulated hernia. She wasn't feeling too well for a while afterwards, so her GP recommended that she went to Temple Street Centre for rehabilitation therapy. Whilst there, she was shown how to make many different toys including intricate cuddly teddy bears with flexible moving arms. Other things included bags, purses, fancy blankets and many other things. All these articles were made by elderly or handicapped people to aid a charitable organisation. Winifred was so impressed by the whole situation that she wrote an article about it in the local newspaper:

WHY I THANK GOD FOR THE 'SAINTS WITHOUT A HALO'

I had been ill for quite a while following major surgery and was referred to the Temple Street Centre to help me recover my composure and to mix again in the world.

At the time I didn't want to go, but it has been one of the most wonderful things that has ever happened to me in all my long life.

At the centre I have met and mixed with the deaf, the dumb, the blind, the disabled and with people, both young and old, suffering from all kinds of crippling illnesses.

I have also met some very young beautiful people confined to wheelchairs, some of whom have never walked and never will walk in their lives.

I have met people who were actually children in adult bodies, so sad yet so uplifting.

When you meet these people you begin to count your blessings, you realise how small is your own affliction and you realise the mercy of God and how selfish man can become.

At Christmas, Temple Street gave a party, a Christmas meal with turkey and all the trimmings and Christmas pudding. We all pulled crackers and wished a Merry Christmas toast with a glass of sweet wine, then we had a cup of tea and mince pies, all followed by a wonderful concert with marvellous singers and fun entertainment.

After the curtain closed, someone called out in a loud voice, "Who'd like to see Father Christmas?" And in unison, more than one hundred voices answered, "I do! I do!"

Father Christmas and his helper came down from the stage to distribute presents to all in the beautifully decorated Christmas room, and it was then that I looked around.

I saw all those handicapped people and I realised what miracles are all about, for no one was different to the other.

We all became as one, the happiness and joy was unanimous, for we were all children again, bearing in mind that some of those enjoying this Christmas revelry were well over ninety years old.

Let us give thanks to God for those in Temple Street, who work so hard to keep these souls going in both body and mind.

The handicapped are taught many skills according to the extent of their disability, but everyone is allowed to have a go at something or other, either in the workshop or craft room, including pottery where many beautiful objects are made by these handicapped people.

The people who take care of the handicapped are patient, tolerant and caring. If there are saints without a halo, these people are my idea of them.

God bless them all and God bless Temple Street. I wish I was wealthy, what a lot I'd give them all – the blind, the deaf, the dumb and the young ones who spend their lives in wheelchairs.

I've never met God but I know how I feel and it's Temple Street people who make God so real, for where there is love there is God

Mrs W. Cowell,
(Aged 78)
Moorland Road,
Burnley

Time passed and by now, all Winifred's children were in their fifties. She was seventy-nine years old, the arthritis was really taking its toll of her, but still she battled on relentlessly. Not being quite as sprightly now, she wasn't able to keep on top of the house, but would not give up her sales.

She could have gone and lived at any one of her children's homes but adamantly refused; she'd go there for a short break but no more. Both Maureen and Barbara lived in Blackpool whereas Barry lived in London. Jimmy, John and Mary were still living locally, which meant she had a wide choice being able to call on any one of them at any time. Despite where they lived though, every one of the family kept in constant touch, keeping an eye on her and helping out in any way they could. Just a few months before her eightieth birthday, she had to go into Wrightington Hospital to have a hip replacement on her other leg. After the operation, she went to convalesce at Barbara's house in Blackpool where she stayed approximately three months. She'd no sooner got home though than she was on the phone calling upon everyone to help out again with the jumble sales and the events she was planning.

She wasn't one for special events but all the same, the family put one on for her eightieth birthday at the Burnley Cricket Club and a good do it was too. Mary and Jimmy's wife Shirley did most of the preparations and between them they arranged a fantastic running buffet. Shirley, being a good singer also, arranged a Karaoke set-up, and together with Jimmy and Winifred's nephew Tony, they put on a great show. Winifred enjoyed it all the more so because many of her family came from Bacup, including her brother Mat and her sister Mary. Everyone was a little concerned that Winifred wouldn't last the pace, so constantly kept an eye on her. But they needn't have worried; she was still going strong right at the end of the night when everybody was ready for going home. Despite Winifred not liking publicity, many write-ups have been written about her in the *Burnley Express* and other newspapers. On this occasion, there was an article written about it under the 'Women's Scene' column along with her photograph:

Supergran Winifred's work goes on.

Meet supergran and fundraiser extraordinary Mrs Winifred Cowell – who has just celebrated her eightieth birthday but still spends all her spare time raising money for charity.

The front room of her Moorland Road home has

become a workroom bursting at the seams with clothes, toys and anything else that can be recycled to raise money for needy causes.

The likeable lady has become so well known for her charitable work that friends pass on items so she can re-sell or use them in some way for charity.

She's always been interested in helping others but since her retirement from Bellings she has devoted the past thirty years to charity work.

Her family has long since given up asking her to slow down and she says she carries on because it "keeps her brain active".

She said, "It helps me as well as helping others, I suppose it's my therapy, it helps me too."

She has never sought the limelight and was embarrassed to find herself the centre of attention on Friday night when her large family of six sons and daughters, grandchildren and great grandchildren organised a huge birthday party at the Burnley Cricket Club and more than one hundred people went along.

She first became involved in charity work when she met the late Sister Mary Veronica of the Convent of Mercy in Yorkshire Street. A great friendship developed between them and she began helping the nuns in their work. Then she started using the church hall to hold sales of all the goods she acquired, using her own home as a storeroom and workroom.

She says she couldn't have managed without the support of St Mary's Church and the Knights of St Columba.

In this way she has raised thousands of pounds over the years, which has gone to dozens of charities for the deaf, blind, children's causes, cancer and other medical charities, handicapped people, animal charities and at Christmas, she sent donations to help starving children in Somalia.

She has just recovered from a hip operation so she can no longer organise the church hall sales as she used to, so all her work is now done from home.

A real unsung hero, she's young in spirit and kind of heart despite having suffered the lean years bringing up her family during the Depression.

"We had nothing, bare stone floors, hardly enough food to survive and no handouts. I used to wonder how I could feed the children when they came home from school, but we managed somehow," she says.

It is probably these hard times that have made her the strong woman she is today. She never forgets that people need to help each other.

After her eightieth birthday, Barry took her on a pilgrimage to Lourdes in the South of France. Since then, she has returned there twice, and on both occasions went with the organisation A.C.R.O.S.S. This is a special group that takes handicapped people and helpers to various destinations on specially designed coaches called Jumbulances, which cater to the needs of the afflicted. Her son John drove her to the picking-up point on Charnock Richards' filling station on the M6 Motorway taking her wheelchair and other aids.

It was on one of these trips that Winifred met and befriended a very special man. Their relationship was only to last fourteen months but a definite affinity was struck up between them. It was on the first journey, and Winifred happened to be sat just behind him on the coach. He was a very smart slim-looking gentleman and her first impression was that he was rather aloof. However, as the journey progressed, she soon discovered this was not the case. She felt the need to rest, so went to lie down on one of the special bunk beds, which happened to be directly facing his seat. On returning to her seat she felt rather dizzy, so he offered her his assistance. It was then that she noticed a light around his waist and being inquisitive, she asked him what it was.

He replied in a very kind gentle voice, "Let's just say, it's to help keep me alive." He introduced himself as Brendan Murphy and from that moment on they became constant companions throughout the whole pilgrimage. Despite not being a well man, he treated her with courtesy and respect, helping to push her wheelchair and other things. He was quite a lot younger than Winifred but in spite of this, they had a great liking for each other.

When she went down to breakfast, he quietly teased her from his table across the room for everyone to hear, "I'll bet you were a cracker when you were younger, Winifred."

"No, you're wrong there," she replied, quite bashful, "I've never had claims to beauty."

"That's only because you've never had the time to look at yourself, have you?" This was the type of friendly banter which characterised their relationship throughout the excursion.

After the crusade they both kept in touch by letter and actually visited each other's homes. On the occasion when Brendan came to Burnley, he arranged to take both Winifred's family and his own for a meal at Rosehill House. Shortly after this, it was his sixty-fifth birthday and a big party was given at his home in Chesire. Her son John drove her there along with his fiancée Ann Burnett and his sister Mary. Before leaving, Brendan insisted on escorting Winifred to the gate and helping her into the car.

Winifred's family really took to Brendan, and Brendan's family to Winifred. Sadly, his condition quickly deteriorated having to spend periods in hospital. Still, they kept in touch by phone, although at times he was too ill to speak.

The last time Winifred saw him was just a week before he died. On Saturday morning, John drove her to Brendan's home where he had prepared a small meal. They didn't stay too long, as it was obvious that he wasn't feeling very well. One striking thing was that his hands were blistered appearing so red they looked as if they'd been dipped in boiling water. They were smothered in some sort of white barrier cream and he was wearing thin protective transparent plastic gloves. The hands were obviously very painful causing lots of discomfort but still he remained the perfect host. Before leaving, he walked Winifred to the gate and gently embraced her giving her a little peck on her cheek.

the *broken biscuit*

"God bless you, Winifred, please remember me in your prayers." They both sensed that this would be their last sighting of each other.

"Yes, Brendan, and me too in yours; God bless you and all your loved ones."

John, who also sensed the situation, felt very emotional. He then helped his mother into the car and they both waved Brendan goodbye as his frail lean figure stood at the gate.

Brendan died shortly after that and the funeral took place within a few days from his home and he was buried in the local Catholic churchyard. Winifred and two of her sons were in attendance.

One Saturday in June 1998, Winifred decided to go on a coach trip with Rosehill Baptist Church to Chester Zoo. It started out like any other ordinary day but something very extraordinary happened that could have had devastating consequences. Jimmy and his wife Shirley drove to Winifred's home to collect her and her wheelchair. When they reached the house Winifred annnounced quite nonchalantly that she was also taking the next door neighbour's three children with her, who were aged eight, seven and six years respectively. This was quite unexpected for Jimmy; he hadn't relished the idea of pushing a wheelchair around a zoo for six hours in the first place, but now he had three kids in tow as well. Spending a day at the zoo was definitely not his idea of a good day out; the weather didn't help either, it was overcast and quite dismal for the time of the year. Still, Shirley and he accepted the situation in good spirits, so off they went with a full carload to the church, from whence the coach departed.

On arriving at the zoo, they settled Winifred in her wheelchair, then gave the children strict instructions to keep close by and not to wander off. The young children were hungry, so the first place they all headed for was a café for a warm drink and a bite to eat. The day worsened, becoming blustery and cold, but at least it didn't rain. Luckily, Winifred was wearing a thick woolly coat, which protected her from the elements. Because of the weather, they spent quite a long time inside the café before venturing around the zoo. Jimmy, not being the most patient bloke in the world, wasn't looking forward to spending a few hours wandering around looking at the animals.

Nevertheless, Shirley was jovial about everything, and like always, she lifted his spirits. Little did Jimmy know that something was going to happen to break the monotony for him.

The paths and walkways around the zoo were level, apart from two hump back bridges, or so they thought. Stopping to watch the sea lions precipitated an event that Winifred will remember until the day she dies. Shirley set off pushing the wheelchair with the three children close at hand leaving Jimmy a little way behind still enthralled by the antics of the sea lions. Shirley and Winifred were chatting away merrily to each other when little Maria, the eight-year-old, started pestering Shirley.

"Can I push Mrs Cowell for a little bit please?" she urged. Shirley was a little apprehensive at first but Winifred pointed out that she was a very sensible child. Seeing no harm, they both agreed; however, Shirley walked just a step behind. Nobody could have foreseen what happened next; it was funny in a way, yet deadly dangerous. They approached a junction that was hidden by thick bushes; the little girl turned right with the wheelchair and then let out a loud scream. Shirley was on the scene immediately only to see the wheelchair careering down a steep incline. She sprinted after it, actually touching the handle but it got away from her; all she could do was watch in horror as it gathered speed. With little Maria wailing loudly, Shirley tried to catch the runaway wheelchair; it looked like a scene out of the Keystone Cops. The hill was very steep and long and if Winifred had been carried to the bottom, then that would have been it. Luckily though the chair veered sideways hitting the raised stones on the edge of the path which slowed it down considerably. Finally it came to an abrupt halt as it hit a large rock and tipped over, throwing Winifred on to the gravel path. She was quite shaken up suffering lots of cuts and abrasions with blood in abundance. On reaching her, Jimmy was most concerned about a rather large lump on the side of her head. Both he and Shirley made her comfortable treating her for shock and administering basic first aid.

When the ambulance arrived, Winifred was taken to Chester Casualty Department where she was informed just how lucky she'd been not to have sustained more serious injuries. The nurses joked with her calling her the Bionic woman saying that the two replacement hips she had were actually stronger than normal joints. They pointed out that but for them she would probably have broken both hips. Another factor that saved her from further injury was because she was wearing the thick woolly coat. They discharged her from hospital the same afternoon, and that was the end of a very trying day. She couldn't get out of bed for three weeks, needing someone to stay with her all the time. But all the same, it wasn't long before she was back to her normal self, getting on the phone and issuing orders to everybody.

Although Winifred is not quite as resilient, she is still as determined as she was thirty years ago; the body is weak but the spirit is still strong. She can't walk very well now but she has a loving family and many friends around her to encourage her. Not only do they keep her going; she has them on the run all the time. According to the write-up in the *Burnley Express* following her eightieth birthday she only does work from her own home now. That was true at the time of going to print, which is now almost six years ago; however, since getting over her second hip operation, she has done several more sales using various venues. At the age of eighty-three her passion for doing the sales was still undiminished and despite not wanting publicity, Winifred just seemed to be always in the headlines.

Quote from the *Burnley Express*:

WINIFRED IS A CHARITY QUEEN.

A PENSIONER is defying her age and illness to be the centre of a vast fund-raising body.

Mrs Cowell of Moorland Road, Rosehill, is aged 83 and suffers with angina and arthritis. But for 25 years she has been the hub of a community, which has raised money for cancer research, handicapped people, a variety of children who need help and people in war-torn areas, such as Bosnia.

Her most recent venture, held at St Mary's Church, Burnley, raised £230 for people fighting to protect unborn children.

The event was Mrs Cowell's first big fundraiser for six years. She has had six operations for her illnesses, which have forced her to take it easier. Though she could not attend the church for the whole event, she turned up for the last 10 minutes.

Mrs Cowell acts as the organiser, but she is modest about her contribution. She said, "The credit for this should not go to me. The best organisation can't work without the help of a good team. My children, neighbours and people from church all help. We are all linked in a chain and every link must be perfect."

The mother of six, who is a grandmother and great-grandmother, has now turned her attentions to a new venture. She has made contact with a priest in India who is trying to keep children off the streets.

Her latest sale was actually on May 16th, 1998 in St Mary's Church Hall; it happened to be the same day as the cup final. Cup final or not, she still called on her family and friends to assist with the running of the sale. It was quite a pleasant day all round as tea and homemade cakes were on sale for a nominal fee of twenty pence. After this particular sale though, she was exhausted, simply worn out, and she told everyone there that it would probably be her last. That's what she said but within a couple of weeks, the odd bag of jumble started appearing again in her home.

"Come on, Mum," one or other of the family would say, "you promised that the sale at St Mary's Hall was your last."

"Oh well, I just thought I could happen do a little private sale."

"That's what you always say, Mum, then before you know it the house is full of jumble again."

"Yes, I know but it keeps me going and makes me feel alive."

"Look, Mum, we all realise that, but we're all a bit concerned that it's getting too much for you; we'd just like you to slow down and relax a little."

The family doesn't mean to get on to her; the simple fact is she is nearly eighty-six years of age, and they are all rather concerned for her welfare.

Reflecting on her own family, Winifred reckons that things have worked out pretty well despite the Depression years and other trying times she has experienced. Every single one of her children is quite healthy and of good character, each having done very well in their own chosen profession. Maureen and Barbara are at present living in their own homes in Blackpool. Maureen is semi-retired running a small block of flats, whilst Barbara is totally retired after successfully running a large hotel. Jimmy and John are also enjoying early retirement after successfully operating their own little business ventures in the building trade. Both Barry and Mary have worked in the nursing profession for most of their working lives and are on the verge of retirement. In 1978, John felt that he had done very well in the building trade so decided that he wanted to give a little back to society. So he too, went into the nursing profession where he spent the latter part of his working life. Retirement has given him the time and scope to write his mother's life-story.

Now in her latter years, Winifred is still a well-known and much-loved character throughout Rosehill Estate. Her house is always full at any time of the day with children from all around and they all truly love her, freely running errands or doing any other little thing that she asks of them. Besides the children on the estate, she has sixteen grandchildren and twenty-one great-grandchildren plus one great-great-grandchild of her own.

She still refuses to give up her independence altogether though, as she counts this as one of her blessings. Every day, she struggles to walk to the bottom of her garden where she likes to say a little prayer thanking God that her family came through it all with smiles on their faces. She has achieved the goal that she so ardently laboured for; all her children still love one another deeply besides having families of their own. Without fail, she looks at the sky, the sun, the flowers, the trees and loves to listen to the sound of the birds. She gives thanks for still having her faculties and the ability to live on her own.

"Oh what a beautiful world it is," she quietly mutters to herself. "Thank God for a new day, a new life and most of all ... my family."

Winifred, now eighty-eight years old, still lives on Moorland Road. All her siblings are now deceased and she is the sole surviving member of that generation.

Burnley Town Council created a new award – the Certificate of Honour – which she received for exceptional voluntary work on June 6th 2000. The Barnados Foundation, at a presentation ceremony at the Gibbon Bridge Hotel near Longridge, picked her as Lancashire Woman of the Year 2000 on October 10th 2000.

Her children have prospered; some have remained in and around the town of their birth, and others have moved further afield and have put down roots in Blackpool and London. But each will always carry within their hearts a little bit of Burnley, a town which they still love and visit regularly. Their lives have not been without tragedy, however the indomitable spirit they have all inherited from their mother has enabled them to weather the storm and stress, which is the lot of all human beings in life.

Winifred's body is now old and frail but her mind is as fresh and vibrant as it was when she was a young girl. She is still doing what she has always done – caring for others – and continues to work tirelessly for various charities, both locally and internationally. Wherever suffering is to be found in what is sometimes a cruel world, Winifred's humanitarian spirit and love for her fellow creatures will also be found. She is an inspiration to each and everyone of us, including her grandchildren, great-grandchildren and great-great-grandchildren.

This is a poem written by John for his mum on Mother's Day.
He was 10 years old at the time.

MUM
You've been there right from the start,
Doing everything with the kindest heart.
You teach us the difference from right and wrong,
Though on occasions, you have to be strong.
Although our home is small and dire,
You make sure there's always a cosy fire.
Despite conditions caused from above,
Our home is always filled with love.
For Sunday dinner you try to please,
With potatoes, cabbage, meat and peas.
Every night you teach us to pray,
And now it is my time to say.
"Of all the mothers put to the test,
From all of them you are the best.
When I grow up and a father I be
I'd like to think I'll be as good as thee."

MY LIFE

Born in Bank Hall, my first day of life,
Given a twin sister, just like a wife.
In a way it was great, but much to my loss,
Right from the start, she was to be boss.

At seven in the morning, I arrived on the scene,
Mary arrived later, she wasn't too keen.
The nurses were nice but nigh to our peril,
They wanted Mum to call us Bobby and Beryl.
Jack and Jill was mentioned but Mum was quite wary
Anf finally settled for plain John and Mary.
On arrival home, waiting at the door,
Our two older siblings, now we were four.
Maureen was four, Jimmy not quite two,
How exciting it was, this adventure new.

Jimmy made it quite clear he was the older brother,
Maureen responded more like a mother.
My dad was not there, nor by the sink,
He was down at the pub, an excuse for a drink.

Twenty months later, our hopes came alive,
Our Barry was born, now we were five.
Poor but loved, Mum kept us all nice and neat,
In a small council house on Dalton Street.

Because of Dad's habits, money was rare,
He'd five little kids, but just didn't care.
He kept up his drinking, the money he spent,
Mí poor óle mum just couldn't pay the rent.

The council was cruel and stuck to the law,
The Bailiff's arrived; we all had to go.
An Albion Street house allayed some of her fears,
It was to be our home for the next twenty years.

When I was four, I felt like a mister,
As Mum gave us a new baby sister.
Yes! Barbara was born, quite a nice mix,
Now our Maureen was the eldest of six.

We used to fight like any sister and brother,
But Mum always taught us to love one another.
She ran the home like running a vessel,
But made each one feel very special.

She had to be strict but treated us fine,
But lo and behold if we didn't toe the line!
She had to be strong with a guiding hand,
In order to teach us the way of the land.

She toiled and strived through all kinds of weather,
In order that we would all remain together.

John W Cowell

the **broken biscuit**

JUNIOR SCHOOL

St Thomas's was the name of our school,
All the kids were poor but ever so cool.
Wearing steel bottom clogs that made a great sound,
Creating bright sparks by kicking the ground.
At nine on the dot into single file we fell,
Then marched into class to the sound of the bell.
Paraded like soldiers dressed in our togs,
Clip clop, clip clop, went the sound of our clogs.
At playtime we used to play in the yard,
One soon learnt that you had to be hard.
The yard was concrete, and much to one's plight,
In that very yard, one had their first fight.
Sparks from clogs, shouts and jeers,
Left many a black eye filled with tears.
It was a hard life, but not quite so cruel,
No kicking! No biting! One stuck to the rule.
Life is quite strange, and through all this strife,
Lots of those kids became friends for life.

John W Cowell

acknowledgements

I would like to thank my brothers and sisters, who have contributed with their own recollections of events described within this book. Also my special thanks to Ann Burnett, whose endless patience and encouragement inspired me to continue writing when my spirit was flagging.

I would also like to record my gratitude personally to my brother Jimmy and his wife Shirley, who also proofread my story and supported me in every way they could. A special thanks is also due to my brother, Barry, for his heart-rending account of the events dealt with in chapter fifteen. My heartiest thanks go to my sisters Maureen, Mary and Barbara for their unstinting support and encouragement. I wish to thank the whole of my family personally for their permission to include in this book events, some of them painful, which touched all of us personally.

Many thanks also to my brother-in-law Jack Heyes, who put a lot of time and effort into designing the book's cover and processing the photographs. I express my gratitude to Michael Walsh, my cousin, who also proofread the book. He also helped me with the editing and gave me lots of advice and encouragement.

I want to thank personally my friends Mr Malcolm Davis and his wife Ivy for their encouragement and for having faith in me.

I wish to acknowledge Bacup Library, Blackburn Library and Burnley Central Library for their kind permission to reproduce certain rare photographs from their archives, and for the use of their technical resources which proved invaluable for my research. Towneley Hall and Burnley Heritage Centre also supplied precious photographs. I am indebted to the *Burnley Express* for their kind permission to reproduce quotations from the *Express* in my book.

I extend my gratitude to my publisher Eddie Mercer of Cremer Press, Blackburn and his editor Madeleine Fish, who gave me help, information and much valued guidance.

My heartfelt thanks to the late Winifred Clark, to whom I owe the title of my book. She was like one of the family as quoted within the chapters.

And, of course, a very special thanks is due to my mother, the subject of this book and without whose vivid memory it could not have been written.